Feminist Legal Theory

CRITICAL AMERICA

General Editors: Richard Delgado and Jean Stefancic

Recent titles in the Critical America series include:

*Legal Education and the
Reproduction of Hierarchy:
A Polemic against the System,
A Critical Edition*
Duncan Kennedy,
with commentaries by Paul Carrington,
Peter Gabel, Angela Harris and
Donna Maeda, and Janet Halley

*America's Colony:
The Political and Cultural Conflict be-
tween the United States and
Puerto Rico*
Pedro A. Malavet

*Alienated: Immigrant Rights, the
Constitution, and Equality in America*
Victor C. Romero

*The Disability Pendulum:
The First Decade of the Americans
with Disabilities Act*
Ruth Colker

*Lawyers' Ethics and the Pursuit
of Social Justice: A Critical Reader*
Edited by Susan D. Carle

*Rethinking Commodification: Cases and
Readings in Law and Culture*
Edited by Martha M. Ertman
and Joan C. Williams

The Derrick Bell Reader
Edited by Richard Delgado
and Jean Stefancic

*Science for Segregation: Race, Law,
and the Case against Brown v. Board
of Education*
John P. Jackson Jr.

*Discrimination by Default:
How Racism Becomes Routine*
Lu-in Wang

*The First Amendment in
Cross-Cultural Perspective:
A Comparative Legal Analysis
of the Freedom of Speech*
Ronald J. Krotoszynski, Jr.

For a complete list of titles in the series,
please visit the New York University Press
website at www.nyupress.org.

Feminist Legal Theory

A Primer

Nancy Levit and
Robert R. M. Verchick

Foreword by Martha Minow

NEW YORK UNIVERSITY PRESS

New York and London

NEW YORK UNIVERSITY PRESS
New York and London
www.nyupress.org

Library of Congress Cataloging-in-Publication Data
Levit, Nancy.
Feminist legal theory : a primer / Nancy Levit and
Robert R.M. Verchick; foreword by Martha Minnow.
p. cm. — (Critical America)
Includes bibliographical references and index.
ISBN–13: 978–0–8147–5198–5 (cloth : alk. paper)
ISBN–10: 0–8147–5198–9 (cloth : alk. paper)
ISBN–13: 978–0–8147–5199–2 (pbk. : alk. paper)
ISBN–10: 0–8147–5199–7 (pbk. : alk. paper)
1. Feminist jurisprudence—United States. 2. Feminist theory—
United States. 3. Women—Legal status, laws, etc.—United States.
I. Verchick, Robert R. M. II. Title. III. Series.
KF478.L48   2006
342.7308'78—dc22   2005034711

New York University Press books are printed on acid-free paper,
and their binding materials are chosen for strength and durability.

Manufactured in the United States of America

c 10 9 8 7 6 5 4 3 2 1
p 10 9 8 7 6 5 4 3 2 1

To Tim, Aaron, and Dylan,
with love and gratitude.
N.E.L.

To my mother, Sue,
and my wife, Heidi.
R.V.

Contents

*Foreword: Feminist Legal Theory, Primed
for Action* xiii
      Martha Minow

Acknowledgments xix

Chapter One. Introduction 1

  A. Feminism and Law 1

  B. A Brief History of Women's Rights and
     Early Concepts of Equality 2

  C. The Equal Rights Amendment 6

  D. Varieties of Contemporary Feminist Legal Theory 8

  E. Unifying Themes and Divisions 12

Chapter Two. Feminist Legal Theories 15

  A. Equal Treatment Theory 16

  B. Cultural Feminism 17

  C. Dominance Theory 22

  D. Critical Race Feminism 26

  E. Lesbian Feminism 29

  F. Ecofeminism 31

  G. Pragmatic Feminism 34

H. Postmodern Feminism 36

I. Questions for Discussion 39

Chapter Three. Feminist Legal Methods 45

A. Unmasking Patriarchy 45

B. Contextual Reasoning 48

C. Consciousness-Raising 49

D. Pulling It Together 50
1. Telling a story 50
2. Analyzing the story 51

E. Questions for Discussion 53

Chapter Four. Workplace Discrimination, Wages, and Welfare 57

A. Defining Workplace Discrimination 58
1. The history of Title VII 58
2. Suing under Title VII 59
3. Pregnancy, maternity leave, and the
work-family conflict 61

B. Feminist Legal Theory in the Courtroom 63

C. Sexual Harassment 66

D. Occupational Segregation and Equal Pay 73

E. Employment in the Military 77
1. GI Jane 77
2. "Don't Ask, Don't Tell" 79

F. Welfare Reform and Economic Independence 80

G. Questions for Discussion 80

Chapter Five Education and Sports 86

A. Educational Opportunities 86
1. The historical path to coeducation 86

2. Contemporary inequalities 89

B. Single-Sex Education 92
   1. The constitutional backdrop: equal protection 93
   2. The statutory backdrop: Title IX 98
   3. The evidence concerning single-sex education 100

C. Charter Schools and Vouchers 104
   1. Charter schools 104
   2. Vouchers 106

D. Athletics and Title IX 107
   1. The importance of school athletics 107
   2. Empirical evidence: the good, the bad,
      and the ugly 109
   3. Complying with Title IX 110
      a. The "interests and abilities" three-step 111
      b. *Cohen v. Brown University* 111
      c. "Boys against the girls" 114

E. Sexual Harassment in Schools 115

F. Questions for Discussion 119

Chapter Six. Gender and the Body 128

A. Abortion 128
   1. Abortion and the Constitution 129
   2. Legislation and political strategies 135
      a. The "partial birth" abortion controversy 136
      b. RU-486 138
      c. Antiabortion violence and clinic access 138
      d. Fathers' rights 140
   3. Reproductive rights and feminist legal theories 141
      a. Tensions of cultural feminism 141
      b. Women's stories and reproductive rights 141
      c. Multicultural perspectives 143
      d. Pro-life feminism 143
      e. Antiessentialism 144

B. Contraception 145
   1. Contraceptive information 145

2. Emergency contraception 147
3. Birth control costs and insurance coverage 147

C. Surrogacy 148
1. Surrogacy arrangements 148
2. Freedom or slavery? 149
3. *In re Baby M* and *Johnson v. Calvert* 151
4. Regulating surrogacy 153

D. The Pornography Debate 153

E. Questions for Discussion 156

Chapter Seven. Marriage and Family 163

A. Marriage and Its Alternatives 163
1. Something old, something new 163
2. The pros and cons of tying the knot 165
3. Same-sex marriage 166
4. Domestic partnerships 168
a. Rules between domestic partners 169
b. Rules between a domestic couple and
third parties 170

B. Divorce and Its Economic Consequences 170
1. The divorce revolution 171
2. Dividing property upon divorce 171
3. What about my law degree? 173

C. Child Custody 174

D. Questions for Discussion 175

Chapter Eight. Sex and Violence 179

A. Rape 181
1. The criminal law rules 181
2. Rape myths 183
3. Special evidence requirements 184
4. Public perceptions, media coverage, and
legal theory 185
5. Acquaintance rape 187

B. Domestic Violence 189
   1. Understanding abusive relationships:
      "Why didn't she just leave?" 190
   2. Battered women who kill their abusers 192
   3. Intimate violence at the intersections of identity 194

C. Legal Intervention 195
   1. Police responses 195
   2. Mandatory reporting, arrest, and
      prosecution policies 198
   3. The Violence against Women Act 201

D. Questions for Discussion 202

Chapter Nine. Feminist Legal Theory and Globalization 212

A. Introduction 212

B. Globalization and Its Discontents 213

C. In Search of a Global Feminist Theory 214
   1. Defining equality and women's well-being 215
   2. The public-private distinction 215
   3. Feminism and multiculturalism 217

D. Case Studies 218
   1. Female genital cutting 218
   2. International trafficking in women and girls 221
   3. Economic development 223

E. Questions for Discussion 227

Index 229

About the Authors 235

Foreword

Feminist Legal Theory, Primed for Action

Martha Minow[1]

This primer is welcome for many reasons. First, it is a model of clear and accessible prose—no small feat in the world of law. Second, it integrates legal doctrine, legal practice, empirical study, and political analysis, and thus exemplifies the two-way bridge between theory and practice that law at its best enacts. As the third and most important reason, *Feminist Legal Theory: A Primer* offers a thorough introduction to the topic of feminist legal theory that will be a valuable resource both for those beginning and for those pursuing inquiry into the subject. Students, scholars, community organizers, and voters are among the lucky audiences for this book.

Actually, it is worth pausing to celebrate the very fact that such a primer is needed. For it was not long ago that "feminist," "legal," and "theory" simply did not come together as a subject warranting an introduction. Only 4.9 percent of the legal profession in 1970, women then started to enroll in larger numbers.[2] That reflected the women's movement but also affected the movement, the profession, and legal education. The emergence of "second-wave feminism" in the 1960s and 1970s reinvented arguments for women's rights first pressed in the nineteenth century. The second-wave movement for women's rights created institutions and changed political debates before it began to influence legal doctrine. When the word "feminist" first appeared in American judicial opinions, it modified the names of health care and advocacy organizations that appeared as parties or players in litigation.[3]

Advocates for women proceeded to challenge traditional treatments of contexts of rape, abortion, workplace discrimination, pornography, and women's health care.[4] New generations of lawyers—women and men—began to take on gender bias in the judiciary, in law firms, in the military, in the relationships between employment and families, and in society. In the 1970s, Ruth Bader Ginsburg led the American Civil Liberties Union ("ACLU") Women's Rights Project in a brilliant campaign to challenge gender-based exclusions throughout the law.[5] Catharine MacKinnon's pathbreaking book, *Sexual Harassment of Working Women* (1979), condemned both employer requests for sexual favors in exchange for employment benefits and hostile working environments and in so doing introduced both new legal doctrinal ideas and new theoretical approaches.

Academic work connecting gender and law began during the 1980s, but it surely did not amount to enough to warrant a primer. It took several more years for "feminist legal theory" to emerge in the legal academy and the law reviews,[6] and the work grew but still faced some barriers to acceptance.[7] As special journals addressing women and the law emerged, so did fights over whether women's legal issues required a particular method or ideology.[8] By 2005, hundreds of articles debating ways to analyze gender, power, and law have filled academic journals, informed litigation strategies, and undergirded statutory and regulatory reforms. Much of the work reflects direct engagement with the lives and struggles of girls and women and a commitment to understand and change practices. Here, feminist work reflects Professor Mari Matsuda's insight: "A casual effort to say, 'Okay, I'll add gender to my analysis,' without immersion in feminist practice, is likely to miss something."[9]

What makes any of this work "theory"? I once heard a journalist say that he could tell that the study of literature was in trouble by the flood of books about literary theory. Theory may reflect trouble, and it also can make trouble by probing behind conventions and day-to-day practice. In law, theory is academic work that seeks to dig deep rather than offer short-term reforms or evaluations of individual cases or practices. What makes a theory "feminist" is itself a subject of considerable scholarly debate, but a pretty good starting point identifies a focus on women, gender relations, power, and inequality.[10] *Feminist Legal Theory: A Primer* comprehensively surveys a broader array of feminist legal theories than most other commentators. Thus, the book includes sustained treatments of equal treatment theory, cultural feminism, dominance theory, antiessentialist theories (critical race feminism and lesbian feminism), ecofeminism, pragmatic feminism, and postmodern feminism.

Each of the coauthors of this book has pioneered forms of feminist legal theory. Nancy Levit deploys feminist tools to challenge stereotypes of maleness.[11] Robert Verchick has traced feminist consciousness-raising methods in environmentalism while arguing for attention to the racial and class dimensions of environmental reforms.[12] The very persistence of multiple strands within feminist legal theory contributes to its emergence as a field, deserving continuing study.[13] The authors here bring original ideas and cogent synthesis to make this primer a terrific resource and a darn good read.

Legal theory should hold promise of making a difference to the understanding and practices of norms made and enforced by the government. Feminist legal theory then must address the urgent situations of violence and oppression domestically and globally, where too often being born female sets an individual on an especially arduous and difficult path. Effectively identifying concrete problems and proposed legal reforms, the primer addresses employment, military service, public assistance, education, reproduction, pornography, sexual violence, marriage and divorce, dependency and caretaking, trafficking in women and girls, genital cutting, and microcredit and other tools for economic development.

This book is called a primer, and when pronounced with a short "I", the work can fairly be described as "a small introductory book on a subject."[14] With a long "I" in the first syllable, the book can become a device for priming, the first step before acting. Indeed, the dictionary defines a "primer" as a container of "percussion powder or compound used to ignite an explosive charge."[15] Feminist legal theory indeed has the capacity to ignite explosive social and legal changes when, as in this book, it invites readers to bring themselves—their "I"—into it.

NOTES

1. Jeremiah Smith, Jr. Professor, Harvard Law School.
2. *See* HEDDA GARZA, BARRED FROM THE BAR: A HISTORY OF WOMEN IN THE

LEGAL PROFESSION (1996); KAREN BERGER MORELLO, THE INVISIBLE BAR: THE WOMAN LAWYER IN AMERICA, 1638 TO THE PRESENT (1986). For a vivid description of the experiences some of the earliest women at one law school that excluded women until the 1960s, see JUDITH RICHARDS HOPE, PINSTRIPES & PEARLS: THE WOMEN OF THE HARVARD LAW SCHOOL CLASS OF '64 WHO FORGED AN OLD-GIRL NETWORK AND PAVED THE WAY FOR FUTURE GENERATIONS (2003).

3. *See* Chico Feminist Women's Health Ctr. v. Scully, 208 Cal. App. 3d 230 (Cal Ct. App. 1989); Hinfey v. Matawan Reg'l Bd. of Educ., 371 A.2d 78 (N.J. Super. Ct. App. Div. 1977) (National Organization for Women filed complaint against sex discrimination in education). Before the 1970s, "feminist" occasionally appeared in opinions in reference to the movement for rights for women in the late nineteenth and early twentieth century. *See* State v. Arnold, 235 N.W. 373 (Minn. 1931).

4. *See* Chapter 1. B. (A Brief History of Women's Rights and Early Concepts of Equality; DAVID A.J. RICHARDS, WOMEN, GAYS, AND THE CONSTITUTION: THE GROUNDS FOR FEMINISM AND GAY RIGHTS IN CULTURE AND LAW (1998).

5. Kathleen M. Sullivan, *Justice Ruth Bader Ginsburg Distinguished Lecture on Women and the Law: Constitutionalizing Women's Equality*, 56 THE RECORD [of the Association of the Bar of the City of New York] 22 (2001).

6. Feminist work seemed to appear earlier in philosophy, literature and other academic departments than in law schools. *See Symposium: Feminist Moral, Social, and Legal Theory: An Introduction*, 56 U. CIN. L. REV. 459 (1987). Martha Fineman started annual workshops on feminism and legal theory in 1985. *See* Martha Albertson Fineman, *Celebrating Twenty Years of Feminist Pedagogy, Praxis and Prisms: Feminist Legal Theory*, 13 AM. U. J. GENDER SOC. POL'Y & L. 13 (2005).

7. *See* Marjorie E. Kornhauser, *Moving the Margins: Assimilation and Enduring Marginality*, 12 COLUM. J. GENDER & L. 478 (2003); Jean Stefancic & Richard Delgado, *Outsider Scholars: The Early Stories*, 71 CHI.-KENT L. REV. 1001 (1996).

8. *See* Linda E. Fisher, *I Know It When I See It, or What Makes Scholarship Feminist: A Cautionary Tale*, 12 COLUM. J. GENDER & L. 439 (2003). Over time, specialty journals increasingly used the word "gender" rather than "women" or "feminist" to refer to the subject matter. *See* Laura A. Rosenbury, *Feminist Legal Scholarship: Charting Topics and Authors, 1978–2002*, 12 COLUM. J. GENDER & L. 446 (2003).

9. Mari J. Matsuda, *Beside My Sister, Facing the Enemy: Legal Theory Out of Coalition, in* FEMINIST LEGAL THEORY: AN ANTI-ESSENTIALIST READER 77 (Nancy E. Dowd & Michelle S. Jacobs eds., 2003).

10. Others have distinguished liberal feminism, Marxist feminism, radical feminism, and socialist feminism. ALISON M. JAGGAR, FEMINIST POLITICS AND

HUMAN NATURE (1983). Unifying them are concerns about equality for men and women and commitments to connect theory with efforts to change practice and social understandings. *See* Katherine T. Bartlett, *Feminist Legal Methods,* 103 HARV. L. REV. 829 (1996) (identifying feminist legal methods as asking the women question, pursuing practical reason about law in context, and raising consciousness).

11. NANCY LEVIT, THE GENDER LINE (1998); Nancy Levit, *Feminism for Men: Legal Ideology and the Construction of Maleness,* 43 UCLA L. REV. 1037 (1996).

12. Robert R.M. Verchick, *In a Greener Voice: Feminist Theory and Environmental Justice,* 19 HARV. WOMEN'S L.J. 23 (1996).

13. Katherine T. Bartlett, *Cracking Foundations as Feminist Method,* 8 AM. U.J. GENDER SOC. POL'Y & L. 31, 53 (2000).

14. WEBSTER'S SEVENTH NEW COLLEGIATE DICTIONARY 676 (1971).

15. *Id.*

Acknowledgments

We are extremely grateful for the support of our colleagues and friends—Elaine Christensen, Barbara Glesner Fines, Rob Garda, Tim Geary, Heidi Molbak, Colin Picker, Allen Rostron, Cameron Rostron, and Dan Weddle—who gave generously of their time and talents to read and comment on portions of the manuscript.

We thank Debra Banister and Gwen Hammond for their excellent secretarial and editorial assistance, as well as the research assistants and library personnel who contributed to this project: Ann Aylward, Nona Beisenherz, Billy Guste, Kathleen Hall, Lawrence MacLachlan, Meredith Moser, Jennifer Warden, and Lorri Wilbee-Kobe.

We are particularly indebted to Richard Delgado for his enthusiasm and superb editing, and for inspiring us through his work.

N.E.L.

R.V.

1

Introduction

Now you have touched the women, you have struck a rock.
Song by South African women protesting
racial apartheid in the 1980s

A. Feminism and Law

What is feminism? The rote answer is that feminism stands for the idea that women and men should have equal economic, political, and social rights. Surely this is true, but there are many aspects to the story. For some, feminism suggests the numerous dramatic and historical examples of female activism and defiance of social conventions: Elizabeth Cady Stanton firing up the suffragist crowds at the Seneca Falls Convention in 1848; the "Million Mom March" on Washington, calling for reproductive freedom and better child care; Katharine Hepburn starring in those fabulous 1940s films—in slacks. Feminism has a quiet side, too. Think of Jane Austen, alone in the parlor, scribbling out *Pride and Prejudice* in between cross-stitches. Or the more than ten million single American moms who today rear their children in the shadows of drugs and poverty. Whether deserved or not (and we think not), feminism also suffers from a hard-to-shake "bad-girl" image of selfishness and militancy. Pat Robertson, the founder of the Christian Coalition, once called feminism a "socialist, anti-family political movement that encourages women to leave their husbands, kill their children, practice witchcraft, destroy capitalism, and become lesbians."[1] Say what you want, there is no escaping this conclusion: feminism is an extremely powerful political and social force.

Feminism is also an influential legal force. Feminism, at its root, is about equal rights. One can talk philosophically about "equality" and "rights," but for those concepts to be *actualized,* to be stamped onto the fabric of everyday life, feminist goals must be incorporated into

1

law and made enforceable by the government. The struggles for enfranchisement, family-planning services, and parental support are all legal battles in the most fundamental sense. To be a student of feminism is to be a student of law, too. Thus we begin this chapter with a brief history of feminist efforts to define and "equalize" the legal rights between the sexes.

B. A Brief History of Women's Rights and Early Concepts of Equality

It is not easy to pinpoint when feminist *legal* theorizing began, since many of the initial arguments for women's equality involved legal and political issues. Some of the earliest arguments for equal legal treatment—such as the rights to vote, make contracts, and own property—were first voiced in social and political tracts. The battle for suffrage saw women speaking in public for the first time in American history. Women reached out to supporters through written tracts, pamphlets, and books, such as Sarah Grimké's *Letters on the Equality of Sexes and the Condition of Women* (1838), in which she pleaded, "I ask no favors for my sex. . . . All I ask of our brethren is that they will take their feet from off our necks."

Early strategies for women's suffrage were tied to the abolitionist movement and racial enfranchisement. When female representatives of antislavery societies Elizabeth Cady Stanton and Lucretia Mott were denied admission as delegates to the World Anti-Slavery Convention in London in 1840 and forced to watch from a balcony, they decided to organize the first women's rights convention. Eight years later, Stanton and Mott published a newspaper advertisement that called a meeting on the rights of women. Three hundred or so women and men gathered in Seneca Falls, New York, and developed the Declaration of Sentiments, a manifesto modeled after the Declaration of Independence, that proclaimed, "We hold these truths to be self-evident: that all men and women are created equal." The Declaration of Sentiments listed "injuries and usurpations . . . on the part of man toward woman" and claimed women's natural rights to equality in political, religious, social, and public spheres, including the right to vote. The declaration's most radical and controversial provision was its demand for women's suffrage: "Resolved, therefore, That it is the duty of the women of this country to secure to themselves their sacred right to the elective franchise."

The Seneca Falls Convention sparked the beginning of the first wave of the women's rights movement. Word of Seneca Falls spread, and organizers began to hold local, state, and national women's suffrage meetings. It was at the second National Women's Suffrage Convention in Akron, Ohio, in 1851 that former slave and gifted orator Sojourner Truth drew parallels between the enslavement of blacks and the servitude of women in her speech, "Ain't I a Woman?":

> That man over there says that women need to be helped into carriages, and lifted over ditches, and to have the best place everywhere. Nobody ever helps me into carriages, or over mud-puddles, or gives me any best place! And ain't I a woman? Look at me! Look at my arm! I have ploughed and planted, and gathered into barns, and no man could head me! And ain't I a woman? I could work as much and eat as much as a man—when I could get it—and bear the lash as well! And ain't I a woman? I have borne thirteen children, and seen most all sold off to slavery, and when I cried out with my mother's grief, none but Jesus heard me! And ain't I a woman?

Whether Truth actually spoke these precise lines is a matter of some dispute.[2] Yet historians agree, based on contemporary reports, that Truth delivered a powerful speech at the Akron convention, making the points that black women were doubly burdened, and their concerns were in part different from those of white women.

An interesting schism occurred among early suffragists between those who believed the causes of emancipation and female suffrage were related and those who believed the causes were at odds. During the Civil War, organizations such as the Women's National Loyal League collected signatures on petitions calling for the emancipation of slaves. When the Fifteenth Amendment conferred the right to vote only on black men in 1870, some later suffrage groups, such as the National Woman Suffrage Association, led by Stanton and Susan B. Anthony, campaigned for women's suffrage on the theory that the white female vote was needed to counter the votes that would be exercised by black males.

Apart from the internal rifts, the very process of fighting for abolition taught women how to labor on their own political behalf. When women were excluded from all-male antislavery organizations, they formed their own abolitionist societies and gradually became used to political activity. Individuals and groups started to petition legislatures for basic rights to make contracts and hold property. Under the common law, the doctrine of coverture said that wives had no independent legal existence from their husbands—upon marriage, the woman's legal identity merged with that of her husband. Husbands had control of their wives' property, wages, and children; and they could physically discipline their wives. Beginning in the mid-nineteenth century, states began to enact statutes, called Married Women's Property Acts, to allow women to make contracts, execute wills, sue and be sued, own their wages, and control their real and personal property. These statutes were passed by male legislators principally to protect their daughters' estates.

Women's rights advocates took the demand for constitutional equality to the Supreme Court. Beginning in 1872, with *Bradwell v. Illinois*,[3] the Supreme Court heard several claims that the recently enacted Fourteenth Amendment (1868) prohibited discrimination against women. The Fourteenth Amendment provided that no state shall deprive any person of the "equal protection of the laws" or of the "privileges and immunities" of federal citizenship. Myra Bradwell had applied for admission to the bar and was rejected by the Illinois Supreme Court based on an Illinois state law that made no provision for admitting women to practice. Bradwell appealed to the U.S. Supreme Court, arguing that one of the privileges the new Fourteenth Amendment guaranteed was the right to practice a profession. A majority of the Court upheld the Illinois decision, ruling that the right to practice law was not one of the privileges of federal citizenship. In a concurring opinion, Justice Bradley elaborated on the Court's rationale, which was based on the "separate spheres" of life occupied by men and women:

> Man is, or should be, woman's protector and defender. The natural and proper timidity and delicacy which belongs to the female sex evidently unfits it for many of the occupations of civil life. The constitution of the family organization, which is founded in the divine ordinance, as well as in the nature of things, indicates the domestic sphere as that which properly belongs to the domain and functions of womanhood. The harmony, not to say identity, of interests and views which

belong or should belong to the family institution, is repugnant to the idea of a woman adopting a distinct and independent career from that of her husband. . . . The paramount destiny and mission of woman are to fulfill the noble and benign offices of wife and mother. This is the law of the Creator.[4]

Without a federal right to practice in the legal profession, women were left to fight repeatedly for the right to be lawyers in individual states and territories. (Several of the first to succeed were Lavinia Goodell, who practiced in the trial courts of Wisconsin before being denied admission to the Wisconsin Supreme Court bar in 1875; Clara Shortridge Foltz, who was admitted to practice in California in 1878; and Belva Lockwood, who became the first female member of the bar of the U.S. Supreme Court in 1879.)

In 1875 the Supreme Court in *Minor v. Happersett*[5] held that the Fourteenth Amendment did not confer on women the right to vote. Just as the right to practice a profession was not a privilege of federal citizenship, neither was the right to vote. The *Minor* Court determined that the Fourteenth Amendment did not extend voting rights to women. Women would need an independent constitutional amendment guaranteeing that right.

The movement for that separate amendment encompassed a sweep of several generations of effort. The battle for suffrage included countless meetings, newspaper articles, grassroots initiatives, organization of suffrage associations, conventions, lectures, and speeches. Elizabeth Cady Stanton and Susan B. Anthony, for instance, traveled across the country by stagecoach and train to give addresses on the public lecture circuit. Early media events, such as the trial of Anthony for unlawfully voting (for Ulysses S. Grant) in the 1872 election, drew attention to the cause of suffrage. Later suffragists protested and organized pickets at the U.S. Capitol.

Passage and ratification of the suffrage amendment took an extraordinary amount of sustained energy on the part of individuals and organizations. Suffragist Carrie Chapman Catt described the more than half century of political campaigns that culminated in the ratification of the Nineteenth Amendment in 1920:

Hundreds of women gave the accumulated possibilities of an entire lifetime, thousands gave years of their lives, hundreds of thousands gave constant interest, and such aid as they could. It was a continuous, seemingly endless, chain of activity. Young suffragists who helped forge the last links of that chain were not born when it began. Old suffragists who forged the first links were dead when it ended. . . . During that time they were forced to conduct fifty-six campaigns of referenda to male voters; 480 campaigns to urge Legislatures to submit suffrage amendments to voters; 47 campaigns to induce State constitutional conventions to write woman suffrage into State constitutions; 277 campaigns to persuade State party conventions to include woman suffrage planks; 30 campaigns to urge presidential party conventions to adopt woman suffrage planks in party platforms, and 19 campaigns with 19 successive Congresses.[6]

Voting rights for women were only the initial step in a still-continuing battle for equal rights.

C. *The Equal Rights Amendment*

In 1923, three years after ratification of the Nineteenth Amendment, Alice Paul, of the National Woman's Party, first proposed an equal rights amendment ("ERA") to Congress: "Men and women shall have equal rights throughout the United States and every place subject to its jurisdiction." The ERA was proposed in Congress every year for the next fifty years until the last version of it—"Equality of rights under the law shall not be denied or abridged by the United States or by any State on account of sex"—finally passed both chambers in 1972. The ERA failed to achieve the constitutionally required ratification by three-fourths of the states. Only thirty-five of the necessary thirty-eight states ratified the ERA during its seven-year (later congressionally extended by three more years) deadline, and the amendment lapsed in 1982.

Commentators speculate on why the ERA failed. In addition to deep attachments to the status quo on the part of both men and women, a constitutional amendment seemed unnecessary to many people who saw no urgent social problem but instead believed equality was being achieved. America had just witnessed the expansion of women's educational and employment rights with the passage of Title VII in 1964. Conservatives viewed recent decisions of the Warren

Court—particularly *Roe v. Wade*[7] in 1973—as much too liberal, and this crystallized additional opposition to the ERA. This relatively rapid progress for women was coupled with uncertainties about what the ERA would mean. Some women feared that husbands' obligations to support their wives would lapse, and they shivered away from unisex bathrooms and the prospects of military service. (The argument of ERA supporters that women were small and would fit well in tanks had little appeals.) The role played by entrenched opposition to equality should not be underestimated: fundamentalist religious groups such as Jerry Falwell's Moral Majority, political action groups such as Concerned Women for America and Phyllis Schlafly's Eagle Forum, and other conservative leaders portrayed the amendment as an attack on homemakers.

Even today, constitutional scholars even today debate the significance of the failed ratification: what its consequences might have been; whether the landscape of gender rights would look different if the ERA had passed; whether the symbolic loss of the ERA may have actually galvanized support for more extensive individual rights on a state level. Eighteen states (Alaska, California, Colorado, Connecticut, Hawaii, Illinois, Louisiana, Maryland, Massachusetts, Montana, New Hampshire, New Mexico, Pennsylvania, Texas, Utah, Virginia, Washington, Wyoming) have state equal rights amendments, many of which were adopted during the 1970s. But their provisions vary widely. Pennsylvania's mirrors the federal ERA: "Equality of rights under the law shall not be denied or abridged in the Commonwealth of Pennsylvania because of the sex of the individual." Connecticut's law is more elaborate: "No person shall be denied the equal protection of the law nor be subjected to segregation or discrimination in the exercise or enjoyment of his or her civil or political rights because of religion, race, color, ancestry, national origin, sex or physical or mental disability." California's, adopted in 1879, states: "A person may not be disqualified from entering or pursuing a business, profession, vocation, or employment because of sex, race, creed, color, or national or ethnic origin."

As with the suffrage movement, the ERA campaign gained an importance beyond its specific objectives. The project helped build networks and organizations whose work continues today. The converse is also true—without a unifying goal like the ERA, some alliances in the feminist movement are beginning to crumble.

D. *Varieties of Contemporary Feminist Legal Theory*

Feminism has been described as a house with many rooms. Theorists have offered a variety of ways to classify these chambers, or schools, of feminist theory. This book will focus on feminist *legal* theory. It will not address schools of feminism sometimes encountered in political or social theory, such as Marxist feminism, humanist feminism, third-wave feminism, psychoanalytic feminism, or French feminism. Feminist legal theories emphasize the role of law in describing society and in prescribing change, while other types of feminist theory might de-emphasize or even question the role of law in these areas. Despite the difference, there has been some free exchange among nonlegal feminist scholars and legal feminist scholars. The principal categories of feminist legal theory we will introduce are equal treatment theory, cultural feminism, dominance theory, lesbian feminism, critical race feminism, postmodern feminism, pragmatic feminism, and ecofeminism. Of course, these divisions are not discrete, and many feminists defy categorization. Some of these theories are overlapping. At times people may disagree as to what kind of feminist a particular writer is. It is important to keep in mind that these are loose categories that help feminists manage discussion, not memberships into particular clubs.

Most early feminist litigation relied on **equal treatment theory,** which says that the law should treat people who are similarly situated exactly alike. Perhaps in part as a reaction to the historical treatment of women as in need of special protection, equal treatment theorists stressed the ways women were similar to men and used this as the platform for claiming equal employment and economic benefits. In the 1970s and 1980s, organizations such as the ACLU Women's Rights Project and the National Organization for Women ("NOW") won a series of lawsuits in the Supreme Court that helped dismantle barriers for women as breadwinners, property owners, and economic players. In the 1971 case of *Reed v. Reed*,[8] the Court struck an Idaho law that gave an automatic preference to male relatives over female relatives as administrators of decedents' estates. Two years later, in *Frontiero v. Richardson*,[9] the Supreme Court held unconstitutional a benefits policy in the military that presumed all wives of servicemen were financially dependent on their husbands, but that did not make the same presumption in the case of *husbands* of *servicewomen*. In his opinion for the Court, Justice Brennan observed that "our Nation has had a long and unfortunate history of sex discrimination . . . rationalized by an attitude of 'romantic paternalism' which, in practical effect, put women, not on a pedestal, but in a cage." In *Taylor v. Louisiana,*[10] the Court struck down a Louisiana statute that excluded women from serving on juries unless they specifically opted into the pool. In 1982, in *Mississippi University for Women v. Hogan,*[11] the Court ruled that a state nursing school's policy of limiting its enrollment to women denied males equal protection under the Constitution. Many suits during this time also began to enforce the anti-sex discrimination mandate of Title VII of the Civil Rights Act of 1964.

Cultural feminists criticized the sameness model as male-biased, serving women only to the extent they could prove they were like men. Purely formal equality of opportunity did not lead to equality of results. People judged women harshly based on their inability to conform to the male norm. Much of cultural feminism, including its legal adaptations, is based on the work of educational psychologist Carol Gilligan, who noted in her 1982 book, *In a Different Voice: Psychological Theory and Women's Development,* that women and men display different emotional and cognitive traits and social skills. Women reason with an ethic of care, emphasizing connections and relations with other people, while men reason with an ethic of rights, stressing rules and autonomy concerns. Advocates of special treatment urged a model that focuses on differences between the sexes—whether rooted in culture or biology: differences in reproductive functions, caretaking responsibilities, and even emotions and perceptions, such as the ways women perceive rape, sexual harassment, and various aspects of reproduction. Cultural feminists say that significant differences between men and women should be acknowledged and compensated legally where they disadvantage one sex. They have favored special maternity leaves, flexible work arrangements, or other workplace accommodations for women.

Dominance theory rejects the sameness-difference debate, noting that both used the male standard as the primary benchmark—with equal treatment theorists emphasizing how similar women are to men, and cultural feminists celebrating how different women are from men. These feminists focus instead on the difference in *power* between women and men. They study the subordination of women and the domination of men in every sphere: social, political, and economic.

Law is complicit with other social institutions in constructing women as sex objects and as inferior, dependent beings. Dominance theorists cite the lack of legal controls on pornography and sexual harassment, excessive restrictions on abortion, and inadequate responses to violence against women as examples of the ways laws contribute to the oppression of women.

Postmodern feminist legal theory presents another attempt to move beyond the categories of sameness and difference. Postmodern feminists argue the comparative approaches of equal treatment ("women are like men") and cultural feminism ("women are *not* like men") inaccurately assume that *all* women are roughly the same, as are *all* men. This assumption is particularly false—and damaging—when speaking of women or men across the lines of race, economics, or country of origin. Postmodern feminist legal theorists therefore reject notions of single truths and recognize instead that truths are multiple, provisional, and thus linked to individuals' lived experiences, perspectives, and positions in the world.

Feminists influenced by postmodernism view gender not as natural, fixed, or objective, but as socially constructed, relative, dependent on experiences, and mutable over time and according to situations. They stress that individuals have multiple identities and play multiple roles. Gender is performed or presented (through, among other things, clothing, work, and mannerisms) differently each day. Some question the usefulness of analysis based on the identity category "women" because it is a category without any unified content—few experiences are shared by all women, differences among women trump their similarities, single individuals may have multiple viewpoints—and because what content exists in the category of "women" already carries with it a picture of the world embedded with traditional conceptions of women's abilities and characteristics.

Critical race feminists make the political point that feminism has for decades centered on the lives and stories of white women. By pointing the spotlight only on gender, traditional white feminists ignore important differences that exist *among* women, most notably, differences of race. In their rejection of a universal female experience, critical race feminists share a feature with postmodern feminists. Critical race feminists emphasize the ways racism, sexism, and classism often intersect in the lives of men and women of color. In the job market, poor women of color must overcome a "triple" disadvantage, as they confront challenges of income, sex, and race. Immigrant women suffer intimate violence at higher rates than other populations; and, faced with threats of deportation, they lack support services, shelters, and legal representation. Men of color are prosecuted more often, convicted more readily, and sentenced more harshly than white men or women. Critical race theorists reject formal equality as being empty, because formal guarantees of equality accept current measures of merit, such as one-dimensional standardized tests and traditional employment credentials. Critical race feminists sometimes employ a more personal kind of storytelling or narrative scholarship to explain how multiple forms of oppression shape the lives of people of color.

Lesbian legal theory focuses on the legal issues confronted by lesbians, gay men, bisexuals, transsexuals, and the transgendered (collectively "LGBT"). Beginning in the 1970s, some lesbian feminists wrote that sexual orientation is more about politics than desire. Lesbian theorists rejected the portrayal of LGBT people as deviant by drawing on scientific evidence about sexuality that showed the prevalence of same-sex inclinations and the spectrum of different sexualities. In law, numerous gay and lesbian theorists cataloged the basic civic rights that the government denies to nonheterosexuals: rights to marry, to serve openly in the military (the "Don't Ask, Don't Tell" policy), to adopt children, and to hold jobs without discrimination. In more than two-thirds of the states, it is still legal to fire lesbians, gay men, bisexuals, and transfolk because of their sexuality. To escape the oppression, subordination, and exclusion, gay and lesbian legal theorists have tried a range of arguments, from constitutional (debating whether gays and lesbians are a suspect class deserving heightened scrutiny under the equal protection clause) to communitarian (emphasizing the common humanity of all people).

Pragmatic legal feminism offers as a primary insight that a search for contextual solutions is typically more useful than abstract theorizing. Different times and contexts may necessitate different approaches or outcomes. Many feminist issues are presented in concrete, specific settings. For example, the issue might be whether a particular law firm should institute a nonpartnership track to allow parents more family time with their children. A concern of some feminists might be that this would become a "mommy track," a form of second-class citizenship utilized primarily or even exclusively by female lawyers. A pragmatic feminist might view the parent track not as a perfect outcome (a more ideal outcome might be to modify billable hour requirements for all the lawyers in a firm), but as the best possible among less-than-ideal choices: a way of expanding the choices and assisting in the reconciliation of family-work conflicts for some individuals who are most affected at that place and time. Pragmatic feminists recognize the danger of universals and look for context-specific solutions.

Ecofeminism emphasizes gender inequality within the context of environmental destruction. Its analysis begins with the premise that the oppression of nature and the oppression of women are intrinsically connected. In this view, sexism and environmental degradation are both preceded by a duality in Western thought that puts the "masculine" features of mind and soul (abstract reasoning, judgments about risk taking, quantitative methods, technology) in charge of the "feminine" features of nature and the body (plants, animals, reproduction, intuition). Most ecofeminists challenge this dominance of masculine ideals by promoting greater respect for the feminine "nature-based" values, a strategy reminiscent of cultural feminism. Other ecofeminists argue that the duality between male and female is overemphasized and should give way to a more unified attack on oppression in general. This strategy is reminiscent of dominance theory. While the ecofeminist movement appears to have its strongest following outside of the United States, its American advocates have proved to be very enthusiastic and creative. In the United States, ecofeminists have campaigned for animal rights, security for migrant farmworkers, better health care for women, and environmental protection for Native Americans.

E. Unifying Themes and Divisions

While the different strands of feminist legal theory have their distinct features, they are generally committed to a similar goal: equal and fair gender relations. All feminist legal theories are mindful of power differences between the sexes. And they all work to make such differences visible to citizens and policymakers. They typically lean toward inclusive, rather than exclusive, arrangements. Most tend to favor collective rather than individualist solutions. Nearly all challenge the public-private distinction, seeing much greater room for state responsibility in matters (such as intimate violence) that formerly had been thought of as purely private.

These schools of feminist legal theory are also drawn together by the methodologies they use, such as consciousness-raising, revealing gendered assumptions and unmasking patriarchy, the use of stories and the political implications of personal experiences, an emphasis on voices not represented in the dominant tradition, contextual reasoning that focuses on particulars of experience, and asking questions about the gendered impact of policies or laws.

Much feminist legal theory is interdisciplinary. Feminists writing in law have drawn on works in philosophy and educational psychology to evaluate legal rules that emphasize rights over relationships. They use understandings from sociolinguistics about patterns of dominance and subordination in discourse—the ways men often speak authoritatively while women often speak deferentially—to assess the treatment of female attorneys in courtroom presentations. They make use of a vast array of empirical evidence, such as sociological studies about occupational segregation by sex to develop theories like comparable worth to remedy pay disparities between men and women. Central to all branches of feminist legal theory are the ideas that women are socially, politically, and legally subordinated and undervalued.

This book will also highlight some of the divisions, contradictions, and tensions in feminist legal theory and litigation. For instance, in the debate regarding whether pornography should be censored, celebrated feminists Catharine MacKinnon and Andrea Dworkin drafted an antipornography ordinance, which was passed by the City of Indianapolis. In subsequent litigation over its constitutionality, the Feminist Anti-Censorship Task Force, a group opposing the regulation of pornography, submitted an amicus brief to the Seventh Circuit, arguing that its protective approach would promote sexist stereotypes and undermine efforts toward equality between the sexes. In *California Federal Savings & Loan Association v. Guerra*,[12] feminist organizations submitted amicus briefs to the Supreme Court on both sides of the question whether a California statute that granted paid maternity leave to women discriminated against men. On the equal treatment side were NOW and the League of Women Voters, who argued that California should be required to provide parallel disability leave for all workers incapacitated for a similar period of time, not just pregnant women. The Supreme Court agreed with the law professors and groups who supported the statute because women physically and socially bear a greater burden from childbirth and newborn care. In *EEOC v. Sears, Roebuck & Co.*,[13] each side hired a feminist historian to act as an expert witness on the question of whether women lacked interest in higher-paying commissioned sales jobs that sold fencing and automotive supplies and just naturally gravitated toward "the softer side of Sears" to sell cosmetics, linens, and clothing. These tensions between competing visions of equality replay themselves throughout feminist legal history and litigation. We take no positions on these issues, but believe the ultimate instructional value of these debates is immense.

NOTES

1. Howard Fineman, *Some Hard Right Turns for the GOP*, NEWSWEEK, June 20, 1994, at 38.

2. *See, e.g.*, CARLETON MABEE, SOJOURNER TRUTH: SLAVE, PROPHET, LEGEND 67–82 (1993).

3. 83 U.S. (16 Wall.) 130 (1872).

4. *Id.* at 141 (Bradley, J., concurring).

5. 88 U.S. (21 Wall.) 162 (1874).

6. CARRIE CHAPMAN CATT & NETTIE ROGERS SHULER, WOMAN SUFFRAGE AND POLITICS: THE INNER STORY OF THE SUFFRAGE MOVEMENT 107–08 (1923).

7. 410 U.S. 113 (1973).

8. 404 U.S. 71 (1971).

9. 411 U.S. 677 (1973).

10. 419 U.S. 522 (1975).

11. 458 U.S. 718 (1982).

12. 479 U.S. 272 (1987).

13. 628 F. Supp. 1264 (N.D. Ill. 1986), *aff'd*, 839 F.2d 302 (7th Cir. 1988).

2

Feminist Legal Theories

*Feminism is a dirty word. . . . Misconceptions abound. Feminists
are portrayed as bra-burners, manhaters, sexists, and castrators.
Our sexual preferences are presumed. We are characterized as
bitchy, . . . aggressive, confrontational, and uncooperative, as well
as overly demanding and humorless.*   Leslie Bender[1]

[W]oman is the Other.   Simone de Beauvoir[2]

What is distinctive about feminist *legal* theory? Do criteria exist for
who can be a "feminist"? Are there compulsory feminist beliefs?
What is the meaning of equality?

Feminist legal theory grew out of the general feminist movement.
Many of the first rights the women's movement fought for were political rights, like the right to vote. Some of the early strategies—such as
Sojourner Truth's claim to equal treatment because she had
"ploughed and planted" just like a man—foreshadowed visions of
equality that would emerge as important *legal* theories in later years.
Often, feminist political action preceded feminist legal theory. While
feminist lawyers were urging courts in the 1960s and early 1970s to
address gender inequalities, it was not until the later 1970s and early
1980s that legal scholars developed distinct branches of feminist legal
theory.

All feminist theories share two things—the first an observation, the
second an aspiration. First, feminists recognize that the world has
been shaped by men, particularly white men, who for this reason pos-
sess larger shares of power and privilege. All feminist legal scholars
emphasize the rather obvious (but unspoken) point that nearly all

public laws in the history of existing civilization were written by men. If such laws give men a leg up, this news can hardly come as a surprise. Second, all feminists believe that women and men should have political, social, and economic equality. But while feminists agree on the goal of equality, they disagree about its meaning and on how to achieve it.

A. Equal Treatment Theory

Sex-based generalizations are generally impermissible whether derived from physical differences such as size and strength, from cultural role assignments such as breadwinner or homemaker, or from some combination of innate and ascribed characteristics, such as the greater longevity of the average woman compared to the average man.

Wendy W. Williams[3]

The first wave of feminist legal theory began in the early 1960s with the emergence of equal treatment theory (also referred to as liberal or sameness feminism). Equal treatment theory is based on the principle of formal equality that inspired the suffrage movement, namely, that women are entitled to the same rights as men. The theory drew from liberal ideals in philosophy and political theory that endorse equal citizenship, equal opportunities in the public arena, individualism, and rationality.[4] The equal treatment principles were simple: the law should not treat a woman differently from a similarly situated man. Also, the law should not base decisions about individual women on generalizations (even statistically accurate ones) about women as a group.

Early efforts to attain equal treatment for women pursued two goals. The first was to obtain equivalent social and political opportunities, such as equal wages, equal employment, and equal access to government benefits. The second was to do away with legislation intended to protect women by isolating them from the public sphere. Examples of such protectionist legislation included limiting women's career options or employment hours.

In the 1970s, the ACLU created a Women's Rights Project ("WRP") to bring sex discrimination lawsuits. Under the direction of Ruth Bader Ginsburg, the WRP followed the strategy of civil rights pioneers in seeking formal equality. To obtain equal treatment under the Constitution, women had to establish that they were "similarly situated" to men, so WRP lawyers argued that women did not differ from men in ways that should matter legally. They persuaded the Supreme Court that men and women were equally qualified to administer estates, so a law that preferred males was unconstitutional,[5] and that female members of the military deserved the same family benefits as male service members.[6] The WRP initially adopted a strategy that used male plaintiffs to challenge laws that, at least superficially, favored women. WRP lawyers surmised that since most judges were men, they would see discrimination best if they could see themselves as its possible victims.

The strategy produced mixed results. The Court upheld a law giving widows, but not widowers, a property tax exemption. The state tax exemption, in the Court's view, was an appropriate equalizing measure for the discrimination that women encounter in the job market, because the law was "reasonably designed to further the state policy of cushioning the financial impact of spousal loss upon the sex for which that loss imposes a disproportionately heavy burden."[7] On the other hand, the Court struck down a law that prohibited the sale of low-alcohol beer to females under the age of eighteen and males under the age of twenty-one, based on the supposedly greater traffic safety risks posed by underage males.[8] When the state presented only weak evidence of a correlation between gender and driving drunk, the Court rejected the stereotype that young men were more reckless than young women.

One of the strengths of Ginsburg's approach in litigating the equal treatment cases was that she directly attacked the notion that "natural" differences justified dissimilar treatment under the law. She showed that many of these differences were socially constructed—that social norms prescribed different roles for men and women. She also argued that if biological differences distinguished the sexes, discrimination based on these immutable differences justified a higher level of judicial scrutiny.

During the late 1970s and 1980s, the formal equality tactic was usually successful in eliminating explicit barriers to equal treatment. The Supreme Court found that a statute imposing obligations only on husbands to pay alimony violated equal protection, as did a congressman's discharge of a female administrative assistant because of her sex.[9] Nursing schools could not reject potential students because they were male; attorneys could not reject potential jurors because they were female.[10] In some cases, though, the Court permitted women to recoup such benefits as extra Social Security allotments as compensation for market disadvantages they experienced.[11]

Equal treatment theory opened many doors for women, particularly in the areas of education and employment. Its rationale was easy to understand and accepted by the mainstream. Part of the reason the strategy won public support was that it targeted individual instances of inequality and sought only gradual change. But theory was incremental and slow-moving. In addition, equal treatment lawsuits remained focused on public activities—such as taxes, liquor sales, and education, rather than the more controversial realm of personal behavior.

Equal treatment theory accepts male experience as the reference point or norm. Women attain equality only to the extent that they are similarly situated with men. One flaw in this approach is that its emphasis on similarity disadvantages women on issues related to pregnancy and childbirth. A new camp of thinkers, cultural feminists, criticized equal treatment theory for failing to protect women when they are not similarly situated to men.

B. Cultural Feminism

I will never be in a man's place, a man will never be in mine. Whatever the possible identifications, one will never exactly occupy the place of the other—they are irreducible the one to the other. Luce Irigaray[12]

Cultural feminism (also called difference theory or, sometimes pejoratively, special treatment theory) argues that formal equality does not always result in substantive equality. Gender-neutral laws can keep women down if they do not acknowledge women's different experiences and perspectives. This theory emphasizes the differences between men and women, whether the biological differences related to childbearing or the cultural differences reflected in social relationships. Cultural feminists note that many institutions, such as the workplace, follow rules based heavily on male-dominated experiences, which can disadvantage women. For instance, the voluntary quit rules of unemployment compensation typically disqualify from receiving benefits people (predominantly women) who leave their jobs because of work-family conflicts. Damages in most tort cases are based on anticipated losses of future earning capacity, so female plaintiffs often receive damage awards discounted by anticipated work absences during child-rearing years. Traditional self-defense rules in criminal law, which require an imminent threat before a defense is allowed, offer limited protection to a battered woman who, though she lives in constant fear of a domestic attack, is unable to predict exactly when her partner will strike.

Cultural feminists argue that men and women should not be treated the same where they are relevantly different and that women should not be required to assimilate to male norms. They urge instead a concept of legal equality in which laws accommodate the biological and cultural differences between men and women. Some cultural feminists see the connectedness of women as rooted in biological as well as cultural origins. They maintain that women are "essentially connected" to other humans, through the physical connections of intercourse, pregnancy, and breastfeeding, and to humanity, through an ethic of care. The problem with legal theory, then, is that it "is essentially and irretrievably masculine" because it treats humans as distinct, physically unconnected, and separate from others.[13]

Cultural feminist theory in law drew on the "different voice" scholarship of educational psychologist Carol Gilligan.[14] Gilligan challenged the dominant theory in psychology, associated with Lawrence Kohlberg, that use of abstract concepts of justice and rights was correlated with higher stages of moral development. She advanced the theory that boys and girls learn different methods of moral reasoning. Girls are taught to value empathy, compassion, preservation of harmony, and a sense of community, while boys are taught to privilege abstract moral principles, rights, autonomy, and individualism. Girls grow into women who reason with "an ethic of care," and boys become men who reason with "an ethic of justice." Men value abstract rights, while women appreciate human relationships.

Some feminists have criticized Gilligan's methodology as anecdotal, arbitrary in its assignment of characteristics as masculine or feminine, and based on an inadequate sample of privileged subjects. A number of these critics deny that many differences exist along gender lines, pointing out that more variation exists among women than between men and women.[15] Others say that creating social policies with an emphasis on differences will reinforce gender stereotypes. Gilligan has replied to these methodological critiques, and others have supported her findings, although the empirical support has not been strong.[16] But, intriguingly, these criticisms have not diminished the general acceptance of her theories.

Cultural feminism does more than identify women's differences; it applauds them: "Cultural feminists, to their credit, have reidentified these differences as women's strengths, rather than women's weaknesses. Women's art, women's craft, women's narrative capacity, women's critical eye, women's ways of knowing, and women's heart, are all, for the cultural feminist, redefined as things to celebrate."[17] In other words, "Viva la différence!"

Legal theorists argued that this distinctively feminine approach to moral and legal reasoning had been omitted, or at least discounted, in law. Feminist legal theorists used Gilligan's work to argue for a rethinking of some long-accepted rules of law. For instance, under traditional tort law, which values individual autonomy, citizens have no obligation to assist strangers in need, even when they can do so without putting themselves in any jeopardy. In almost all states, one can watch a blind person walk into traffic with no legal obligation even to yell out a warning. (It is not nice, but it is not tortious.) Using the idea that law ought to encourage communal responsibilities of care, feminist legal scholars advocated the creation of tort duties to assist strangers who are in peril. Some cultural feminists argued that women, who more often organize their lives around caregiving relationships, have been harmed by gender-neutral custody standards. Others have advocated less adversarial, more cooperative styles of lawyering, such as a greater use of mediation as opposed to litigation. More generally, cultural feminists argued for a movement away from a male-oriented rights model and a greater incorporation into law of an ethic of care.

A primary criticism of cultural feminism is that it values women only if they adopt conventional social roles. In celebrating attributes associated with women—empathy, nurturing, caretaking—cultural feminism reinforces women's stereotypical association with domesticity. Another objection is that it characterizes women as needing special protection. As the Supreme Court observed, protectionist laws historically have disadvantaged women by putting them "not on a pedestal, but in a cage."[18]

The question of which model—formal equality or celebration of difference—leads to more fairness is known as the "equal treatment–special treatment" or "sameness-difference" debate. A key disagreement between equal treatment theorists and cultural feminists concerns pregnancy and maternity leave. A 1987 Supreme Court case, *California Federal Savings & Loan Association v. Guerra ("Cal Fed")*,[19] illustrates the positions of the two camps. In *Cal Fed* a California statute required employers to provide women up to four months of unpaid maternity leave, but it did not require similar leave for other temporary disabilities. Cultural feminists and equal treatment theorists filed "friend of the court" briefs on opposite sides of the case. Equal treatment theorists, including the ACLU's Women's Rights Project and NOW's Legal Defense and Education Fund, argued that the state law violated federal Title VII provisions, because employers refused similar leaves to workers with other temporary "disabilities." They contended that special treatment for pregnant women reinforced stereotypes that women in the workforce need protective legislation. In support of the state law, a cultural feminist group, the Coalition for Reproductive Equality in the Workplace ("CREW"), argued that biological differences between men and women justified different leave policies and that accommodation of pregnancy would actually promote Title VII's goal of workplace equality: "[W]ithout the statute, women were forced to choose between having children and maintaining job security—a choice not imposed on men."[20]

Thus, equal treatment theorists maintained that pregnancy should be treated the same as other disabilities, while cultural feminists countered that a pregnancy-specific disability policy was constitutional and sensible because pregnancy is a unique condition that burdens only women. The Supreme Court upheld the state law, noting that "[b]y 'taking pregnancy into account,' California's pregnancy disability leave statute allows women, as well as men, to have families without losing their jobs."[21]

Following the *Cal Fed* debate, the sameness and difference camps attempted to join hands in support of the Family and Medical Leave Act ("FMLA"). Recent scholarship, though, demonstrates the recurrent divide between equal treatment and cultural feminist groups. For example, with respect to the FMLA, theorists have observed that, in practice, "only mothers take leave," which means that the statute "only accommodates women's caretaking, protection that gives them a measure of job security but at the same time preserves employers' incentive to prefer male employees."[22] One possible resolution is to require paid family leave, which would remove part of the disincentive for men to assume primary caregiving responsibilities.

Theorists continue to argue about which model better promotes true equality: the assimilation model that emphasizes the sameness between women and men or the accommodation model that stresses their differences. The debates continue with respect to such issues as a parent track that permits working parents to work less than full-time so that they can devote time to child rearing; custody rules that favor the "primary caregiver" (or whether that presumption discriminates against men); and whether the principles of formal equality that underlie dramatic decreases in maintenance (alimony) result in poverty for nonworking mothers. Some feminists have tried to move beyond the equal treatment–special treatment divide by questioning basic institutional structures and the social ideas that perpetuate them. Joan Williams, for example, asks whether the work world needs to be built around the norm of an "ideal worker" who can work full-time plus overtime and has no child care responsibilities.[23] Theorists have recognized that equal treatment poses difficulties by ignoring real differences, while different treatment "is a double-edged sword permitting unfavorable as well as favorable treatment against an historic background of separate spheres ideology."[24] For law professor Martha Minow, the difference dilemma boils down to a single question: "When does treating people differently emphasize their difference and stigmatize and hinder them on that basis, and when does treating people the same become insensitive to their differences and likely to stigmatize or hinder them on that basis?"[25]

C. Dominance Theory

Take your foot off our necks, and then we will hear in what tongue women speak.   Catharine A. MacKinnon[26]

First introduced in 1979 by Catharine MacKinnon, dominance theory (or radical feminism) focuses on the power relations between men and women. Dominance theory argues that the inequalities women experience as sex discrimination in the economic, political, and familial arenas result from patterns of male domination. This theory says that men are privileged and women are subordinated, and this male privileging receives support from most social institutions, as well as a complex system of cultural beliefs.

Dominance theory departs from equal treatment theory and cultural feminism, criticizing both sameness and difference approaches for allowing men to be the metric or norm: "Under the sameness standard, women are measured according to our correspondence with man, our equality judged by our proximity to his measure," while "[u]nder the difference standard, we are measured according to our lack of correspondence with him."[27] The goal of both equal treatment theory and cultural feminism is equivalence between women and men; the goal of dominance theory is liberation from men.

In particular, dominance theory provided a different perspective on violence against women in areas such as rape, intimate violence, and sexual harassment. Equality theories were ill equipped to address these experiences, since they "failed to address the patriarchal structures of power that led to and perpetuated them."[28] Patriarchy means the rule or "power of the fathers." It is a system of social and political practices in which men subordinate and exploit women. The subordination occurs through complex patterns of force, social pressures, and traditions, rituals, and customs. This domination does not just occur in individual relationships, but is supported by the major institutions in society.

Within the family, men, as "heads of the household," control women. Domestic violence is domination in an extreme form. This dominance is tolerated, since the criminal justice system imposes lenient sentences on people who perpetrate violence against women. In the employment sphere, a gendered division of labor occurs whereby women are segregated into inferior-status jobs at lower wages. Dominance theorists have demonstrated the ways that laws, most of which have been drafted by men, assist in reinforcing male domination. For instance, in most states, a rape victim must prove she did not consent, even where violence occurs. As another example, in the law of unemployment insurance, if women are forced to quit jobs for family reasons (such as a lack of child care), they are not eligible for compensation.

Patriarchy is created and reinforced by a system of beliefs that says men should be superior in education, employment, politics, and religion. It is "a political structure that values men more than women."[29] Women are relegated to the status of second-class citizens. Catharine MacKinnon describes the ways men are dominant and privileged:

> Men's physiology defines most sports, their needs define auto and health insurance coverage, their socially designed biographies define workplace expectations and successful career patterns, their perspectives and concerns define quality in scholarship, their experiences and obsessions define merit, their objectification of life defines art, their military service defines citizenship, their presence defines family, their inability to get along with each other—their wars and rulerships—defines history, their image defines god, and their genitals define sex.[30]

The media display degrading images that treat women as possessions, while the legal system supports these demeaning depictions as protected speech. Women are forced into stereotypic molds that demand they present themselves as feminine and deferential, and assume a disproportionate share of the responsibility for housework, child care, and elder care. Patriarchy gives men control of women's sexuality, their reproductive freedom, and their lives.

Patriarchy includes sexual domination by men and sexual submission by women. Sexuality in this society focuses on men's desires and satisfaction. Women live with the fear of rape and sexual abuse. They learn to trade on their sexuality for advancement. Women are treated in the work environment as objects of attraction rather than professional peers. Women are represented, in everything from fashion ads to pornography, as sexual objects or commodities.

In 1983 Andrea Dworkin and Catharine MacKinnon proposed an antipornography ordinance that created a cause of action for sex discrimination for pornography that showed "the graphic sexually explicit subordination of women, whether in pictures or in words," and women being "presented as sexual objects."[31] The outcome of the antipornography campaign is discussed in Chapter 6, but for present purposes, this attempt to translate one type of feminist legal theory into law is an example of dominance theory's sweeping critique of patriarchy and the search for systematic and institutional remedies.

Patriarchy shapes men, too, when it values characteristics associated with traditional definitions of masculinity, so that men learn to reject intimacy and repress emotions. Both men and women are socialized toward stereotypic gender behaviors characteristic of their sex. Men who do not conform to traditional images of manliness and who act in effeminate ways are considered a threat to masculinity and are not only subordinated like women, but often punished for their gender transgressions.[32]

One method of promoting the traditional patriarchal structure is to discourage same-sex relationships and compel heterosexuality. "Compulsory heterosexuality"[33] occurs through legal rules, such as the military's "Don't Ask, Don't Tell" policy, and through much more subtle forms of cultural indoctrination, ranging from the male fear of all things pink to the epidemic use of "faggot" among high school boys (just as popular in our day). Politicians, better than most, understand our subconscious attraction to the alpha male. Thus, in the 2004 Republican National Convention, California governor Arnold Schwarzenegger mocked critics of his party's economic plan by calling them economic "girlie men."[34]

When women live in a patriarchal society, they may internalize the beliefs of the dominant group. They may seek out, choose, and even enjoy dependent or submissive relationships or caretaking roles. "Women value care," according to MacKinnon, "because men have valued us according to the care we give them. . . . Women think in relational terms because our existence is defined in relation to men."[35] This psychological aspect of oppression is called "false consciousness."

To create awareness of oppression and expose this system of internalized beliefs, MacKinnon suggests that women engage in "consciousness-raising"—that they join women—only groups and discuss their experiences with housework, sexuality, caregiving, and menial jobs. Through this process women will make visible to themselves and each other the daily micro-inequities that are the product of male privilege and build collective knowledge about their experiences of oppression.

Other feminists have criticized the idea of false consciousness—that women cannot make independent choices—as "infuriatingly condescending," and the remedy of consciousness-raising as unworkable because relating personal experiences will not inevitably lead to political solutions.[36] Dominance theory has also drawn criticism for "gender essentialism"—the assumption that all women share the same experience—namely, that of victims. Critics have also charged that dominance theory mistakenly "universalize[s] the experience of white women as the experience of all women, ignoring differences of race, class, and ethnicity," and that it devalues women's experiences as mothers.[37] Nonetheless, the theory has powerfully influenced legal thinking—particularly on the subjects of rape, sexual harassment, and pornography.

D. Critical Race Feminism

> [I]n feminist legal theory, as in the dominant culture, it is mostly white, straight, and socio-economically privileged people who claim to speak for all of us.   Angela P. Harris[38]

In the 1980s, a number of legal theorists, principally women of color and lesbians, complained that feminist legal theory omitted their experiences and concerns. They charged that feminist legal theory doted excessively on the needs of privileged white women. Mainstream feminists made universal assertions about women's experiences (for example, that all women experienced subordination or that women are generally more nurturing and compassionate than men). This phenomenon of "feminist essentialism"—that "a unitary, 'essential' women's experience can be isolated and described independently of race, class, sexual orientation, and other realities of experience"—stifled the voices of lesbians and minority race women "in the name of commonality."[39]

Opponents of essentialism—who call themselves *antiessentialists*—argue that discrimination is best understood not from the center of an oppressed group's membership (meaning for women, white, middle-class, and heterosexual), but from the margins. In other words, discrimination functions differently depending on a person's combination of personal characteristics. Sexism surely affects all women, from the sweatshop seamstress to Martha Stewart. But it is the *intersection* of characteristics like sex, race, wealth, and sexual orientation that really suggests how people will treat you.[40]

Critical race feminists argue that legal doctrines in various areas, such as rape, sexual harassment, and domestic violence, do not adequately address discrimination based on the intersections of these categories. As just one example, the requirement in employment discrimination for a black woman to identify either as a woman or as a racial minority and to claim either sex or race discrimination ignores the ways racism and sexism intertwine.

The multiple categories of human identity suggest another insight of critical race feminism—that people see themselves as having multiple identities. The cashier at your grocery store is not *just* a cashier. She is a mother, perhaps, a Latina, a breast cancer survivor, and much more. This kaleidoscope of roles means not just that people feel oppression at different pressure points, but that, with practice, people can begin to understand oppression from perspectives other than their own. This ability, which law professor Mari Matsuda calls "multiple consciousness," is more than (to use her words) "a random ability to see all points of view, but a deliberate choice to see the world from the standpoint of the oppressed."[41]

Multiple consciousness is important to the study and practice of law: it enables outsiders to use formal legal discourse without losing their empathic understanding—their consciousness—of oppression. This way of thinking makes it possible for lawyers to contemplate laws beyond current rigid doctrines that do not acknowledge powerlessness: to think about tort damages for racial hate speech, to understand the needs of same-sex clients who want to adopt, to envision reparations for slavery. Critical race feminism draws from the critical legal studies movement the idea that many laws are not neutral or objective, as they purport to be, but are actually ways that traditional power relationships are maintained. For example, traditional First Amendment law prohibits people who have been the victims of virulent hate speech from suing for damages. In allowing the vilification of women and people of color, law has been instrumental in continuing hierarchies of gender and race.

The experiences of women of color are not the experiences of most women. One way to blend minority experiences into legal analysis is to tell "stories." Such stories, or personal narratives, introduce readers to challenges and emotions that might otherwise not be considered by majority group members.

When law professor Patricia Williams went Christmas shopping in New York City one year, a white teenager (chomping bubble gum) refused to press the buzzer to admit her to a Benneton store. In a well-known essay, Professor Williams later used this experience to explore the social connections among race, sex, crime, and commerce.[42] Adele

Morrison tells stories of lesbian victims seeking shelter from intimate violence but having their batterers admitted to the safe house because they are also women.[43] Law professor Anthony Alfieri, a former legal aid lawyer, recalls an interview he once had with a woman seeking food stamps. In addition to legal need, the woman's story revealed to him the dignity and pride she felt in caring for children and foster children.[44] As Richard Delgado observes, "Stories, parables, chronicles, and narratives are powerful means for destroying mindset—the bundle of presuppositions, received wisdoms, and shared understandings against a background of which legal and political discourse takes place."[45] The idea is to make law acknowledge the experiences of these outsiders.

Critical race theorists challenge the view that race is a biological phenomenon. Of course, if biological differences among races lead to innate performance differences, this would undermine affirmative-action measures as an instrument in the movement toward equality. It also affirms Bell Curve concepts of educational tests as reflective of "merit." Flatly, it justifies racism as a benign product of naturally occurring differences.

Race theorists have demonstrated that the traits that define races are not biological or genetic categories with much scientific significance.[46] Race is a social construct—a belief system about the importance of skin color. This process of social construction means that the inferior and negative meanings attached to darker races are also social inventions. The biological view of race led to laws in the not distant past prohibiting interracial marriage and justifies contemporary resistance to transracial adoption. Critical race feminists have extended this critique of biological race to demonstrate its continuing influence on laws and legal decisions. They have shown how this belief in genetic race influences courts to make surrogacy decisions that view black women acting as gestational surrogates simply as breeders. They have also exposed how pregnant women of color who use drugs are more likely than white women to be prosecuted on drug charges or for child endangerment, abuse, or neglect.[47]

Critical race feminists believe that a jurisprudential method recognizing "that differences are always relational rather than inherent" can lead to liberation.[48] They also emphasize the instrumental value of storytelling or narrative. Because legal cases always begin with

human stories, making sure the stories of oppression are told—
"speaking truth to power"—is a first step toward equality.[49]

E. Lesbian Feminism

Like critical race feminists, lesbian feminists are antiessentialists, opposing the idea of a universal female experience. Denounced in the
1970s by Betty Friedan, then-president of NOW, as the "lavender
menace," lesbians have long been dismissed by the mainstream feminist movement. This marginalization is an example of the larger phenomenon of dominant subgroups excluding a subordinate one in
order to leverage their own acceptance. Other theorists have made the
point that lesbian feminists have excluded gay men and bisexuals
from their analyses, given minimal attention to the voices of poor lesbians and gays and those of color, and entirely omitted the impact of
laws on transsexuals.[50]

Early lesbian and gay legal theorists revealed the links between heterosexism and sexism. They showed how traditional ideas of masculinity demanded segregation of the sexes, repression of feminine
traits in men, and the exclusion, harassment, and vilification of those
assumed to be sexually deviant. This promoted the supremacy of
"masculinity over femininity as well as the elevation of heterosexuality over all other forms of sexuality."[51] They traced the penalties law
imposes on lesbians and gay men and explained that this condemna-
tion was tied to social meanings of gender that approve only of traditional familial arrangements (think: Ward, June, Wally, and the
Beave).

Concerns of lesbian feminists in law may differ from those of
straight feminists—the latter may be trying to get male partners to assume more child care responsibilities, while the former are fighting to
obtain custody of their children. The daily lives of lesbians are affected in myriad ways by state exclusions from basic benefits, familial
arrangements, and employment rights that straights take for granted.
If you are gay or lesbian, disclosure of your sexual orientation can justify termination from employment. If you have a same-sex partner,
you are not entitled to the same insurance, property, inheritance, custody, or adoption rights as straight couples. The General Accounting

Office has identified 1,049 federal laws in which "benefits, rights and privileges" are dependent upon marriage.[52] For this reason, gays and lesbians generally disfavor the Defense of Marriage Act, a federal bill passed by Congress that limits marriage to opposite-sex couples only. We will look more at the Defense of Marriage Act in **Chapter 7**. A second example involving the military's "Don't Ask, Don't Tell" policy will come in for discussion in **Chapter 4**.

Some legal theorists have written on whether sexual orientation has a biological basis. They have drawn on evidence from the sciences concerning the genetic and biological origins of sexuality: Simon LeVay's autopsy study revealing that a part of the brain, the hypothalamus, was twice as large in heterosexual men as in homosexual men; twin studies showing that if one twin is gay, a 50 percent chance exists that the other is as well; research showing that gays and lesbians who undergo "conversion therapy" or "reparative counseling" for the purpose of changing their sexual orientation experience a high failure rate.[53] Lesbian, gay, bisexual, and transgender ("LGBT") legal theorists have used these scientific findings to argue that if sexual orientation exerts a strong biological influence, it should be a suspect classification, like race and gender, and command heightened constitutional scrutiny. If sexuality originates in biology, how can a legal blame system be justified? Others, like law professor Sam Marcosson, argue that sexual orientation is "constructively immutable"—it is a characteristic that is immutable for "all relevant legal and political purposes . . . even if it is a product of social construction."[54] The point is that sexual orientation, perhaps like religious orientation, is so intimately connected to personal identity that, even if not purely biological, it must be treated as something beyond voluntary choice. The social meanings attached to sexual orientation are so powerful at maintaining a disfavored social class that LGBT individuals need constitutional protection from discrimination.

In one sense, the structure of lesbian and gay legal theory has followed a pattern reminiscent of the sameness-difference debate in feminist legal theory. Some formal equality theorists have tried to show that LGBT couples are similar to the "ideal"—the heterosexual norm—as committed partners and loving parents. They try to demonstrate that LGBT identity is not just about sexuality and that differences in sexual orientation should not make a difference, socially or legally. Difference theorists (called, in this context, antisubordination theorists) critique the heterosexual norm as they challenge the ways society has artificially constructed sexual nonconformists as deviants. But perhaps it is not surprising at all that discussions of equality often return to concepts of sameness and difference, since one version of equality is treating similarly situated people alike.

F. Ecofeminism

My first step from the old white man was trees. Then air. Then birds. Then other people. But one day when I was sitting quiet . . . it come to me: that feeling of being part of everything, not separate at all. I knew that if I cut a tree, my arm would bleed.   Alice Walker[55]

Ecofeminism describes women's rich and varied relationships with society and nature. First advanced in the 1970s,[56] ecofeminism has since flowered into a stunning array of variations, with emphases ranging from economics to spiritualism, from animal rights to international human rights. The most recent and, perhaps, most promising version of ecofeminism emphasizes the intersections of human oppression (sexism, racism, and so on) and environmental destruction. The analysis begins where all ecofeminism begins: with the premise that the oppression of nature and the oppression of women are closely connected.[57] In this view, sexism and environmental destruction flow from the same problem: a false duality in Western thought that favors the human mind and spirit over the natural world and its processes. Because Western culture often associates the masculine with mind and spirit (science, reason, Descartes) and the feminine with the natural world (sex, instinct, Mother Nature), this dualism casts a double whammy, subordinating nature and women at the same time. This hierarchy—as old as Adam[58]—has been used to explain everything from the country's obsession with damming rivers to the pope's opposition to premarital sex.

For many ecofeminists, the dynamics of separation and control that enable sexism and environmental destruction also perpetuate other forms of oppression. This leads to a multilayered analysis of sexism and the abuse of power. As Ellen O'Loughlin explains, because most women "experience [discrimination] in more than one way (that is, through the dynamics of racism, classism, heterosexism, and ageism, as well as sexism), ecofeminism, in order to fight the oppression of women and nature, must look at more than just the ways in which sexism is related to naturism."[59]

Some of the affirmative contributions of environmental philosophy are its appreciation of aesthetics, its contemplation of equal access to natural resources, and its valuing of ecological ethics over human-centered utilitarianism. These ideas inform environmentalists' projects, such as efforts to preserve the Arctic National Wildlife Refuge for future generations, instead of drilling it now in hopes of oil discovery. These same considerations of connections among living things and valuation of community over self dovetail in ecofeminism with feminist principles of respect, inclusion, and compassion for others.

One might be tempted to see ecofeminism as just a "green" interpretation of antiessentialism, but the ecofeminist view of compound oppression contributes something new. First, ecofeminism holds *as its core principle* a recognition of shared oppression between women and nature. This principle not only encourages the examination of other shared oppressions, but makes avoidance of compound oppressions conceptually impossible: to take the "eco" or the "feminism" out of ecofeminism negates the whole idea.

Second, ecofeminism provides an important metaphor for understanding shared oppression: the ecological system. In fact, the concept of ecology provides us with an almost poetic image for understanding many difficulties that women face. Ellen O'Loughlin writes:

> An ecologist cannot just add up the parts of a pond and think she is coming close to describing that ecosystem and how it functions. A fish in a pond and a fish in an ocean, looked at ecologically, must be understood as inhabiting different, maybe similar but not the same, places. Likewise women are in different places. Whether I am in a field or an office, what I do there, my niche, is at least partially determined by the interconnection of societal environmental factors.[60]

It is precisely this emphasis on compound oppressions in the context of an ecological whole that makes the theory so useful in building coalitions among legal organizers.

Some good examples come from the environmental justice ("EJ") movement, a grassroots movement concerned with environmental dangers affecting the poor and people of color. In the United States, the EJ movement is mainly populated and directed by women. This was a grassroots movement that began, in part, around kitchen tables across the country, as women compared notes on the illnesses their children were suffering and traced these shared ailments to contaminated well water or landfills that leached toxins into the ground.[61] As a result, EJ advocates emphasize pollution problems affecting families and children—childhood asthma in the inner city (which is aggravated by air pollution), lead-based paint in old houses, or contaminated drinking water. Flexible collaborators, EJ advocates have joined forces with mainstream environmentalists, public health advocates, and poverty lawyers. The factor that holds these groups together is not necessarily love of nature, although that may be a part, but rather love of justice—the commitment to fight oppression in all its forms.

A social justice perspective enables these new environmentalists to draw connections between contamination and discrimination. When national studies show correlations between neighborhood pollution and wealth or race,[62] EJ advocates question zoning laws that perpetuate the segregation of poor single mothers and minorities. When the federal government warns women of childbearing years to lower their intake of tuna because of mercury contamination,[63] EJ advocates question pollution limits that were made strict enough to protect men but not women.

The ecofeminist movement received a *global* boost when, in 2004, Kenyan activist Wangari Maathai won the Nobel Peace Prize for leading thousands of African women in crusades against deforestation, poverty, and authoritarian government. Each of these problems posed important challenges to women. Deforestation, for instance, deprived rural communities of firewood, requiring women and girls to trek miles in search of cooking fuel. In addition, many legal and social traditions limit African women's participation in the workforce and public life, making them particularly vulnerable to poverty and corrupt autocrats. Describing that year's choice, a representative of the Nobel Committee said, "We have added a new dimension to the concept of peace. We have emphasized the environment, democracy building, and human rights and especially women's rights."[64]

G. Pragmatic Feminism

> We must look carefully at the nonideal circumstances in each case and decide which horn of the dilemma is better (or less bad), and we must keep redeciding as time goes on. . . . [We must] confront each dilemma separately and choose the alternative that will hinder empowerment the least and further it the most. The pragmatic feminist need not seek a general solution that will dictate how to resolve all double bind issues.
>
> Margaret Jane Radin[65]

Feminist legal pragmatists draw on the works of the classical pragmatists in philosophy, such as John Dewey and Charles Sanders Peirce, especially their understanding that "truth is inevitably plural, concrete, and provisional."[66] This means that pragmatists reach tentative conclusions and know that their truths are usually incomplete and open to change.

Pragmatists generally steer away from abstractions: for them, abstract concepts do not dictate real-world practical solutions. Feminists as pragmatists do not look for solutions in formal legal rules, but instead view legal rules as partial explanations for outcomes in individual cases. Pragmatic feminists recognize that many of the debates among feminists are about different visions of an ideal means to reach the goal of equality. They also recognize that subordinated groups often face a "double bind," and that an outcome along ideal dimensions may leave individuals without a remedy. For instance:

> When we single out pregnancy, for example, for "special treatment," we fear that employers will not hire women. But if we do not accord special treatment to pregnancy, women will lose their jobs. If we grant special treatment, we bring back the bad old conception of women as weaker creatures; if we do not, we prevent women from becoming stronger in the practical world.[67]

Feminist legal pragmatists criticize the universalism (for example, all men dominate women) of some of the other types of feminist legal theories and stress instead the importance of context and perspective. They recognize that "all observations are relative to a perspective," including "the time and place where they occur . . . [and] the set of prior beliefs and attitudes that are held by the observing party."[68]

Some have criticized pragmatism generally for its emphasis on individual perspective, its uncertainty, and its refusal to commit to abstract theorizing. "Being a legal pragmatist," jokes law professor Jack Balkin, "means never having to say you have a theory."[69] The serious challenge, though, is finding, in the absence of any foundational theory, a workable standard of morality.

Consider, for example, how a pragmatic feminist's approach might differ from that of an equal treatment theorist. In some tribal societies, land is generally inheritable only by male heirs, but customary norms impose an obligation on families to care for unmarried daughters by giving them a piece of land. An unmarried or divorced daughter who has children of her own to care for might argue for an extension of those cultivation or occupancy rights to her situation—not on the basis that she should have rights equal to those of her brothers, but on the basis that families have an obligation to care for all their daughters. The latter strategy has a much better chance of success in this culture than the former approach. This pragmatic approach may produce a favorable outcome in the individual case, but might not contribute to theoretically satisfactory or lasting egalitarian results: "For long-term gender equality, however, this recognition of customary rights is not a real victory. It is premised on the perception that women's interests in property belonging to their natal families are contingent. . . . Daughters are only accommodated in exceptional circumstances, namely when they fail to marry, or when their marriages fail."[70]

Pragmatism comes with no firm convictions, but it does offer perhaps an improved set of methods for coming to conclusions—tentative and partial though they might be. Feminist pragmatism contributes less in the way of concrete legal solutions and more in terms of methodological suggestions. Since one aspect of feminist methodology is to look at the realities of experience, pragmatic feminists find truths in the particulars of women's daily realities. Thus, for pragmatists, personal experiences help build theories, and theories need to incorporate the concrete situations of diverse individuals.

H. Postmodern Feminism

I am in favor of localized disruptions. I am against totalizing theory.

Mary Joe Frug[71]

We have been thinking about different feminist legal theories as if they were so many flavors of ice cream. Some swear by vanilla; others like rocky road. But postmodern feminist theory (and to a lesser extent pragmatism) is more of an interpretive tool than a uniform flavor. It's an ice cream scoop.

Postmodern feminism shares with critical feminist theories and with pragmatism a rejection of essentialism—the idea that all women share any single experience or condition. But postmodernists play on a whole different level of abstraction. Unlike antiessentialists, who find truth in a harmony of many voices, postmodernists think harmony is impossible. And truth, well, that's a figment of your imagination.

As the name implies, postmodernism emerged as a response to *modernism,* an intellectual movement that rejected the formal structures of Victorian art (narrative in literature, realism in painting) in hopes of capturing a more immediate, less stylized picture of human experience. Modernists wanted truth boiled down to the bone. Postmodernists also reject traditional styles and forms, but go one further by rejecting the very notion of objective knowledge or experience. Postmodernists challenge the very possibility of truth or objectivity. In the postmodern view, knowledge can never be certain or empirically established, since, as Peter Schanck explains, "[W]hat we think is knowledge is always belief"—and "[b]ecause language is socially and culturally constituted, it is inherently incapable of representing or corresponding to reality."[72] Boil truth down to the bone, and all that's left is steam.

Postmodern analysis begins with a technique called "deconstruction." Developed in the 1960s and 1970s by French philosopher Jacques Derrida, deconstruction entails taking a hard look at historical, artistic, or linguistic details to reveal the political messages and biases hidden within. Textual accounts always encode hidden messages because language is unavoidably packed with explicit and implicit information that changes with context. Consider the "Whites Only" signs of the Jim Crow South. One could say (as some politicians did) that the message was one of separation only, not subordination; but most people today would agree that the stronger, hidden message was about class power. This is the postmodern thesis: that when you get down to it, there is no such thing as justice, beauty, or truth—only power and the quest to maintain it. Pull up the floorboards of any opera, treatise, or constitution, and you will find a foundation built on the geometry of power. Every document, text, piece of language, work, or discussion contains hierarchies. Justice (or what passes for justice) belongs not to the ages but to today's ruling class, who define and shape it to their advantage, until, of course, a new class topples the first and imposes its own version. (If this reminds you of the French Revolution, you are getting the idea.) The trick for postmodernists is to identify these power structures through deconstruction and then to reverse those structures through political action.

Postmodern feminists use the tools of deconstruction to challenge the modernist idea of an unchangeable rule of law. Laws are not objective or impartial—they are crafted from political biases, so reliance on laws, and on traditional ways of practicing law, can reinforce inequalities. Postmodern practices critique many subtle hierarchies of power—even power hierarchies between lawyers and their clients. These strategies are intended to reveal the nonobvious ways that power works in relationships.

Postmodernism reveals that language, knowledge, and power are connected in ways that transmit cultural norms of gender. Because postmodernism focuses on oppression, it is especially concerned with how hierarchies are created and passed on in culture. Postmodernists suggest that we create and transmit hierarchies such as gender oppression by subtle and pervasive systems of speech and action (discourse and so-called discursive practices). For instance, women may internalize the expectations of advertisements that depict them as anorexically thin, perfectly coifed, and able to expertly wield cleaning products, just as they understood the messages of some older protectionist laws that limited the number of hours women could work to protect women from strenuous labor.

The postmodern strategy of understanding the connections between discourse and power is used to prompt rethinking of traditional gender identities so that they are more fluid and less attached to biological sex or to cultural norms. As an example of the ways language constructs identities, consider Judith Butler's postmodern explanation of how gender identity is "performatively constituted" by expressions:

> If I claim to be a lesbian, I "come out" only to produce a new and different "closet." The "you" to whom I come out now has access to a different region of opacity. Indeed, the locus of opacity has simply shifted . . . so we are out of the closet, but into what? What new unbounded spatiality? The room, the den, the attic, the basement, the house, the bar, the university, some new enclosure. . . . For being "out" always depends to some extent upon being "in"; it gains its meaning only within that polarity. Hence, being "out" must produce the closet again and again in order to maintain itself as "out."[73]

Sometimes postmodern analysis, like the preceding paragraph, looks more like performance art than legal critique. The response is that such "transgressive" rants, or riffs, are riffs of *resistance*. By challenging the language of social relationships, and resisting proper forms of speaking and writing, postmodernists say they can neutralize subliminal messages of inequality transmitted by the dominant culture. Perhaps. Still, it is hard to locate and fight injustice if we cannot even agree on the meaning of "out" or "in." In the words of Catharine MacKinnon, "Postmodernism as practiced often comes across as style—petulant, joyriding, more posture than position. . . . Postmodernism imagines that society happens in your head."[74]

Some feminists find postmodernism neither liberating nor effective. For them, the postmodern challenge of foundational truths undermines the stark realities of discrimination, intimate violence, and subordination that women have been trying to document. They worry that the emphasis on multiple perspectives reduces the realities of rape, sexual abuse, prostitution, and sexual harassment to just another set of "narratives." Furthermore, critics say that postmodernism operates at too a high a level of theory to be of political use:

> According to postmodernism, there are no facts; everything is a reading, so there can be no lies. Apparently it cannot be known whether the Holocaust is a hoax, whether women love to be raped, whether Black people are genetically intellectually inferior to white people, whether homosexuals are child molesters. To postmodernists, these

factish things are indeterminate, contingent, in play, all a matter of interpretation.[75]

Postmodernists and dominance theorists have also battled over whether women have "agency"—free will to choose, for example, sadomasochistic sex. In the postmodern view, S/M might be "a potentially pleasurable and subversive sexual practice,"[76] while a dominance theorist might dismiss whether the S/M practices can ever be freely chosen, or whether any such "choice" is actually a product of false consciousness.

This is just one example of the larger debate about postmodern approaches. Postmodernism counsels that people should adopt "subversive practices" and try to escape oppression. It rallies citizens to fight chauvinism and resist autocracy, but shows little interest in what equality or democracy should really look like. When the oppressed have finally broken their chains and slipped through the bars, how will they know they are free?

I. *Questions for Discussion*

1. At the turn of the twenty-first century, the movement for gender equality seems to have stalled. Some of the most significant battles, such as the fight for suffrage, *Roe v. Wade,* basic equal pay cases, and men's rights to sue for sexual harassment, have already been fought. Many of the issues that remain are second-generation discrimination issues—such as the glass ceiling in employment, the absence of paid family leave, women doing a disproportionate share of unpaid domestic work, or simply societal beliefs about appropriate gender roles. Can you identify some others of these smaller second generation issues: the more subtle forms of discrimination that are not clearly proscribed by existing laws, and the micro-inequities that it is difficult for law to even reach? Do any major or landmark legal issues still remain to be fought?

2. The diversity among feminist legal theorists raises the difficulties of building coalitions among oppressed groups. Some antiessentialists call for greater coalition-building. Others caution against it, be-

cause alliances among minorities or between minority and dominant groups usually operate to serve the more powerful groups, whose interests may diverge. Choose one of the issues you identified in question 1. Would coalition-building be a critical strategy in addressing that issue?

3. Are some of these philosophies of feminism too bleak to gain many adherents or too critical to provide a positive platform? For instance, dominance theory seems to suggest that most, if not all, women are subordinated in many ways—and that they may not even know it, the problem of false consciousness. Individuals, in the postmodern view, are almost purely social and cultural creations. If, as postmodernism seems to suggest, women's experiences are not "homogeneous," this raises the question whether they "can ever ground feminist theory."[77] Will dominance theory gather supporters, or will it be perceived as relegating women to permanent victim status? Will postmodernism lead to more fluid gender roles or create such anxiety over ambiguity that the status quo remains the preferred model of interpreting gender roles? Even if neither theory gains more adherents, how does its presence in the field of feminist theory affect other, more generally accepted theories?

Suggested Readings

Kathryn Abrams, *Sex Wars Redux: Agency and Coercion in Feminist Legal Theory*, 95 Colum. L. Rev. 304 (1995).

All the Women Are White, All the Blacks Are Men, But Some of Us Are Brave (Gloria Hull et al. eds., 1982).

Ruth Colker, Hybrid: Bisexuals, Multiracials, and Other Misfits Under American Law (1996).

Critical Race Feminism: A Reader (Adrien Katherine Wing ed., 2d ed. 2002).

Ruth Bader Ginsburg & Barbara Flagg, *Some Reflections on the Feminist Legal Thought of the 1970s*, 1989 U. Chi. Legal F. 9.

bell hooks, Feminist Theory: From Margin to Center (1984).

Darren Lenard Hutchinson, *Identity Crisis: "Intersectionality," "Multidimensionality," and the Development of an Adequate Theory of Subordination*, 6 Mich. J. Race & L. 285 (2001).

New Perspectives on Environmental Justice: Gender, Sexuality, and Activism (Rachel Stein ed., 2004).

Joan Chalmers Williams, *Dissolving the Sameness/Difference Debate: A Post-Modern Path Beyond Essentialism in Feminist and Critical Race Theory,* 1991 DUKE L.J. 296.

NOTES

1. *A Lawyer's Primer on Feminist Theory and Tort,* 38 J. LEGAL EDUC. 3, 3 (1988).

2. THE SECOND SEX 33 (1949).

3. *Equality's Riddle: Pregnancy and the Equal Treatment/Special Treatment Debate,* 13 N.Y.U. REV. L. & SOC. CHANGE 325, 329 (1984–85).

4. *See* MARY WOLLSTONECRAFT, A VINDICATION OF THE RIGHTS OF WOMEN (Carol H. Poston ed. 1988) (1779); JOHN STUART MILL, THE SUBJECTION OF WOMEN (Mary Warnock ed. 1986).

5. Reed v. Reed, 404 U.S. 71 (1971).

6. Frontiero v. Richardson, 411 U.S. 677 (1973).

7. Kahn v. Shevin, 416 U.S. 351 (1974).

8. Craig v. Boren, 429 U.S. 190 (1976).

9. Orr v. Orr, 440 U.S. 268 (1979); Davis v. Passman, 442 U.S. 228 (1979).

10. Mississippi Univ. for Women v. Hogan, 458 U.S. 718 (1982); J.E.B. v. Alabama, 511 U.S. 127 (1994).

11. *See* Califano v. Webster, 430 U.S. 313 (1977).

12. ETHIQUE DE LA DIFFERENCE SEXUELLE 19–20 (1984).

13. Robin West, *Jurisprudence and Gender,* 55 U. CHI. L. REV. 1, 2 (1988).

14. CAROL GILLIGAN, IN A DIFFERENT VOICE: PSYCHOLOGICAL THEORY AND WOMEN'S DEVELOPMENT (1982).

15. *See, e.g.,* Catherine G. Greeno & Eleanor E. Maccoby, *How Different Is the "Different Voice?"* 11 SIGNS 310, 315 (1986); Carol Stack, *The Culture of Gender: Women and Men of Color,* 11 SIGNS 321, 322–24 (1986).

16. *See* NEL NODDINGS, CARING: A FEMININE APPROACH TO ETHICS AND MORAL EDUCATION 2, 128–30 (1984); Carol Gilligan, *Reply by Carol Gilligan,* 11 SIGNS 324 (1986); Sara Jaffee & Janet Shibley Hyde, *Gender Differences in Moral Orientation: A Meta-Analysis,* 126 PSYCHOL. BULL. 703 (2000).

17. *See* West, *supra* note 13, at 18.

18. Frontiero v. Richardson, 411 U.S. 677, 684 (1973).

19. 479 U.S. 272 (1987).

20. Martin H. Malin, *Fathers and Parental Leave,* 72 TEX. L. REV. 1047, 1060 (1994).

21. 479 U.S. at 289.

22. Joanna L. Grossman, *Job Security Without Equality: The Family and Medical Leave Act of 1993,* 15 WASH. U.J.L. & POL'Y 17 (2004).

23. JOAN WILLIAMS, UNBENDING GENDER: WHY FAMILY AND WORK CONFLICT AND WHAT TO DO ABOUT IT 213 (2000).

24. Jane L. Dolkart, *Hostile Environment Harassment: Equality, Objectivity, and the Shaping of Legal Standards,* 43 EMORY L. REV. 151, 171 (1991).

25. MARTHA MINOW, MAKING ALL THE DIFFERENCE: INCLUSION, EXCLUSION, AND AMERICAN LAW 20 (1990).

26. CATHARINE A. MACKINNON, FEMINISM UNMODIFIED: DISCOURSES ON LIFE AND LAW 45 (1987).

27. *Id.* at 34.

28. Cynthia Grant Bowman & Elizabeth M. Schneider, *Feminist Legal Theory, Feminist Lawmaking, and the Legal Profession,* 67 FORDHAM L. REV. 249, 252 (1998).

29. West, *supra* note 13, at 4.

30. CATHARINE A. MACKINNON, TOWARD A FEMINIST THEORY OF THE STATE 224 (1989).

31. American Booksellers Ass'n v. Hudnut, 771 F.2d 323, 324 (2nd Cir. 1985), *cert. denied,* 475 U.S. 1132 (1986).

32. Francisco Valdes, *Queers, Sissies, Dykes, and Tomboys: Deconstructing the Conflation of "Sex," "Gender," and "Sexual Orientation" in Euro-American Law and Society,* 83 CAL. L. REV. 1 (1995).

33. Adrienne Rich, *Compulsory Heterosexuality and Lesbian Existence, in* POWERS OF DESIRE: THE POLITICS OF SEXUALITY 177 (Ann Snitow et al. eds. 1983).

34. Arnold Schwarzenegger, *Remarks Prepared for Delivery at the 2004 Republican National Convention,* delivered Aug. 31, 2004, http://www.usatoday.com/news/politicselections/nation/president/2004-08-31-schwarzeneggerfulltext_x.htm.

35. MACKINNON, FEMINISM UNMODIFIED, *supra* note 26, at 39.

36. Mary Becker, *Caring for Children and Caretakers,* 76 CHI.-KENT L. REV. 1495, 1515 (2001).

37. April L. Cherry, *A Feminist Understanding of Sex-Selective Abortion: Solely a Matter of Choice?,* 10 WIS. WOMEN'S L.J. 161, 214 n.241 (1995).

38. Angela P. Harris, *Race and Essentialism in Feminist Legal Theory,* 42 STAN. L. REV. 581, 588 (1990).

39. *Id.* at 585, 589–90.

40. *See* Kimberlé Crenshaw, *Demarginalizing the Intersection of Race and Sex: A Black Feminist Critique of Antidiscrimination Doctrine, Feminist Theory and Antiracist Politics,* 1989 U. CHI. LEGAL F. 139.

41. Mari J. Matsuda, *When the First Quail Calls: Multiple Consciousness as Jurisprudential Method,* 11 WOMEN'S RTS. L. REP. 7, 8 (1989).

42. PATRICIA J. WILLIAMS, THE ALCHEMY OF RACE AND RIGHTS 44, 45 (1991).

43. Adele M. Morrison, *Queering Domestic Violence to "Straighten Out" Criminal Law: What Might Happen When Queer Theory and Practice Meet Criminal Law's Conventional Responses to Domestic Violence,* 13 S. CAL. REV. L. & WOMEN'S STUD. 81, 94 (2003).

44. Anthony V. Alfieri, *Reconstructive Poverty Law Practice: Learning Lessons of Client Narrative,* 100 YALE L.J. 2107 (1991).

45. Richard Delgado, *Storytelling for Oppositionists and Others: A Plea for Narrative,* 87 MICH. L. REV. 2411, 2413 (1988).

46. ROBERT L. HAYMAN, JR., THE SMART CULTURE: SOCIETY, INTELLIGENCE, AND LAW 127–29 (1997).

47. *See, e.g.,* Dorothy E. Roberts, *The Genetic Tie,* 62 U. CHI. L. REV. 209, 261–65 (1995); Dorothy E. Roberts, *Unshackling Black Motherhood,* 95 MICH. L. REV. 938 (1997).

48. Harris, *supra* note 38, at 608.

49. ANITA HILL, SPEAKING TRUTH TO POWER (1997).

50. *See, e.g.,* Darren Lenard Hutchinson, *Out Yet Unseen: A Racial Critique of Gay and Lesbian Legal Theory and Political Discourse,* 29 CONN. L. REV. 561 (1997).

51. Valdes, *supra* note 32, at 125.

52. General Accounting Office, Memo from Office of the General Counsel to The Honorable Henry J. Hyde, Jan. 31, 1997, http://www.gao.gov/archive/1997/og97016.pdf. at 2. Note that this count includes only those laws enacted prior to the passage of the Defense of Marriage Act precluding federal recognition of same-sex marriages on September 21, 1996.

53. Judy Foreman, *The Basis for Sexual Orientation,* L.A. TIMES, Dec. 8, 2003, at F8.

54. Samuel Marcosson, *Constructive Immutability,* 3 U. PA. J. CONST. L. 646 (2001).

55. ALICE WALKER, THE COLOR PURPLE 178–79 (Harcourt Brace Jovanovich 1982).

56. French writer Françoise d'Eaubonne coined the term, *ecofeminisme,* in 1974. Carolyn Merchant, *Ecofeminism and Feminist Theory, in* REWEAVING THE WORLD: THE EMERGENCE OF ECOFEMINISM 100 (Irene Diamond & Gloria Feman Orenstein eds. 1990).

57. Janis Birkeland, *Ecofeminism: Linking Theory and Practice, in* ECOFEMINISM: WOMEN, ANIMALS, NATURE, 13, 18 (Greta Gaard ed. 1993).

58. "And the LORD God took the man, and put him into the garden of Eden to dress it and to keep it." Genesis 2:15 (King James).

59. Ellen O'Loughlin, *Questioning Sour Grapes: Ecofeminism and the United Farm Workers Grape Boycott, in* ECOFEMINISM, *supra* note 57, at 148.

60. *Id.* at 149–50.

61. Robert R. M. Verchick, *In a Greener Voice: Feminist Theory and Environmental Justice,* 19 HARV. WOMEN'S L.J. 23 (1996).

62. *See, e.g.,* COMMISSION FOR RACIAL JUSTICE OF THE UNITED CHURCH OF CHRIST, TOXIC WASTES AND RACE IN THE UNITED STATES 15 (1987).

63. U.S. DEPARTMENT OF HEALTH AND HUMAN SERVICES AND U.S. ENVIRONMENTAL PROTECTION AGENCY, WHAT YOU NEED TO KNOW ABOUT MERCURY IN FISH AND SHELLFISH (March 2004) (EPA-823-R-04-005), *available at* http://www.cfsan.fda.gov/~dms/admehg3.html.

64. Fred Barbash & Emily Wax, *Kenyan Environmental Activist Wins Nobel Peace Prize,* WASH. POST, Oct. 8, 2004, at A1.

65. *The Pragmatist and the Feminist,* 63 S. CAL. L. REV. 1699, 1700, 1704 (1990).

66. *Id.* at 1706.

67. *Id.* at 1701.

68. Catharine Pierce Wells, *Why Pragmatism Works for Me,* 74 S. CAL. L. REV. 347, 357 (2000).

69. J. M. Balkin, *The Top Ten Reasons to Be a Legal Pragmatist,* 8 CONST. COMMENT. 351, 361 (1991).

70. Celestine I. Nyamu, *How Should Human Rights and Development Respond to Cultural Legitimization of Gender Hierarchy in Developing Countries?,* 41 HARV. INT'L L.J. 381, 416 (2000).

71. *A Postmodern Feminist Legal Manifesto (An Unfinished Draft),* 105 HARV. L. REV. 1045, 1046 (1992).

72. Peter C. Schanck, *Understanding Postmodern Thought and Its Implications for Statutory Interpretation,* 65 S. CAL. L. REV. 2505, 2508 (1992).

73. JUDITH BUTLER, GENDER TROUBLE: FEMINISM AND THE SUBVERSION OF IDENTITY 33 (2d ed. 1999).

74. Catharine MacKinnon, *Points Against Postmodernism,* 75 CHI.-KENT. L. REV. 687, 2700-01 (2000).

75. *Id.* at 703.

76. Brenda Cossman, *Gender, Sexuality, and Power: Is Feminist Theory Enough?,* 12 COLUM. J. GENDER & L. 601, 620 (2003).

77. Maxine Eichner, *On Postmodern Feminist Legal Theory,* 36 HARV. C.R.-C.L. L. REV. 5, 3 (2001).

3

Feminist Legal Methods

*To take what there is, and use it, without waiting forever in vain
for the preconceived—to dig deep into the actual and get something
out of that—this doubtless is the right way to live.*   Henry James[1]

Context is all.   Margaret Atwood[2]

Feminist theory is, at its core, an exploration of the actual. Whatever
the appeal of broad principles or abstract rules, such tools cannot lead
to justice unless they are understood and applied in ways that acknowledge the real-life experiences of those affected. While its gar-
dens burst with variety, legal feminism has been held together by a set
of "feminist methods" developed by women's rights activists and feminist scholars in the late 1960s and early 1970s. Rather than develop
any substantive theory of sex inequity or how to remedy it, feminist
legal methodology focuses on the tools of how to practice feminist
legal thinking and the ways of documenting the experiences of gender.
Although descriptions vary, the fundamentals of feminist methods
generally include (1) unmasking patriarchy, (2) contextual reasoning,
and (3) consciousness-raising.[3]

A. Unmasking Patriarchy

Legal feminists begin their critique with a series of questions designed
to uncover male biases hidden beneath supposedly "neutral" laws.
This technique, called "unmasking patriarchy," helps identify the gender-based consequences that law creates. Having identified these consequences, feminist legal theorists then work to show that the tradi-

tional legal underpinnings are not inevitable, but can be changed. The method assumes that even the most ordinary aspects of law conceal what Catharine MacKinnon calls "the substantive way in which man has become the measure of all things."[4]

To start the process, legal scholar Katharine Bartlett recommends asking "the woman question." In her words,

> [A]sking the woman question means examining how the law fails to take into account the experiences and values that seem more typical of women than of men, for whatever reason, or how existing legal standards and concepts might disadvantage women. The question assumes that some features of the law may be not only nonneutral in a general sense, but also "male" in a specific sense. The purpose of the woman question is to expose those features and how they operate, and to suggest how they might be corrected.[5]

Bartlett's description suggests two points. First, it is difficult to locate gender bias without understanding women's personal experiences in the real world. Already, feminist *men* are at a disadvantage. But we all have ground to make up. The experiences of women vary, sometimes dramatically, according to class, age, race, and sexual orientation. Putting yourself in another's shoes is a skill all feminists must cultivate.

Second, the goal of understanding women's personal experiences is to show how law's unequal consequences "might be corrected." Corrective action will usually involve some form of enfranchisement, that is, the transfusion of women's outside experiences into the mainstream political or legal process. Enfranchisement can occur in formal ways (the right to vote, the right to organize in the workplace) or less formal ways (seminars, protest marches, demonstrations).

Asking the woman question is in part an empirical assessment— using data to reveal how seemingly neutral laws contain a gender bias. The questions that should be asked concern whether particular laws consider women's experiences, whether legal rules implicitly favor one sex, and whether social practices promote illegitimate gender stereotypes. Examples of assessing the influence of gender include tallying the numbers of males and females selected for promotion by a particular employer; documenting whether mothers or fathers are more likely to win custody of children in contested cases; or accumulating data about the treatment of girls and boys in school classrooms. The outcome of the inquiry is not always favorable to women, because men, too, can be disadvantaged by gendered tilts in the law.

Through careful inquiries, feminists try to expose unfairness by attacking law's reliance on the differences between men and women as a means of distributing social benefits. This effort can occur on one of two levels. On the first level, feminists seek to prove that the relied-upon difference is empirically false. On the second level, feminists concede that an actual gender difference exists, but they challenge the way in which the difference is used to benefit men at the expense of women.

How does all this work in real life? Think of Myra Bradwell from **Chapter 1,** who unsuccessfully fought the stereotype of female "timidity and delicacy" to pursue a legal career. Or Sally Reed, who buried the "only men can handle money" myth by protesting a law preferring men as estate administrators. Both cases are examples of this first level of unmasking, which rejects stereotypes on the grounds of accuracy.

Where underlying gender differences are real, feminists seek to discredit not the assumption of differences, but the assumption that differences justify burdening women in relation to men. This is the second level of unmasking. Consider the real difference of childbearing. In the 1970s, women began challenging employee benefit plans that covered almost all potential disabilities *except* pregnancy.[6] Defenders of the policies argued that because pregnancy leaves were more costly than many other disability leaves, their omission was justified. The burden to women, under this view, resulted not from the *policy* (which was just a way to contain costs) but from a real *difference* (the ability to become pregnant). Indeed, to offer pregnancy leave, knowing that only women could take it, would amount to a *special benefit* to women that would discriminate against men.

In the feminist view, the argument's flaw is that such disability policies are not based on gender-neutral principles. They are based on a set of moral and economic obligations that acknowledge an employer's responsibility toward an employee who is assumed to be a man. What the "typical man" needs for his minimum peace of mind (disability leave for prostate cancer, weekends to care for his children) he might get. What the "typical woman" needs (pregnancy leave, flexible weekday hours to care for her children) are "extras." The second level of unmasking urges that both men and women be used as benchmarks.

Unmasking provides a dramatic alternative to simply blaming the victim for social inequalities. Widespread social disparities are properly viewed as structural problems, requiring public, rather than private, solutions. The absence of women lawyers in the nineteenth century was not the result of their lack of abilities, but of sexist attitudes that did not acknowledge those abilities. The awkward balance between childbearing and wage earning is not an indictment of motherhood or working moms, but an indictment of the male-centered workforce.

This focus on the structural bias of institutions suggests a lesson from the second level of the unmasking process: that bias, although real, may not always be intentional. Thus, while it may be true that the absence of better pregnancy benefits as a whole results from a historical devaluation of motherhood in the workplace, it does not follow that an individual employer who refuses to offer a better policy is acting out of intentional sexism. This point is important because some discrimination laws target only intentional rather than institutional or unconscious, discrimination.

Finally, the process of unmasking cautions against assumptions of neutrality in nearly any area. As law professor Martha Minow notes, feminists have exposed the dominance in "field after field of conceptions of human nature that take a male as the reference point and treat women as 'other,' 'different,' 'deviant,' 'exceptional,' or baffling."[7] Unmasking is a method of revealing that laws, social institutions, or areas of research are not unbiased or impartial. Imagining a new version of American society requires a new appreciation for social context.

B. Contextual Reasoning

When examining discrimination, feminists pay special attention to the personal and social history of the parties, relative perceptions among the parties, and overall context. Implicit in this vision is the belief that the daily lives of real people matter, or, as the bumper sticker says, "The Personal *Is* Political." Capturing this idea, law professor Mari Matsuda writes, "[W]ho makes breakfast, who gets a paycheck, who gets whistled at in the street—all the experiences of daily life are a part of the distribution of wealth and power in society."[8]

Some believe that sensitivity to experience and context is empirically associated with women.[9] Feminists have long invoked the realities of private life to spur legislative and social change for women. Suffragists argued that the right to vote would improve government by allowing women to bring their personal insight and morality into public discourse. Some feminists lent aid to the temperance movement out of concern for families threatened by drinking husbands who squandered household income and abused their wives and children. More recently, feminists have prompted often dramatic changes in the legal treatment of divorce and domestic violence by documenting the unfair and sometimes tragic consequences experienced by women and children in such situations.[10] Today one can find accounts of personal experience in legal scholarship, courtroom briefing, and even judges' opinions.

C. Consciousness-Raising

Consciousness-raising describes the process by which individuals share personal experiences with others in an effort to derive collective significance or meaning from those experiences.[11] Its catalysts are what Virginia Woolf called "the arts of human intercourse; the art of understanding other people's lives and minds, and the little arts of talk."[12] Through consciousness-raising women begin to view what otherwise might appear as isolated instances of insensitivity or chauvinism as symptoms of broader societal oppression. This exercise also enables participants to more easily unmask hidden biases and to identify appropriate personal contexts in which to examine issues. A consistency in accounts of women's harm and misfortune, for instance, leads participants to question the supposed neutrality of governing rules. Women's stories challenged the myth that law operates fairly and neutrally. Mari Matsuda offers the following concrete example: "Women who are currently told that strict enforcement of the legal guarantee of equal pay for equal work has created an abstract condition called 'equality' look at their own experience as underpaid workers, and then redefine 'equality' as equal pay for work of equal value."[13] Drawing general conclusions about institutional oppression from private observation grounds social theory in actual experience and affirms the union between the personal and the political. In addition, sharing stories through consciousness-raising assures participants that they are not misguided or alone in their observations. Rather, such collaboration infuses the group with a sense of collective identity and power to rewrite "the meaning of women's social experience."[14]

For many people, consciousness-raising suggests a small interactive group—book clubs, exercise classes, knitting circles (or, as they say nowadays, "stitch and bitch" sessions). Yet the process can also operate on a larger scale, through the popular media (think: Oprah), in books (think: *Our Bodies, Ourselves*), comics (think: Guerilla Girls), paintings, photographs (think: Robert Mapplethorpe), and music.[15] In this sense, female artists from Sappho to Billie Holiday can be seen as early consciousness raisers.[16] As noted in **Chapter 2,** some legal scholars artfully employ personal stories to facilitate feminist consciousness-raising. Others characterize more formalized settings like trials, hearings, or interviews as opportunities for deliberative discussion in which personal perspectives are shared in a way that resembles feminist consciousness-raising. **Chapter 6** discusses the ways reproductive rights advocates have used storytelling techniques in amicus briefs filed in the Supreme Court. To be effective as a transformative practice, consciousness-raising may need to be national in scope in order to illuminate the effect of law on all women' lives.

Whether consciousness-raising is intimate or global, formal or informal, its underlying values remain the same: a commitment to collective engagement, the public significance of private life, and an acceptance of individual perspective. As with the methods of unmasking patriarchy and contextual reasoning, the process—not the result—is the top priority. Sharing stories is good per se and helps build "spiritual and humane value[s]" in itself.[17]

D. Pulling It Together

1. Telling a story

To show how feminist methods can coalesce into a legal movement, we will tell a story. Imagine Gloria, a single mother who has just moved into a rented house in the industrial part of her new city. She has an hourly day job as a server at a local restaurant. Her son, Marcus, attends the neighborhood elementary school where he has just enrolled. Things go well for the first few weeks, but their good fortune does not last. Toward the middle of autumn Marcus develops a breathing problem. He coughs and wheezes and cannot catch his breath. On some days his problem is so bad Marcus must stay home from school. That means Gloria stays home from work to care for Marcus, which, in turn, means she gives up a day's wages. The doctor says Marcus has asthma and prescribes medication. It helps, but not all the time, so Marcus continues to miss school occasionally and Gloria continues to miss work, since reliable child care, especially for a sick child, is hard to find.

One day in Gloria's women's Bible study group, talk turns to children's health. Gloria learns that several mothers in her neighborhood also have young children with asthma who are also missing school, often on the same days. Gloria and the other mothers decide to research this problem on the Internet. They learn that childhood asthma rates are at an all-time high and that the condition can be significantly aggravated by pollutants in the air. Some of the most irritating pollutants are emitted daily from a city power plant in Gloria's neighborhood. When the temperature and humidity are just right, those chemicals can pose a threat to neighborhood asthma sufferers. Other chemicals emitted from the power plant present other harms. Some evidence suggests, for instance, that mercury fallout from the plant may be responsible for new warnings about locally caught fish, which hold that all women of childbearing age should limit their diets to one fish meal per month.

When Gloria and the other mothers complain to state officials and to the power plant operators, they are dismissed by some as "nervous Nellies," or worse, "hysterical housewives." A spokesperson at the plant hypothesizes that the children's respiratory attacks might instead be related to poor housekeeping, lax pest control, or the improper use of medication. As for the fish warnings, as long as people are provided clear instructions on how to protect themselves, that sacrifice is small compared with the significant cost that stricter rules would place on state power generators.

2. Analyzing the story

This account—which we made up, but which is based on real data[18]—suggests several opportunities for applying feminist legal methods. Let's start with unmasking patriarchy and Bartlett's "woman question." How does law in this circumstance "fail[] to take into account the experiences and values that seem more typical of women than of men?" As Gloria immediately learns, the laws of employment do not provide much of a safety net when illness strikes a single-parent family. No law requires Gloria's employer to provide paid or unpaid leave while she cares for her son. (The time she has taken off may not be guaranteed by the employer and could reflect badly on her at promotion time.) No public program or statute guarantees drop-in child care for sick children. Health and insurance laws can fail to ensure that children like Marcus get effective preventative care and affordable prescription drugs. Zoning and land-use laws probably played some role in putting Gloria's inexpensive home so close to a toxic power plant (or vice versa). A set of environmental regulations tolerates levels of pollution harmful to asthmatic children and young women who eat fish. Finally, state officials who are charged with enforcing health and safety laws dismiss Gloria as an overemotional woman.

Some of these elements betray an obvious male bias. The "hysterical housewives" comment intentionally employs stereotyping, not logic, to make its point. The pollution standards affecting fish also disadvantage women in relation to men, although that bias is probably unintended. (Does it matter?) But other inequalities require more digging. Lack of paid leave, child care, affordable medical care, progressive zoning, and pollution protection for asthmatic children are not, in themselves, discriminatory on the basis of sex. But when we consider that single parents bear the brunt of leave and child care problems and that most single parents are mothers, an outcome unfavorable to women emerges. Because women are more likely than men to care for ill children, public health laws affecting children also disadvantage more women than men. Finally, single mothers, who as a class are less affluent than single fathers, are more likely to be harmed by policies like zoning and land-use laws that favor wealthier neighborhoods over poorer ones.

Once we see that Gloria's problems are related to laws unfriendly to women, the next step is to contextualize the legal issues. To some extent we have already done this as part of the unmasking process. Uncovering the gendered effects of employment-leave or insurance polices, for instance, required knowing the demographics of single parents and primary caretakers. But contextual reasoning can be taken farther. When Gloria assembles the clues surrounding Marcus's asthma—the nationwide surge in diagnoses, the correlation with certain weather conditions, the evidence of other children missing school on the same days—Gloria is using her own particularized knowledge to draw a connection between pollution and illness, a connection that apparently escaped even health officials. This same knowledge of context will allow Gloria and her fellow activists to frame this "public health" issue as an ecological issue, perhaps leading to coalitions with environmental advocates.

Finally, Gloria's investigation benefited from having friends, what academics call a "social network." In this case, it was a church group. Other feminist projects begin in the grade-school parking lot, the yoga studio, or on Internet listservs. The point is that people get together to share experiences, observations, and hypotheses. Through the sharing and sifting of ideas, a "big picture" is constructed, linking the daily lives of women with larger economic and political forces. Sometimes political movements are born.[19] Gloria's search goes from "me" to "us" and, finally (making the critical shift from object to subject), to "we." Our daily experiences, they find, are shaped by laws maintained for *us;* and if the laws serve us poorly, *we* can change them.

E. Questions for Discussion

1. Feminist methodology calls for a look "beneath the surface of law to identify the gender implications of rules."[20] Various writers have applied feminist methods to seemingly neutral legal standards, such as the laws of self-defense (which may deprive battered women of a defense because violence against them may not be "imminent" in the traditional sense when they respond to their attackers) or the rules of evidence (which may reflect male norms in admitting testimony about the prior workplace sexual relationships of sexual harassment victims). Legal scholars have argued that use of feminist principles would lead to significant revisions of substantive rules in areas such as tort law, contract law, evidence, and criminal procedure. If you applied feminist legal methods to the U.S. Constitution, would the provisions of the document or the ways it is interpreted be different?[21]

2. Do feminist legal methods inevitably lead to the elimination of bias in decision making, or do the decision makers themselves need to have different life experiences? Consider the situation of a male office worker who circulates sexually explicit jokes in e-mails to coworkers or posts a *Sports Illustrated* swimsuit calendar on the wall near his desk. Does that employee risk a sexual harassment lawsuit, or does he have a good free-speech defense?[22] If a judge "asked the woman question" about this situation or applied principles of consciousness-raising to it, would that judge uphold a First Amendment defense to sexual harassment liability?

Will these methods actually be useful to judges—and used by them—or are the strategies of feminist legal methods helpful only if one is, first, a believer in feminist principles? While feminist beliefs do not divide neatly along gender lines, it is important to consider the gender composition of the judiciary. Among federal judges, only 22.2 percent (two of the nine) of Supreme Court justices, 17.4 percent of the U.S. courts of appeal judges, and 16.2 percent of the U.S. district court judges are women.[23] Can nonfeminist decision makers be persuaded to use feminist methods?

SUGGESTED READINGS

Kathryn Abrams, *Feminist Lawyering and Method,* 16 LAW & SOC. INQUIRY 373 (1991).
GLOBAL CRITICAL RACE FEMINISM: AN INTERNATIONAL READER (Adrien Katherine Wing ed., 2000).
Phyllis Goldfarb, *A Theory-Practice Spiral: The Ethics of Feminism and Clinical Education,* 75 MINN. L. REV. 1599 (1991).
Sandra Harding, *Is There a Feminist Method?, in* FEMINISM AND METHODOLOGY 1 (Sandra Harding ed., 1987).
Audre Lorde, *The Master's Tools Will Never Dismantle the Master's House, in* SISTER OUTSIDER 110 (1984).
Catharine A. MacKinnon, *From Practice to Theory, or What Is a White Woman Anyway?,* 4 YALE J.L. & FEMINISM 13 (1991).
Robert R. M. Verchick, *In a Greener Voice: Feminist Theory and Environmental Justice,* 19 HARV. WOMEN'S L.J. 23 (1996).
STEPHANIE M. WILDMAN ET AL., PRIVILEGE REVEALED: HOW INVISIBLE PREFERENCE UNDERMINES AMERICA (1996).
PATRICIA J. WILLIAMS, THE ALCHEMY OF RACE AND RIGHTS (1991).

Heather Ruth Wishik, *To Question Everything: The Inquiries of Feminist Jurisprudence,* 1 BERKELEY WOMEN'S L.J. 64 (1985).

NOTES

1. HENRY JAMES, THE COMPLETE NOTEBOOKS OF HENRY JAMES 52 (1987).
2. MARGARET ATWOOD, THE HANDMAID'S TALE 187 (Ballantine Books 1987) (1985).
3. *See* Katharine T. Bartlett, *Feminist Legal Methods,* 103 HARV. L. REV. 829, 836–37 (1990).
4. CATHARINE A. MACKINNON, FEMINISM UNMODIFIED: DISCOURSES ON LIFE AND LAW 34 (1987).
5. Bartlett, *supra* note 3, at 837.
6. *See, e.g.,* Geduldig v. Aiello, 417 U.S. 484 (1974) (holding that state benefits plan that excludes disabilities arising from pregnancy does not constitute sex discrimination under the Fourteenth Amendment's equal protection clause); General Electric Co. v. Gilbert, 429 U.S.125 (1976) (finding that private benefits plan that excludes disabilities arising from pregnancy does not constitute sex discrimination under Title VII). As a reaction to *Gilbert,* Congress passed the Pregnancy Discrimination Act of 1978, 42 U.S.C.A. § 2000e(k), which explicitly defined conduct that discriminated on the basis of pregnancy as sex discrimination within the meaning of Title VII.
7. Martha Minow, *Foreword: Justice Engendered,* 101 HARV. L. REV. 10, 61 (1987).
8. Mari J. Matsuda, *Liberal Jurisprudence and Abstracted Visions of Human Nature: A Feminist Critique of Rawls' Theory of Justice,* 16 N.M. L. REV. 613, 618 (1986).
9. *See, e.g.,* CAROL GILLIGAN, IN A DIFFERENT VOICE: PSYCHOLOGICAL THEORY AND WOMEN'S DEVELOPMENT 105 (1982).
10. *See, e.g.,* LINDA GORDON, HEROES OF THEIR OWN LIVES: THE POLITICS AND HISTORY OF FAMILY VIOLENCE (1988).
11. Bartlett *supra* note 3, at 863–64.
12. VIRGINIA WOOLF, THREE GUINEAS 34 (1938).
13. Matsuda, *supra* note 8, at 619–20.
14. Catharine A. MacKinnon, *Feminism, Marxism, Method, and the State: An Agenda for Theory, reprinted in* THE SIGNS READER: WOMEN, GENDER & SCHOLARSHIP, 227, 255 (Elizabeth Abel & Emily K. Abel eds., 1983).
15. *See, e.g.,* DONNA FERRATO, LIVING WITH THE ENEMY (1991) (documenting domestic violence through photographs); ANNA QUINDLEN, LIVING OUT LOUD (1988) (collecting newspaper editorial columns); DEFENDING OUR LIVES

(Cambridge Documentary Films, Inc.) (documentary film about domestic violence).

16. *See, e.g.,* Sappho, *I have had not one word from her, in* SAPPHO: A NEW TRANSLATION 42 (Mary Barnard trans., 1986) (examining lesbian love); Billie Holiday, *My Man, in* BILLIE HOLIDAY: THE COMPLETE DECCA RECORDINGS (Verve 1991) (examining domestic violence).

17. Matsuda, *supra* note 8, at 621.

18. *See, e.g.,* Lisa Heinzerling & Rena Steinzer, *A Perfect Storm: Mercury and the Bush Administration,* 34 ENVT'L L. REP. 10297 (2004) (reviewing dangers and sources of airborne mercury); Celene Krauss, *Women of Color on the Front Line, in* UNEQUAL PROTECTION: ENVIRONMENTAL JUSTICE AND COMMUNITIES OF COLOR 256 (Robert D. Bullard ed. 1994) (describing treatment of female grassroots activists by male professionals).

19. *See, e.g.,* Marion Crain, *Between Feminism and Unionism: Working Class Women, Sex Equality, and Labor Speech,* 82 GEO. L.J. 1903, 1938 (1994) (describing how seamstresses united in protest against sexual harassment); Gabriel Gutiérrez, *Mothers of East Los Angeles Strike Back, in* UNEQUAL PROTECTION: ENVIRONMENTAL JUSTICE AND COMMUNITIES OF COLOR 220, 222–27 (Robert D. Bullard ed. 1994) (recalling efforts of Latina women who organized to prevent the building of a prison in their neighborhood); Sally Ward Maggard, *Gender Contested: Women's Participation in the Brookside Coal Strike, in* WOMEN AND SOCIAL PROTEST 75, 79–90 (Guida West & Rhoda Lois Blumberg eds. 1990) (women unite to assist in a strike at their husbands' coal mine and were the instrumental force in getting the miners concessions where the men had been unable); Anne F. Scott & Andrew M. Scott, *One Half the People: The Fight for Women's Suffrage, in* WOMEN'S AMERICA 239, 305 (Linda K. Kerber & Jane De Hart-Mathews eds. 1987) (describing women's suffrage movement).

20. Bartlett, *supra* note 3, at 843.

21. *See* Kenneth L. Karst, *Woman's Constitution,* 1984 DUKE L.J. 447.

22. *See* Eugene Volokh, *Freedom of Speech and Appellate Review in Workplace Harassment Cases,* 90 Nw. U. L. REV. 1009 (1996).

23. American Bar Association Commission on Women in the Profession, *A Current Glance of Women in the Law* (2001), *available at* http://www.abanet.org/women/currentglance.pdf.

4

Workplace Discrimination, Wages, and Welfare

In 2003, the median weekly earnings of white men were $715.00. White women earned 79% of this amount ($567). Black women earned 68% ($491). Hispanic women earned 57% ($410).[1]

In 1998, Mitsubishi Motors Corp. paid a record $34 million settlement of sexual harassment claims to 486 women who alleged they were groped, kissed, called derogatory names, and subjected to lewd jokes and displays of sexual graffiti at the company's manufacturing plan in Normal, Illinois.[2]

[L]ess than 10 percent of women in an organization who say they have experienced harassment say they reported it or talked to a supervisor.[3]

In 2000, only 13.5% of male workers requested leave under the federal Family Medical Leave Act. Of those workers, 57.6% took leaves for personal health reasons. Only 22.8% took leave to care for a newborn, newly adopted or foster child.[4]

In 2002 the General Accounting Office ("GAO") examined the salaries of full-time managers in ten industries from 1995 to 2000. In no industry did female managers earn the same as men, and in most industries women lost ground in the five-year period. How wide is the gap? The 2000 census found that the average earnings for women in management and professional occupations were about $15,000 less than those of men. Many of the rationalizations for these inequalities have been debunked. A 2003 GAO report controlled for several factors—from education level to other family income to work interruptions—and still found a 23 percent gender gap.[5] This chapter explores the reasons the gender wage gap relentlessly endures.

Historically, most challenges to workplace discrimination followed the strategy of debunking myths that women are incapable of performing certain jobs. In 1873 Myra Bradwell fought vigorously, though unsuccessfully, to explode the myth of female "timidity and delicacy" that kept married women from practicing law in Illinois. Nearly a hundred years later, Sally Reed defied the stereotype of men as better business people by successfully challenging a statute that preferred males as estate administrators. In 1973 Sharron Frontiero persuaded the Supreme Court to strike down a military benefits plan that presumed that wives of male officers eligible under the plan were economically dependent on their husbands but that husbands of eligible female officers were not. The Supreme Court has continued to reject false stereotypes about women and their abilities. Where underlying gender differences are *real*, discrimination challenges get more complicated. In these cases, feminists seek to discredit not the assumption of difference but the assumption that differences justify burdening women in comparison to men.

A. Defining Workplace Discrimination

1. The history of Title VII

Title VII of the Civil Rights Act of 1964 is the main federal statute addressing employment discrimination based on sex. The statute provides that "[i]t shall be an unlawful employment practice for an employer . . . to discriminate against any individual with respect to his compensation, terms, conditions, or privileges of employment because of such individual's race, color, religion, sex or national origin."[6]

When Title VII first came into force in the summer of 1963, it did not include a prohibition of discrimination based on sex. Many interest groups tried unsuccessfully to add sex as a protected category in the statute. But it was Representative Howard Smith, a conservative Democrat from Virginia (a supporter of the equal rights amendment, but opponent of the race discrimination provisions of Title VII), who proposed the addition of "sex" on the last day the statute was debated.[7] The statute passed as amended, and President Johnson signed it into law a short time later.

The Equal Employment Opportunity Commission ("EEOC") became the federal agency charged with creating policies to implement and enforce Title VII. In the early years, the commission thought the primary purpose of Title VII was to eliminate race discrimination. Indeed, the first executive director of the EEOC, Herman Edelsberg, called the sex provision a "'fluke' that was 'conceived out of wedlock.'"[8]

Because the EEOC did not take sex discrimination seriously, employers did not change their employment practices with respect to the hiring and promotion of women. In the 1960s and early 1970s, NOW pressured the EEOC to enforce Title VII. NOW members picketed newspapers to end the practice of sex-specific "help wanted" advertisements, filed groundbreaking lawsuits to challenge company rules barring women from jobs that required heavy lifting, and publicly demanded that the EEOC create regulations to set standards for public enforcement and private lawsuits. In 1972 the EEOC finally enacted those regulations.[9]

Armed with these regulations, women and men began to take their grievances to federal court. In the 1970s, discrimination lawsuits mainly involved hiring questions. Could a woman be a construction worker, a prison guard, a cop? Could a man become a nurse, a flight attendant, a receptionist? The 1980s saw a shift to lawsuits charging discrimination in promotion and firing.

2. Suing under Title VII

Title VII prohibits two forms of discrimination: disparate treatment and disparate impact. In a disparate treatment suit, the plaintiff must demonstrate that the employer intentionally treated him or her less favorably than coworkers because of sex. The plaintiff can show the discriminatory motive through evidence that is either direct (the boss refuses to hire young women, saying "they'll start having babies and miss work") or circumstantial (a qualified woman is turned down for a job as a "longshoreman" even though the employer has an available position and continues to seek applications).

In disparate impact cases, the plaintiffs show that a facially neutral employment practice disproportionately harms a protected group. No proof of intent is required for disparate impact suits, but plaintiffs must demonstrate that this neutral employment practice has discriminatory effects—a statistically significant disparity in the way the practice affects the plaintiff class. For example, a plaintiff class might show that an employer's minimum height or weight requirement disproportionately excludes women from job opportunities.

The employer then has a chance to respond. In disparate treatment suits, an employer can defend the decision by demonstrating that sex is a "bona fide occupational qualification," what lawyers call a "BFOQ." In disparate impact suits, an employer must show that the offending neutral practice is a "business necessity," related to successful job performance. According to the U.S. Supreme Court, a BFOQ must be more than a flimsy excuse and "is valid only when the essence of the business operation would be undermined." Easy cases include requirements that airport security workers who pat down female travelers be women, or that the male characters in a drama be played by men. Similarly, courts have easily rejected proposed BFOQs grounded on nothing but customer prejudice. Airlines cannot limit flight attendant positions to perky young women any more than law firms can limit their new hirings to men because male attorneys provide a supposed aura of competence. But the line separating bona fide requirements from bogus ones gets surprisingly thin. What of a television broadcaster's insistence that a news anchor team consist of one male and one female? Or a nursing home's requirement that attendants of elderly women be female if that is what the patient requests? Federal courts have accepted both rationales in past discrimination cases.[10] And in the 1977 decision *Dothard v. Rawlinson*,[11] the U.S. Supreme Court held that an all-male maximum-security prison could refuse to hire women as guards in contact positions because the risk of sexual assault on female corrections officers threatened prison security.

The same issue concerning the relevance of sex to job performance has occurred in other contexts. The Supreme Court decided in *UAW v. Johnson Controls*[12] that a battery manufacturer could not exclude fertile women from certain areas of its plant out of concerns that lead exposure might damage fetal development. The Court reasoned that fertile and infertile workers were equally capable of producing batteries and that the "fetal protection policy" was not a legitimate reason to bar all fertile women from lead exposure jobs. In 1997 Hooters restaurant paid $3.75 million to settle a class action for hiring only women as servers. In 2001 a male obstetrician-gynecologist sued an otherwise all-female ob-gyn practice for refusing to make him a share-holder because he was male and not attracting enough patients. Is this rationale persuasive? How about a battered women's shelter that insists its counselors be women? If you are a believer in equal treatment theory, you might find it hard to permit such practices. On the other hand, a cultural feminist might embrace such restrictions. What would a dominance theorist say?

3. Pregnancy, maternity leave, and the work-family conflict

A major barrier to workforce integration involves the way we handle the physical and cultural differences between the sexes. Women and men *are*, after all, different in some ways. On the physical side, only women carry and bear offspring—a biological reality unlikely to be undone in our lifetimes. In addition, on average, adult women tend to be physically smaller than adult men (though exceptions abound). On the cultural side, women continue to bear the lion's share of child care and housekeeping responsibilities. This division of labor is changing, of course, but not everywhere and usually very slowly. Legal theorists disagree about the extent to which antidiscrimination law should recognize physical and social differences between women and men. When should the law recognize differences in average height or child care obligations, and when should it treat people as if they were exactly alike? To put it another way, when does difference make a difference?

Cultural feminists stress that women's economic marginalization may result from their devotion to caregiving. They argue that caregiving is a laudable objective and that the solution is not gender-neutral rules that promote the full integration of women into the workforce. Equal treatment feminists instead argue that women do not enter the workforce with a set of "preordained preferences," and emphasize instead that employers' practices help structure women's job choices.[13] These theorists also worry that if pregnancy (or breastfeeding or child care) is treated as a category of exception, this will feed the perception of women as less capable or less valuable workers. Dominance theorists, rather than asking whether the workplace should make special family-friendly accommodations, such as a separate partnership track, flexible working hours, or part-time positions, propose more fundamental, structural reforms, such as reduced workweeks for all workers or unemployment compensation laws that provide benefits for job separations based on work-family conflicts.

One branch of this discussion has centered on how pregnancy should be treated in the workplace—given no accommodation, treated like other disabilities, or specially accommodated. The debate between special and equal treatment theorists crystallized in a legal battle leading up to the Supreme Court's 1987 decision in *California Federal Savings & Loan v. Guerra*. A California statute provided special treatment for pregnant workers—up to four months of unpaid pregnancy disability leave and the right to job reinstatement. It did not require equivalent paternity leave for men. Challengers argued that the Pregnancy Discrimination Act ("PDA"), an extension of Title VII that compels employers to treat pregnancy like any other disability, precluded this difference in treatment, and feminists filed amicus briefs on both sides. The ACLU, the League of Women Voters, NOW, and the National Women's Law Center argued that the California law was a discriminatory form of protectionist legislation. They urged the treatment of pregnancy in ways comparable to other temporary disabilities to move away from damaging stereotypes about pregnant women. Other feminist groups supported the statute because pregnancy is a condition unique to women and because inadequate leave policies force pregnant workers to choose between their procreational rights and their jobs, a choice not imposed on males. The Supreme Court ultimately held that the PDA created a floor, but not a ceiling, for disability benefits, and reasoned that the preferential treatment was justified: "By 'taking pregnancy into account,' California's pregnancy disability-leave statute allows women, as well as men, to have families without losing their jobs."[14]

The work-family conflict, of which pregnancy and child care issues are a part, still rankles American households and the feminists who study them. It is in part a conflict between the public and private spheres. In the past, the law tried to keep each in its own corner, but this ideology of separate spheres tended to relegate women to the home and exclude them from the public arenas of higher education, employment, and political life. It still does. According to law professor Joan Williams, the pay differential known as the "gender gap" overshadows an equally important differential called the "family gap."[15] The "family gap" measures the wages of mothers against the wages of other adults. While women without children, for instance, earn 90 percent of the wages of men, women with children earn only 60 percent of the wages earned by men with children. This is because at the key stage of career advancement, many mothers (but not fathers) cut back in the workplace—most working fewer than forty hours a week. Consider that 90 percent of American women become mothers, and you can see where this is headed.

Solutions to the work-family conflict require bridging the public-private divide. Families, for instance, could become more equitable in the distribution of household tasks; more fathers could work part-time, and more mothers could pursue career black belts. This idea—which is essentially about injecting the public values of sexual equality into our private relationships—is appealing, but difficult to engineer through law. Our legal tradition normally disfavors governmental intrusions in our family lives.

A second approach would involve making employers more "family-friendly," that is, injecting the values of the private home into the public workplace. This idea is easier for law to accomplish, since a strong tradition of workplace regulation already exists, governing everything from overtime wages for garment workers to air quality standards in office buildings. In one effort to make employers more family-friendly, Congress enacted the Family and Medical Leave Act of 1993 ("FMLA"). The law requires large employers—those with fifty or more employees—to grant male and female employees up to twelve weeks of unpaid leave during a twelve-month period for the birth and care of a newborn, the arrival of an adopted or foster child, or the care of a family member, or for an employee's own serious medical needs.[16] One criticism of the FMLA is that the leave is *unpaid,* a fact that may explain why FMLA leave is most often used to care for an employee's own medical needs rather than the needs of a family member.[17] In contrast, nearly all other industrialized countries offer *paid* parental leave for an average of thirty-six weeks.[18] And it is not uncommon for such countries to offer unpaid or partially paid leaves of three years or more.

B. Feminist Legal Theory in the Courtroom

Feminist legal theory has strongly influenced employment litigation. Not only has feminist jurisprudence shaped the strategies of civil rights lawyers and legislators who argued the landmark cases and worked toward the enactment of antidiscrimination legislation, it has also fueled a trend toward a less formal and more cooperative process of settling cases, called alternative dispute resolution. Perhaps most important, feminist theory helped show how familiar stereotypes played into the hands of economic oppression. What were formerly thought to be biological differences between men and women are now seen as socially scripted gender roles.

A landmark case from the U.S. Supreme Court that highlights the role of stereotyping in employment decisions is *Price Waterhouse v. Hopkins*.[19] Ann Hopkins was denied partnership by the accounting giant Price Waterhouse. Despite her being one of the best "rainmakers" at the firm, several reviewing partners criticized her dress and demeanor. One stated that she was too "macho" and "overly aggressive" and needed to take a "course at charm school." Another was concerned that Hopkins was "a lady using foul language." A supporter advised her to "walk more femininely, dress more femininely, wear make-up, have her hair styled, and wear jewelry."

The Supreme Court held that Price Waterhouse violated Title VII in its use of gendered comments to deny Hopkins partnership, recognizing for the first time that sex stereotyping could be a form of sex discrimination. *Price Waterhouse,* though, was the easy case of visible discrimination based on failure to conform to gender stereotypes—with explicit statements in Hopkins's partnership file. Most cases entail more subtle forms of discrimination and are more difficult to prove, such as male workers who are not "manly" enough, the dockworker who is offended by coworkers' raunchy insults and rough horseplay, or the effeminate grade school teacher who wears a gold earring.[20] Other cases concern gays and lesbians who endure slurs, taunts, and worse because of their relationships outside the workplace, or the female television news reporter who is told to wear blouses with more "feminine touches" to appeal to more conservative viewers.[21] Imagine the glances, gestures, or code words (Do *you* have "fire in the belly"?) that can doom an employee who does not conform to gender role expectations.

Although legal theorists have made progress in exposing and redressing some forms of social stereotyping in employment, others remain. Employers can enforce sex-specific dress and grooming codes (for instance, requiring women to wear pantyhose or limiting hair length for men) that promote the employer's business image. Courts have explicitly held that Title VII did not intend to change community standards about acceptable dress. Wardrobe emerges as a mere preference about personal presentation, not a matter of autonomy or equal rights. The idea is that "excluding men who wear dresses from the workplace does not keep women down."[22]

Another example of social stereotyping includes employee job choice. Consider, for instance, the choice of which sales department to join in a department store. In *EEOC v. Sears Roebuck & Co.,*[23] the EEOC, using multiple regression analyses that controlled for age, education, and qualification differences among applicants, established a strong statistical case that the company had a pattern of hiring men for higher-paying commission sales jobs. Sears hired men to sell appliances, furnaces, building supplies, and hardware, while it hired predominantly women in lower-paying noncommissioned jobs to sell apparel and cosmetics. Sears defended with survey evidence showing that female sales applicants lacked interest in the commission sales positions because they were competitive, high pressure, and had irregular hours. Women preferred the more feminine tasks of selling accessories and housewares.

A federal court of appeals accepted this "choice" or "lack of interest" defense, holding that women's underrepresentation in commission sales positions was the result of their own job preferences. The court assumed that women naturally gravitate toward "the softer side of Sears," but it omitted any evaluation of the ways employer practices could have shaped women's preferences. Sears, for example, used a "vigor" scale to rate job applicants, and interviewers determined applicants' ratings on that scale according to prepared questions that included whether applicants had played football, had ever hunted, swore often, or possessed a lower-pitched voice. The *Sears* court treated women's choices as if they were completely unaffected by any employer practices, such as a lack of training for nontraditional jobs or the wage structure of commission and noncommission jobs that made selling dresses a lower-paying job than selling fencing.

An interesting dimension of the *Sears* litigation was the way both sides used feminist historians as expert witnesses. Professor Rosalind Rosenberg testified on behalf of Sears that women preferred the lower-stress, less aggressive, less competitive jobs selling apparel and accessories and that they could enter and leave these jobs more easily, thus adapting their work to familial responsibilities. Professor Alice Kessler-Harris testified for the EEOC that women, like men, acted out of economic self-interest, and that employer limitations on job opportunities affected women's preferences, rather than women having inherently different interests than men in selling particular products. She drew on women's acceptance of traditionally male jobs throughout history when those jobs became obtainable. She concluded that women made choices about jobs principally based on "the framework of available opportunity."

The *Sears* case was intriguing on a number of levels. It was a straightforward face-off of feminist theorists in the courtroom—a direct application of theory, in a partisan context, where some subtlety and nuance were necessarily omitted. Sears's strategy represents a successful use of difference theory, with an autonomy twist, to avoid inquiry into its employment practices. The "choice" strategy developed in *Sears*—the idea that women voluntarily choose economic disadvantage to accommodate their family responsibilities, and that women lack interest in jobs traditionally held by men—now represents a well-entrenched Title VII defense to employment discrimination claims. In fact, a study reveals that in cases decided between 1967 and 1989, employers succeeded on this lack of interest defense in sex discrimination cases more than 40 percent of the time.[24]

C. Sexual Harassment

The law of sexual harassment represents one of the most direct translations of legal theory into legal doctrine. In 1979 dominance theorist Catharine MacKinnon wrote a landmark book, *Sexual Harassment of Working Women: A Case of Sex Discrimination*. MacKinnon began with women's stories about the practices of sexual harassment: an eighteen-year-old file clerk whose employer routinely told her about the intimacies of his marriage and asked her opinions about various sexual positions; a secretary who was asked to accompany her boss on an out-of-town trip (the hotel accommodations he made had her staying in the same room with him, and when she refused to have sex with him, upon their return, he deprived her of her job responsibilities); the first female to work as a janitor for a company, who was assigned to clean men's bathrooms on the night shift, where she was repeatedly propositioned for sex, and suffered extreme stress. These episodes were about more than personality conflicts or "men behaving badly." They told a collective story of how sexually charged behavior—from the boorish to the bellicose—altered working conditions nationwide for women. While the male janitor mopped and polished to earn his paycheck, the female janitor had to mop, polish, *and* repel sexual predators. The private cocoon of male-female relations had been reinterpreted as a force in the market economy.

MacKinnon argued that then-existing employment, contract, and tort laws did not provide adequate remedies for certain types of gender-based indignities women suffered at work. She concluded that "the unwanted imposition of sexual requirements in the context of a relationship of unequal power" should be considered discrimination on the basis of sex under Title VII. MacKinnon coined the ideas of "quid pro quo" harassment (conditioning employment benefits on an explicit request for sexual favors) and sexually hostile environment (where the working conditions include gender-based intimidation or hostilities that create an abusive environment). Her book prompted the EEOC the very next year to revise its "Guidelines on Discrimination Because of Sex" to include both quid pro quo and hostile environment harassment as sex discrimination in violation of Title VII.

In 1986 the Supreme Court decided *Meritor Bank v. Vinson,* recognizing both types of sexual harassment. In 1991 the nation received a public education about sexual harassment when the Senate Judiciary Committee held confirmation hearings for Justice Clarence Thomas and heard testimony about Anita Hill's allegations that he harassed her. In 1992 the EEOC handled about 10,500 sexual harassment charges. That number then increased significantly in the late 1990s and has since waned somewhat: from 1995 to 2001, the EEOC received approximately 15,500 sexual harassment charges each year. The number of EEOC charges dropped to 14,396 in 2002 and to 13,566 in 2003.[25] In the decade from 1992 to 2002, the proportion of charges filed by males increased from 9 percent to almost 15 percent.

Finally, in 1998, the Supreme Court clarified when employers would be vicariously liable for harassment by supervisors. If an employee experienced a tangible employment-based loss, such as a demotion, promotion denial, or termination, the employer is strictly liable. Absent such a tangible job action, the employer can raise an affirmative defense to avoid liability by proving that it "exercised reasonable care to prevent and correct promptly" any harassing behavior and that the plaintiff "unreasonably failed to take advantage of any preventive or corrective opportunities provided by the employer or to avoid harm otherwise."[26] Employers are liable for harassment by coworkers if they knew or should have known of the harassment and failed to take prompt and appropriate corrective action.

Quid pro quo harassment is fairly straightforward. It occurs when a supervisor makes an unwelcome sexual advance a term or condition of employment. The proof required in a hostile environment case is more complicated. According to the Supreme Court, the harassment must be both unwelcome and sufficiently severe or pervasive "to create an objectively hostile or abusive work environment—an environment that a reasonable person would find hostile or abusive,"[27] and one that the victim subjectively perceives as abusive as well. Typically, to demonstrate sufficient severity, the plaintiff must show that the workplace "is permeated with discriminatory intimidation, ridicule, and insult." The plaintiff does not have to show a tangible or economic injury.

Requiring the plaintiff to prove that harassment is "unwelcome" implies that sexualized behavior on the job is otherwise normal, or at least consented to. While commentators have suggested making "welcomeness" an affirmative defense, most courts require plaintiffs to prove the negative—that the harassment is unwelcome—as part of their prima facie case.

The test for "unwelcomeness" often focuses on whether the complainant has in some way invited the harassing behavior. Courts investigate whether the plaintiff has engaged in any sexual banter, used sexually explicit or foul language, dated coworkers, participated in practical jokes of a sexual nature, or dressed in a sexually provocative manner. In *Meritor Bank,* the Supreme Court even said that evidence of "a complainant's sexually provocative speech or dress . . . is obviously relevant." Whether a plaintiff has solicited or invited harassment often turns into an investigation of the alleged victim's behavior, habits, appearance, character, or lifestyle.

The unwelcomeness inquiry recalls the old practices in rape law which put the victim "on trial" by focusing on her nonconsent or introducing evidence of her past sexual history. In 1994 Congress amended the Federal Rules of Evidence to extend rape shield protection to civil cases, including sexual harassment suits. Rule 412 excludes evidence about the plaintiff's past sexual behavior unless its probative value substantially outweighs any prejudicial effect. Most courts apply the rule to preclude the introduction of evidence about the complainant's nonworkplace conduct, unless she has discussed that conduct at work.

Even if sexual character evidence is omitted, conclusions about whether the plaintiff welcomed the attention of the alleged harasser still reflect prevailing social norms about appropriate gender behavior. Some of the culturally prescribed ways that women typically respond to difficult situations (such as offensive jokes or a kiss on the cheek from a supervisor)—with silence, an uncomfortable laugh, or attempts to maintain friendly interactions—can be interpreted as consent or encouragement.

Consider the case of Mary Carr. In 1984 she became the first female tinsmith apprentice to work in the gas turbine division at General Motors. All of Mary's coworkers were male and many resented her presence. Over a period of five years, Mary's colleagues continuously harassed her. They painted the word "cunt" on her toolbox; left sexual graffiti and nude pinups in her work areas; told her that they "won't work with any cunt"; referred to her as "whore," "cunt," and "split tail"; cut the seat out of her overalls; stripped to their underwear in front of her on several occasions; urinated off the roof of the building in front of her. One coworker suggested "that if he ever fell from a dangerous height in the shop she would have to give him 'mouth to dick' resuscitation."[28]

Yet, the U.S. District Court for the Southern District of Indiana dismissed Mary's claim for sexual harassment because she had "invited it." The trial court had found evidence that Mary had used the "F" word, told dirty jokes, used vulgar language, engaged in a shouting match with a male coworker, touched the thigh of another male coworker, and pointed out the clitoris depicted in a pornographic picture when coworkers asked her to do so. The trial judge found that she had "provoked" them by engaging in "unladylike" behavior.

The Seventh Circuit Court of Appeals reversed the trial court on the issue of Mary welcoming her coworkers' harassment. The appellate court refused to compare Mary's conduct to that of her coworkers or to justify their behavior based on hers because, as one woman surrounded by many men, her foul language should have been seen as only an attempt to fit in.

In determining whether the harassment in a given case is sufficiently severe or pervasive to constitute a harassing environment, a number of courts have held that the standard varies depending on the work setting. Thus, some federal appellate courts accept a "blue-collar" environment defense to crude language or offensive behavior for rough, working-class jobs.[29] Other courts reject the idea that the standard for harassment depends on the culture of the industry, since this would perpetuate the pattern of gender discrimination in occupations where it has traditionally been accepted. The Sixth Circuit found the industry standard reasoning "illogical, because it means that the more hostile the environment, and the more prevalent the sexism, the more difficult it is for a Title VII plaintiff to prove that sex-based conduct is sufficiently severe or pervasive to constitute a hostile work environment."[30]

The law of sexual harassment requires not only that the plaintiff subjectively perceive the working environment to be abusive, but also that an objective, reasonable person in the plaintiff's position would reach the same conclusion. Some feminist theorists argued that a "reasonable person" instruction invites jurors to think that the person who stands in the plaintiff's shoes is a reasonable man. They pointed out that perceptions may differ based on gender and argued that women are more sensitive to sexually harassing conduct—women are more likely than men to perceive sexual compliments, jokes, innuendo, or propositions as unwelcome and offensive; men are more likely than women to impose responsibility for harassment on the victim. Other feminists argued that the reasonable person standard did not necessarily enforce a male viewpoint and that a gendered standard based on presumed vulnerability risks branding women as overly emotional creatures.

Four circuit courts of appeal and several state courts in the late 1980s and early 1990s accepted the reasonable woman standard. But most federal and state appellate courts continue to use the reasonable person standard. The Supreme Court has not decided the issue.[31] Trial simulation studies from the middle to late 1990s examined the influence of different legal standards on juror decision making. Most concluded that the legal standard had virtually no effect on jurors' conclusions regarding whether sexual harassment had occurred, because jurors used their own criteria.[32]

It was not until 1998 that the Supreme Court held that-same sex sexual harassment was actionable under Title VII. Prior to the decision in *Oncale v. Sundowner Offshore Services,*[33] the federal courts of appeal were split over whether Title VII prohibited same-sex (principally male on male) harassment. A number of courts flatly rejected same-sex claims. They were troubled by the "because of sex" language in Title VII and could not see how harassment between members of the same sex could be "because of sex." Some circuits allowed same-sex claims if the alleged perpetrator was homosexual but not if the perpetrator was heterosexual and the victim homosexual. Several courts held that the language of Title VII did not limit "who may bring suit based on the sex of either the harasser or the person harassed," and that Title VII was intended to eliminate workplace harassment that was sexual in nature, irrespective of the motive or sexual orientation of the perpetrator.[34] In short, many courts had difficulty seeing sexual harassment as anything other than the paradigm case of excessive male-on-female attention motivated by sexual desire.

Joseph Oncale, a crew worker on an offshore oil rig, suffered persistent sexual taunts, physical assaults and rape threats at the hands of coworkers and supervisors. During one incident, his supervisor restrained him while a coworker shoved a bar of soap into his anus. Oncale quit his job and sued for sexual harassment. The Fifth Circuit Court of Appeals held that Title VII did not recognize claims for same sex harassment. The Supreme Court reversed, holding that same-sex harassment was actionable as sex discrimination under Title VII. The Court noted that the "because of sex" requirement could be satisfied by showing sexual desire, hostility to one sex, or "direct comparative evidence about how the alleged harasser treated members of both sexes in a mixed-sex workplace."[35] Unclear after *Oncale* is whether harassment based on the sexual orientation or gender identity of the victim (an effeminate male or a masculine female harassed because of failure to conform to prevailing gender stereotypes) is actionable.[36]

Although the *Oncale* decision was unanimous, the opinion, written by Justice Scalia, left open a number of questions. Despite the progressive holding regarding same-sex harassment, Justice Scalia insisted that Title VII "does not reach genuine but innocuous differences in the ways men and women routinely interact with members of the same sex and of the opposite sex" and that the statute should not become "a civility code." He offered several examples of what he called "ordinary socializing in the workplace" that should not be mistaken for harassment: "male-on-male horseplay," "intersexual flirtation," and "simple teasing or roughhousing among members of the same sex." Scalia wrote, "A professional football player's working environment is not severely or pervasively abusive, for example, if the coach smacks him on the buttocks as he heads onto the field—even if the same behavior would reasonably be experienced as abusive by the coach's secretary (male or female) back at the office."[37] Since *Oncale*, lower courts have addressed the contours of the permissible hazing—"teasing," "roughhousing," or "horseplay"—defense and whether an "equal opportunity harasser" (one who harasses both sexes equally) can be liable.

The law of sexual harassment has evolved rapidly in a relatively short span of time. Feminist theories helped trace the pattern of dominance and desire in the workplace, linking it to hostility toward women in unconventional jobs or toward women in general. Feminist theories also enable critics to explore the mismatched perspectives from which men and women view their behavior. Most important, these theories enabled courts to reconceive some patterns of workplace behavior as legal wrongs that cause economic harm and deserve compensation.

History teaches that once a legal right is won, the specter of political retrenchment is always near. After the Supreme Court handed American Indians a victory for tribal sovereignty in *Worcester v. Georgia*,[38] for instance, neither the state of Georgia nor President Andrew Jackson would do anything to enforce it.[39] Today, some argue that the civil rights victories of the 1950s through the 1970s are being quietly rolled back by lax enforcement officers and hostile judges. The phenomenon can be attributed to a dynamic that law professor Derrick Bell calls "interest convergence."[40] In this view, government does not protect the rights of the powerless simply because "it is the right thing to do." It does so because the practical interests of dominant groups (soothing guilt, impressing the international community, and so on) have suddenly "converged" with the practical interests of the less empowered. When this convergence wanes, so does the commitment to equal rights. After the heady days of Title VII and civil rights activism, public interest in sexual equality wilted, as did political leadership at the EEOC.

D. Occupational Segregation and Equal Pay

Women constitute almost half (47 percent) of the workforce in this country,[41] yet jobs remain sharply segregated by sex. In 1990, almost seventy occupations (including electricians, auto mechanics, plumbers, roofers, carpenters, firefighters, and airplane pilots) were at least 95 percent male, while seven (including secretaries, receptionists, dental assistants, preschool and kindergarten teachers, and child care workers) were 95 percent female. Many other fields are over 90 percent male or female.[42] Women are vastly overrepresented in traditionally female jobs with low pay, low status, and high turnover: 79 percent of administrative support occupations, including clerical jobs, are held by women, whereas 91 percent of jobs in precision production, craft, and repair occupations are held by men.[43] In short, approximately half of all men or all women in the workforce would have to change jobs for there to be equal occupational distributions between the sexes.[44]

Most career choices are probably the result of a complex set of factors. Traditional explanations for the phenomenon of occupational segregation by sex focus on supply-side reasons—that men and women enter the labor market with different education, training, and preferences. Some occupational aspirations are formed early, as boys and girls are channeled educationally into or away from math or science. Social expectations may stake out appropriate career territories for men and women, and people may make vocational choices based on traditional social roles. However, early socialization has played a somewhat lesser role in recent years as women have ventured into traditionally male fields, and recent survey data indicate women consistently have aspirations to work in traditionally male jobs. Conversely, more men are entering traditionally female occupations; however, the absolute numbers remain small, and social pressures still discourage men from working in child care occupations. Contemporary studies by labor economists suggest that employer practices exclude both men and women from occupations not traditional for their genders and shape employee preferences for certain jobs, given workplace cultures, and the description of jobs in masculine or feminine terms. Economists have also demonstrated the self-perpetuating phenomenon of segregation—that women steer away from nonintegrated workplaces because they "rationally use level of diversity as a proxy for discrimination."[45]

Segregation by sex persists not only horizontally across occupations, but also vertically within workplaces. Even where integration exists in certain fields, women are underrepresented in positions of power at work. Fifteen years ago, women held "about 13% of tenured academic posts, 6% of the partnerships of large law firms, 5% of federal elective offices, and 3% of executive positions at publicly traded corporations."[46] The numbers have not changed substantially since then. Women "hold only about 5 percent of the top-level jobs" in the American workforce. "Their representation in senior management positions has risen at a glacial rate, from 3 percent in 1980 to 7 percent today."[47]

Limits on women's or men's entrance into a profession and success in a career that has traditionally been identified with the other sex present one dilemma of formal equality: informal barriers create impediments and construct "glass ceilings" that foil substantive equality. These artificial barriers to advancement include gender stereotypes about roles, abilities, and leadership styles; exclusion of women from informal networks of communication; a lack of company commitment to the advancement of women; and the absence of mentors. The subtle forms of bias—such as not having lunch or playing racquetball with a supervisor, and then not being considered as "a team player"— may be difficult to see in everyday working life. Senior leaders may assume that "women's emotions prevent them from managing effectively," or they may subscribe to deep normative standards that women should not exercise power over men.[48]

Here again, "choice" theory (that women make independent decisions to work in female-dominated industries because they like the work, or forgo promotions to stay in jobs that allow more time for family responsibilities) battles structuralist theories (that attitudinal bias, discriminatory employer practices, and organizational structures without family-supportive plan such as flexible hours hinder women's advancement). The tension between these causal explanations is often internalized: "A quick look at bookstore shelves suggests that middle-tier women who buy books about the glass ceiling are more likely to demand books that tell them how to make better choices than books that describe institutionalized discrimination and/or explain intersections among race, gender and class."[49]

The division of labor by sex relates directly to the gender wage gap. The culture undervalues the kinds of work performed predominantly by women. The labor market devalues caregiving jobs, such as nursing and social work, because they are close to domestic activities and because the qualities and skills those jobs require, such as compassion, nurturing, and empathy, are associated with women.[50] Male-dominated occupations command higher pay. Estimates vary, but labor sociologists and economists who focus on job rather than occupation-level integration estimate that segregation accounts for approximately 80 percent of the pay gap between the sexes.[51] Work patterns also play a role in the wage gap. Female employees "have fewer years of work experience, work fewer hours per year, are less likely to work a full-time schedule, and leave the labor force for longer periods of time than men."[52]

While occupational segregation is tied to wage discrimination, the way current discrimination laws are structured, they cannot reach wage inequalities caused by job segregation based on sex. The Title VII discrimination model is best for individual instances of similarly situated men and women being treated differently. With the success of the lack of interest argument, as in the *Sears* case, Title VII has limited potential to systemically desegregate the workplace. Furthermore, Title VII simply cannot "address what is not there at all: the need for state or employer-provided day care, flex-time to attend to children's needs, or maternity benefits."[53]

The other main federal statute to attack sex-based wage discrimination is the Equal Pay Act. It requires that men and women receive equal pay for equal work in jobs within a given establishment that require "equal skill, effort and responsibility, and which are performed under similar working conditions."[54] The equal pay mandate is not triggered unless the jobs compared are "substantially equal."

In the early 1980s, theorists concerned with substantive, not just formal, equality developed the concept of "comparable worth"—the idea that Title VII's prohibition on wage discrimination should extend beyond the Equal Pay Act's minimum requirement of equal pay for substantially equal work. It was an effort to address a portion of the wage gap attributable to occupational segregation, something the Equal Pay Act would never reach, because that law requires equal pay for men and women only when their jobs are equal in content. Comparable worth theory says "that work perceived as women's work has been downgraded and that the value of work performed in predominantly female jobs—by male and female workers alike—is systematically underrated, given the relative skill, effort, and responsibility involved."[55] Comparable worth proposes that jobs that are comparable—but not substantially equal—in their value to the employer should command equal pay.

In the 1980s, a number of states conducted studies of public jobs, measuring them not by market wages but according to their relative worth to the employer, as signified by characteristics such as time demands, physical effort, skills, supervisory responsibilities, and working conditions. Weights were assigned to each factor, and regression techniques were used to evaluate whether jobs were actually being paid according to their internal value to the employer. In this way, evaluators could compare pay scales for people in dissimilar jobs such as, say, nurses and truck drivers.

Critics question whether jobs actually have any intrinsic or objective value and argue that the techniques of weighting job factors invite subjective assessments. They maintain that evaluating millions of jobs would be costly and that widespread adoption of comparable worth would represent a considerable intervention in the market. Opponents of comparable worth insist that the forces of supply and demand in the labor market provide a neutral standard for evaluating the worth of jobs. Supporters, of course, question the presumption that the market operates in a nondiscriminatory manner. Some challengers, such as Phyllis Schlafly, argue that comparable worth would undermine job desegregation because it would eliminate the economic incentive for women to enter traditionally male fields: "After all, why would a woman want to be a telephone pole repair person, a highway ditch digger or a prison guard if she could get the same pay working in a carpeted climate controlled office?"[56]

Although employers have commissioned comparable worth assessments that documented substantial wage disparities, and those studies have been used by plaintiffs under Title VII, courts have consistently rejected comparable worth suits. The Ninth Circuit held that

"Title VII does not obligate [an employer] to eliminate an economic inequality that it did not create."[57]

In contrast to American law, courts in the European Union have embraced comparable worth theory. Interpretations of the European Economic Community Treaty's Article 119 requires "equal remuneration for equal work as between men and women workers," language that closely approximates the Equal Pay Act. The Council of Ministers has interpreted Article 119 in the Equal Pay Directive to mean essentially equal pay "for the same work or for work to which equal value is attributed," essentially a comparable worth standard.[58] Australia, Canada, New Zealand, and the United Kingdom have also experienced some success revaluing the jobs predominantly held by women with mandatory comparable worth or pay equity programs.

As the experience of other countries shows, comparable worth is capable of remedying some of the sex-based wage disparities resulting from occupational segregation by sex. Resistance stems in part from the same forces that keep occupations sex-segregated: deep-seated cultural beliefs that males and females are inherently suited for fundamentally different kinds of work.

E. Employment in the Military

1. GI Jane

War is man's work. Biological convergence on the battlefield would not only be dissatisfying in terms of what women could do, but it would be an enormous psychological distraction for the male who wants to think that he's fighting for that woman somewhere behind, not up there in the same foxhole with him. It trumples the male ego. When you get right down to it, you have to protect the manliness of war. General Robert H. Barrow, U.S. Marine Corps[59]

In this country, for the most part, men are the soldiers. The Women's Armed Services Integration Act of 1948 allowed women to begin serving in the military (and not just enlist in auxiliary forces) but limited the number of women to no more than 2 percent of the ranks. The act also banned women from serving in combat areas. The Military Selective Service Act mandates draft registration by all males between the ages of eighteen and twenty-six.[60] The U.S. Supreme Court held in 1981 in *Rostker v. Goldberg*[61] that selective service registration for men, but not women, did not violate equal protection guarantees. The Court determined that in the area of military affairs, it should defer to the judgment of Congress, and because women were not eligible for combat positions, by statute, men and women were not similarly situated for purposes of draft registration.

Following the Gulf War, in 1993, Congress repealed parts of the combat exclusion for women, allowing women to serve on combat ships and planes.[62] Military policy, however, still bars women from service on submarines and from units that are likely to directly engage the enemy in ground combat. Although women constitute 14 percent of all soldiers (and about one-fifth of recruits), they are excluded from "infantry, armor, short-range air defense, cannon artillery, combat engineers, and special forces."[63] This means that women are precluded from serving in roughly one-third of jobs in the army. The combat restrictions also exclude women from career paths that lead to the highest-ranking military positions.

Some feminists argue that allowing women to serve in all combat positions in the military—in an environment free of harassment, with career advancement opportunities, where their opinions will be taken seriously on military matters—is essential to full citizenship. Others question whether women should fight to participate in an institution that embraces hierarchy and glorifies brutality, particularly when feminists have more urgent domestic issues to address, such as equal pay, intimate violence, and sexual harassment. Practical arguments against full integration of women into all military positions range from assertions that women lack strength to concerns that they would have special privacy or hygiene needs, or would distract male soldiers and destroy unit cohesion. Supporters respond by noting that war is becoming increasingly technological, making strength less of an issue, and it is increasingly difficult to discern a line between combatant and that noncombatant activity. Since some women can meet physical strength requirements, the military should simply impose those threshold requirements rather than exclude all women; in addition, other countries, such as Canada, Denmark, Germany, Israel, and Norway, allow women to serve in combat roles.

The male-only draft registration and other military exclusions are usually framed in terms of how they disadvantage women. Virtually untold, though, are the stories of the much greater numbers of men who are forced into military service. With required registration, men have no alternative other than to be this country's warriors. In 2003 a group of students, including a brother and sister, Nicole Foley and Samuel Schwartz, filed a lawsuit in a Massachusetts federal district court alleging that the male-only selective service registration violated equal protection guarantees in explicitly burdening men and exempting women. The judge dismissed the suit with reasoning that echoed the Supreme Court's circular rationale in *Rostker:* since the purpose of the selective service registration statute was to create combat troops, and women are still prohibited from serving in ground combat areas, men and women are not similarly situated. The court also noted that since bills were introduced in Congress in 2003 to require women as well as men to register for conscription, the judiciary should defer to the legislature, since it is the body to which the Constitution assigns military powers.[64]

2. "Don't Ask, Don't Tell"

Women are not the only ones impeded from serving in the military. Until 1993, the military had a strict rule prohibiting homosexuals from serving in the armed forces. During Bill Clinton's presidential campaign, he promised to eliminate the prohibition on gays serving in the military. Instead, he signed a purported compromise, the "Don't Ask, Don't Tell" policy, which supposedly relaxed the strict ban.[65] The policy bans homosexual conduct, making statements that one is gay or lesbian, or attempts to marry a same-sex partner.

As of the summer of 2004, the military has discharged 9,682 service members for simply being gay or lesbian under the Don't Ask, Don't Tell policy—more dismissals than under the prior ban. The policy has also led to thousands of cases of harassment and hazing of personnel suspected of being homosexual.[66] Courts have "uniformly" upheld the exclusion of gays and lesbians from the military, often under the rationale that their admission would undermine unit cohesion.[67] An open question is whether the Supreme Court's decision in *Lawrence v. Texas*[68]—holding that a Texas statute criminalizing same-sex sodomy violates the due process clause—overrules the "Don't Ask, Don't Tell" policy.[69]

F. Welfare Reform and Economic Independence

In 1996 Congress passed the Personal Responsibility and Work Opportunity Reconciliation Act ("PRWORA"), a law that promised, as President Clinton put it, to "end welfare as we know it."[70] The act replaced a larger entitlements-based program, known as Aid to Families with Dependent Children ("AFDC"), with a more limited grant-based program designed to move welfare recipients from welfare to work. Under PRWORA, a recipient can receive aid for a maximum of twenty-four consecutive months before his or her grant is terminated. An individual's total lifetime receipt of welfare benefits is limited to five years.

PRWORA dramatically reduced welfare rolls and reintroduced millions of Americans—many of whom are women—into the workforce. But the act did little to increase women's economic independence. Because most former recipients who have taken jobs are paid at or near the minimum wage, many new female workers still cannot support themselves or their families. In addition, former female recipients remain occupationally segregated. Many available, low-skilled jobs are in the clerical and caretaking fields, and studies suggest that government case workers overwhelmingly direct women to these fields over, say, truck driving or construction.[71] There is an irony here: many poor single moms who once stayed home caring for their own young children are now encouraged to join the workforce, where they will instead care for other people's young children. PRWORA offers some child care funds for off-welfare mothers (who would presumably employ yet *another* level of professional caregivers), but critics charge that these funds are often insufficient.

G. Questions for Discussion

1. At the heart of gender and work issues has been societal refusal to value housework and child care. Some feminists, such as Caitlin Flanagan, argue that professional, white women are exploiting third world women as nannies and housekeepers.[72] Some women's ability to enter the workforce depends on their taking advantage of another market to provide child care. This shifts the burden of caretaking from one group of women to another, less economically

powerful group. Do you agree that in order for some women to enter the workforce, they have to subscribe to a system that undervalues the work that women do in the home and with children? Is this necessarily exploitive? Is it possible to be a parent and work outside the home without enforcing these stereotypes? Is it the role of private individuals to address this problem, or is it the responsibility of government to create a system in which people do not have to make Hobbesian choices?

2. A substantial divide separates popular opinion about sexual harassment and legal theory and doctrine. Many people think sexual harassment is only about sexual desire. Legal doctrine recognizes that sexual harassment is not just about sex, but also about power. Members of the public believe that juries are awarding large verdicts for people saying "'Nice ass' once, jokingly, by the water cooler."[73] The law requires that harassment must be severe and pervasive. Why do such differences exist between the law and public opinion?

3. We have argued that the "dress code" cases suggest a relationship between antidiscrimination law and worker autonomy. That is, in upholding regulations on appearance, courts say that Title VII was not intended to promote autonomy over what one looks like. A right to wear tank tops, flip-flops, a nose ring? Forget it. But other cases, like *Sears,* appear to take a more expansive view of worker autonomy. In *Sears,* for instance, when the EEOC argued that the department store was shunting women into dead-end jobs, the court insisted that such women were merely exercising their autonomy, their choice—a choice, which, the court implied, Title VII *protects.* Are the dress code cases inconsistent with *Sears,* or can they be reconciled? Should these cases be seen as disputes over autonomy at all?

SUGGESTED READINGS

Kathryn Abrams, *Cross-Dressing in the Master's Clothes,* 109 YALE L.J. 745 (2000).

Kathryn Abrams, *The New Jurisprudence of Sexual Harassment,* 83 CORNELL L. REV. 1169 (1998).

Katharine T. Bartlett, *Only Girls Wear Barrettes: Dress and Appearance Stan-*

dards, Community Norms, and Workplace Equality, 92 MICH. L. REV. 2541 (1994).

Cynthia Grant Bowman & Elizabeth M. Schneider, *Feminist Legal Theory, Feminist Lawmaking, and the Legal Profession,* 67 FORDHAM L. REV. 249 (1998).

Ruth Colker, *Pregnancy, Parenting and Capitalism,* 58 OHIO ST. L. J. 61 (1997).

Mary Anne C. Case, *Disaggregating Gender from Sex and Sexual Orientation: The Effeminate Man in the Law and Feminist Jurisprudence,* 105 YALE L.J. 1 (1995).

BARBARA EHRENREICH, NICKEL AND DIMED: ON (NOT) GETTING BY IN AMERICA (2001).

Lucinda M. Finley, *Transcending Equality Theory: A Way Out of the Maternity and the Workplace Debate,* 86 COLUM. L. REV. 1118 (1986).

JANET HALLEY, DON'T: A READER'S GUIDE TO THE MILITARY'S ANTI-GAY POLICY (1999).

Diane H. Mazur, *A Call to Arms,* 22 HARV. WOMEN'S L.J. 39 (1999).

Vicki Schulz, *Life's Work,* 100 COLUM. L. REV. 1881 (2000).

NOTES:

1. U.S. Dep't of Labor, Bureau of Labor Statistics, Table No. 37, *Median Weekly Earnings of Full Time Wage and Salary Workers by Selected Characteristics,* ftp://ftp.bls.gov/pub/special.requests/lf/aat37.txt (last visited Apr. 21, 2004).

2. James P. Miller, *Business Brief: Mitsubishi Will Pay $34 Million in Sexual-Harassment Settlement,* WALL ST. J., June 12, 1998, at B4.

3. Gail Schmoller Philbin, *Silent Majority,* CHI. TRIB., Feb. 25, 2004, at 1.

4. U.S. Dep't of Labor, *Balancing the Needs of Families and Employers,* tbls.A2–2.6, http://www.dol.gov/asp/fmla/APPX-A-2-TABLES.htm (last visited June 18, 2004).

5. Marie C. Wilson, *Time to Close Gender Wage Gap,* DET. FREE PRESS, Dec. 22, 2003, *available at* 2003 WL 71423713.

6. 42 U.S.C. § 2000e-2(a)(1) (1964). The statute's use of *his* is meant to include men *and* women.

7. 110 Cong. Rec. 2577-581 (1964) (remarks of Rep. Smith). The lack of legislative history defining "sex" in this context now fuels debate about whether Title VII protects against discrimination based on sexual orientation.

8. JO FREEMAN, THE POLITICS OF WOMEN'S LIBERATION: A CASE STUDY OF AN EMERGING SOCIAL MOVEMENT AND ITS RELATION TO THE POLICY PROCESS 54 (1975).

9. 29 C.F.R. § 1604 (1972).

10. Fesel v. Masonic Home of Delaware, 447 F. Supp. 1346 (D. Del. 1978).

11. 433 U.S. 321 (1977).

12. 499 U.S. 187 (1991).

13. Vicki Schultz, *Telling Stories About Women and Work: Judicial Interpretations of Sex Segregation in the Workplace in Title VII Cases Raising the Lack of Interest Argument,* 103 HARV. L. REV. 1749, 1840 (1990).

14. 479 U.S. 272, 289 (1987).

15. Joan Williams, *Our Economy of Mothers and Others: Women and Economics Revisited,* 5 J. GENDER RACE & JUST. 411, 416 (2002).

16. 29 U.S.C. § 2612 (2001).

17. U.S. DEPARTMENT OF LABOR, BALANCING THE NEEDS OF FAMILIES AND EMPLOYERS: THE FAMILY AND MEDICAL LEAVE SURVEYS, 2000 UPDATE, *available at* http://www.dol.gov/asp/fmla/chapter2.htm.

18. Sheila Kammerman & Shirley Gatenio, Issue Brief: *Mother's Day: More Than Candy and Flowers, Working Parents Need Paid Time-Off,* Clearinghouse on Int'l Developments in Child, Youth & Fam. Policies, Spring 2002, *available at* http//www.childpolicyintl.org/issuebrief/issuebrief5.htm.

19. 490 U.S. 228 (1989).

20. *See, e.g.,* Oncale v. Sundowner Offshore Servs., 523 U.S. 75 (1998); Strailey v. Happy Times Nursery Sch., 608 F.2d 327 (9th Cir. 1979).

21. Craft v. Metromedia, Inc., 766 F.2d 1205 (8th Cir. 1985).

22. Jack M. Balkin & Reva B. Siegel, *The American Civil Rights Tradition: Anticlassification or Antisubordination?,* 58 U. MIAMI L. REV. 9, 25 (2003).

23. 628 F. Supp. 1264 (N.D. Ill. 1986), *aff'd,* 839 F.2d 302 (7th Cir. 1988).

24. Vicki Schultz & Stephen Petterson, *Race, Gender, Work, and Choice: An Empirical Study of the Lack of Interest Defense in Title VII Cases Challenging Job Segregation,* 59 U. CHI. L. REV. 1073, 1097 (1992).

25. U.S. Equal Employment Opportunity Commission, *Sexual Harassment Charges—EEOC and FEPAs Combined: FY 1992–FY2003,* http://www.eeoc.gov/stats/harass.html.

26. Faragher v. City of Boca Raton, 524 U.S. 775, 807 (1998).

27. Harris v. Forklift Sys., Inc., 510 U.S. 17, 21, 23 (1993).

28. Carr v. Allison, 32 F.3d 1007, 1010 (7th Cir. 1994).

29. Gross v. Burgraff Constr. Co., 53 F.3d 1531 (10th Cir. 1995).

30. Williams v. General Motors Corp., 187 F.3d 553, 564 (6th Cir. 1999).

31. *Compare, e.g.,* Ellison v. Brady, 924 F.2d 872, 879–80 (9th Cir. 1991) (approving use of the reasonable woman standard), *with* Morgan v. Massachusetts Gen. Hosp., 901 F.2d 186, 192–93 (1st Cir. 1990) (rejecting its use).

32. *See, e.g.,* Barbara A. Gutek et al., *The Utility of the Reasonable Woman Legal Standard in Hostile Environment Sexual Harassment Cases: A Multimethod, Multistudy Examination,* 5 PSYCHOL. PUB. POL'Y & L. 596 (1999).

33. 523 U.S. 75 (1998).

34. Doe v. City of Belleville, 119 F.3d 563, 572 (7th Cir. 1997).

35. 523 U.S. at 80–81.

36. *See, e.g.,* Rene v. MGM Grand Hotel, Inc., 305 F.3d 1061 (9th Cir. 2002).

37. 523 U.S. at 80–82.

38. U.S. (6 Pet.) 515, 561 (1832).

39. RONALD TAKAKI, A DIFFERENT MIRROR: A HISTORY OF MULTICULTURAL AMERICA 86 (1993).

40. Derrick A. Bell, Jr., Brown v. Board of Education *and the Interest Convergence Dilemma,* 93 HARV. L. REV. 518 (1980).

41. U.S. Dep't. of Labor, Bureau of Labor Statistics, *Employed Persons by Occupation, Sex, and Age,* http://www.bls.gov/cps/cpsaat9.pdf (last visited Sept. 9, 2005).

42. Christine Jolls, *Accommodation Mandates,* 53 STAN. L. REV. 223, 292 tbl.3 (2000).

43. U.S. Census Bureau, *Women and Men in the U.S.: March 2002* (Mar. 2003), http://www.census.gov/prod/2003pubs (last visited June 13, 2004).

44. RONALD G. EHRENBERG & ROBERT S. SMITH, MODERN LABOR ECONOMICS: THEORY AND PUBLIC POLICY 383–84 (8th ed. 2003).

45. Scott A. Moss, *Women Choosing Diverse Workplaces: A Rational Preference with Disturbing Implications for Both Occupational Segregation and Economic Analysis of Law,* 27 HARV. WOMEN'S L.J. 1 (2004).

46. Deborah L. Rhode, *The "No-Problem" Problem: Feminist Challenges and Cultural Change,* 100 YALE L.J. 1731, 1764 (1991).

47. JOAN WILLIAMS, UNBENDING GENDER: WHY FAMILY AND WORK CONFLICT AND WHAT TO DO ABOUT IT 67 (2000).

48. Matt L. Huffman & Philip N. Cohen, *Occupational Segregation and the Gender Gap in Workplace Authority: National Versus Local Labor Markets,* 19 SOC. FORUM 121, 123 (Mar. 2004).

49. Andrea Giampetro-Meyer, *The Power Pyramid,* 24 BERKELEY J. EMP. & LAB. L. 203, 212 (2003).

50. *See, e.g.,* Suzanne Gordon, *Feminism and Caregiving,* 10 AM. PROSPECT 119 (1992).

51. *See, e.g.,* Trond Peterson & Laurie A. Morgan, *Separate and Unequal: Occupation-Establishment Sex Segregation and the Gender Wage Gap,* 101 AM. J. SOC. 329, 344–45 (1995).

52. U.S. General Accounting Office, *Women's Earnings: Work Patterns Partially Explain Difference Between Men's and Women's Earnings,* GAO-04-35 2 (Oct. 2003).

53. Marion Crain, *Confronting the Structural Character of Working Women's Economic Subordination: Collective Action v. Individual Rights Strategies,* 3 KAN. J. L. & PUB. POL'Y 26, 26 (Spring 1994).

54. 29 U.S.C. §§ 201–9 (2004).

55. Martha Chamallas, *The Architecture of Bias: Deep Structures in Tort Law,* 146 U. PA. L. REV. 463, 475 (1998).

56. Rhonda Jennings Blackburn, *Comparable Worth and the Fair Pay Act of 1994*, 84 Ky. L.J. 1277, 1299 (1995–96) (quoting Phyllis Schlafly).

57. Am. Fed'n. of State, County & Mun. Employees, AFL-CIO (AFSCME) v. Washington, 770 F.2d 1401, 1407 (9th Cir. 1985).

58. Ursula R. Kubal, Comment, *U.S. Multinational Corporations Abroad: A Comparative Perspective on Sex Discrimination Law in the United States and the European Union*, 5 N.C. J. Int' L. & Com. Reg. 207 (1999).

59. Michael Wright, *The Marine Corps Faces the Future*, N.Y. Times June, 20, 1982, §6 (Magazine), at 16, 74, *quoted in* Kenneth L. Karst, *The Pursuit of Manhood and the Desegregation of the Armed Forces*, 38 UCLA L. Rev. 499, 534 (1991).

60. 50 U.S.C. app. §§ 451–473 (2003).

61. 453 U.S. 57 (1981).

62. National Defense Authorization Act for Fiscal Year 1994, Pub. L. No. 103-160, 107 Stat. 1547 (1993) (codified as 10 U.S.C. § 6015).

63. Adam N. Wojack, *Integrating Women into the Infantry*, 82 Mil. Rev. 67 (Nov. 1, 2002).

64. Schwartz v. Brodksy, 265 F. Supp. 2d 130, 134 (D. Mass. 2003) (referring to H.R. 163, 108th Cong., § 10; S. 89, 108th Cong., § 10 (Jan. 7, 2003)).

65. 10 U.S.C. § 654 (2000).

66. Center for the Study of Sexual Minorities, *New Data Reveal Extensive Talent Loss Under Don't Ask, Don't Tell*, June 21, 2004, http://www.gaymilitary.ucsb.edu/PressCenter/press_rel_2004_0621.htm.

67. *See, e.g.*, Philips v. Perry, 106 F.3d 1420 (9th Cir. 1997).

68. 539 U.S. 558 (2003).

69. Hensala v. Dep't of the Air Force, 343 F.3d 951, 958 (9th Cir. 2003).

70. President Bill Clinton, Remarks at the Welfare Reform Bill Signing (Aug. 22, 1996), http:// www.acf.dhhs.gov/news/welfare/wr/822potus.htm.

71. Cynthia Negrey et al., *Job Training Under Welfare Reform: Opportunities for and Obstacles to Economic Self-Sufficiency Among Low-Income Women*, Geo. J. on Poverty L. & Pol'y 347, 348, 357 (2000).

72. Caitlin Flanagan, *Dispatches from the Nanny Wars: How Serfdom Saved the Women's Movement*, Atlantic Monthly, Feb. 2004, at 113.

73. Lawrence Grobel, *Playboy Interview: David Duchovny*, Playboy, Dec. 1998, at 63, 70.

5

Education and Sports

A. *Educational Opportunities*

1. The historical path to coeducation

In this country and others, girls have had much more limited access to education than boys. In America's colonial period, formal public schooling was generally available only to boys. Families and towns viewed the education of girls as unnecessary to their primary roles as wives and mothers. Girls, if they were formally educated at all, attended "dame schools," where they learned to read only enough to study Puritan religious principles. In many places, even if a town provided grammar school education for girls, it did so in a sex-segregated setting. Black and Native American girls almost never received public schooling.

Over the next two hundred years, the practice of coeducation gradually developed. Parents' beliefs about the value of education changed, and they began to smuggle their daughters into public schools, sometimes paying the teachers extra tuition to instruct the girls on the side. Even parents who had doubts about educating girls as preparation for employment thought that education would make girls into better mothers and worthier companions to their husbands. In agrarian regions, during summers when older boys did farmwork, some communities hired teachers to supervise young boys and girls in the otherwise empty school buildings. In rural areas, where more than three-fourths of Americans lived as late as the mid-1800s, it made economic sense to teach small numbers of boys and girls together in one building.[1] By the middle of the nineteenth century, most public elementary schools had slowly and quietly become coeducational. Of course, "[a]lmost all of the girls and boys who participated in these schools were white."[2]

Early high schools, particularly in urban areas, were sex-segregated. Wider "acceptance of coeducation in practice had obviously to wait upon more general approval of the idea that girls should have more than rudimentary education."[3] In the 1850s educational theorists began to debate the wisdom of coeducation in secondary schools. Opponents wanted to shield teenage girls "from the contamination . . . of riffraff boys."[4] Supporters argued that girls were entitled to the same rights to public education as boys and that they should be educated under the same conditions. Race and class entered the equation. In Southern states, white secondary schools were separated by sex, while colored schools were mixed. "The civilized upper classes everywhere chose separate sex schools."[5] Ultimately, mixed-sex secondary education prevailed in large part because teaching transformed into a job for women, and city high schools developed a pool of inexpensive prospective teachers. By the late nineteenth century, women held more than 90 percent of teaching jobs in urban schools.[6] This entailed the acceptance of females in classrooms as teachers, which, in part, paved the way for female students.

Institutions of higher education still denied admission to women. Some university administrators insisted that they excluded women "for their own sake; it was to prevent harm to the 'female constitution,' which was poorly equipped for such things as education."[7] Prior to the Civil War, almost all colleges and universities refused to admit women. Before the war, only one out of six women attended a coeducational college or university.[8] The middle to late 1800s saw the establishment of such women's colleges as Mount Holyoke, Vassar, Smith, Wellesley, and Bryn Mawr. Some elite schools, like Harvard and Columbia, established parallel women's colleges, such as Radcliffe and Barnard. By 1867, of the nation's three thousand female students in full-time programs, "[s]lightly over two-thirds were in the nation's thirty-odd women's colleges, while the remainder were dispersed across forty private coeducational colleges and eight state universities."[9]

A variety of forces prompted institutions of higher education to admit women. The suffrage movement pushed for female access to public education. The federal Morrill Acts, in 1862 and 1890, established funds for land-grant schools that provided opportunities for women to obtain higher education. By 1945, 70 percent of all colleges and universities were coeducational. Of course, even within formally coeducational institutions, departments steered female students toward courses in home economics, sewing, nursing, and cooking, and away from classes in engineering, medicine, or law.[10] In the 1960s and 1970s, the most prestigious Ivy League schools finally admitted women: Princeton and Yale began admitting women in 1969; Brown and Dartmouth went coeducational in 1972, Harvard in 1976, while Columbia held out as an all-male school until 1983.[11]

Professional schools also resisted admitting women. In 1893 Johns Hopkins was the first major medical school to admit women—for financial, not egalitarian, reasons. Beginning around 1915 other medical schools, such as Yale, Pennsylvania, and Columbia, admitted a few women, while Harvard refused them admission until 1945.[12] Even when medical schools began to admit women, many set quotas on the number they would accept. The quotas averaged about 5 percent before World War II, rising to between 6 and 8 percent after the war. In 1970 only 7.7 percent of all physicians were women.[13] Following a sex discrimination lawsuit against several medical schools in the mid-1970s, the schools began to change their admissions practices. By 1980 women constituted 23 percent of medical school graduates, by 1990, 35 percent, and by 2003, 46 percent. It was not until 2003 that women made up the majority of applicants to medical school, yet they still account for only one-quarter of all physicians, 19 percent of associate professors in medical school, and 11 percent of full professors.[14]

Law schools followed a similar pattern of exclusion and reluctant admission. No women were admitted to any law school until 1868, and for the next half century, even schools that accepted women might admit only one or a few per year. Some elite law schools, like Columbia and Duke, did not begin to admit women until the late 1920s. Harvard held out until 1950, Notre Dame until 1969, and Virginia until 1970; Washington and Lee, the last accredited law school with an all-male student body, finally began admitting women in 1972.[15] Even after law schools started to admit women, their enrollment levels held at about 3 percent until the 1970s.[16] Once admitted to law schools, women were not welcomed. At some schools, including Harvard, professors did not call on women in class until one day in the spring, "Ladies Day," when they called only on women—and their questions took the form of hazing.[17] In 1968 a law school textbook contained the statement "After all, land, like women, was meant to be possessed."[18]

Today women represent almost 50 percent of most law schools' entering classes, but still only 23 percent of full professors and 13 percent of deans.[19] Some evidence suggests that female students, particularly at elite schools, have different law school experiences than their male counterparts: they participate less often in class discussions, experience a loss of confidence, attain slightly lower grades, and receive fewer law school honors.[20] Even numerical parity between male and female law students has not translated into equality of opportunity.

Until relatively recently in the history of this country, girls have had fewer and more meager educational opportunities than boys. Only grudgingly and gradually did secondary schools, colleges and universities, and professional schools consent to become coeducational.

2. Contemporary inequalities

Continuing inequalities shape the school experiences of males and females at all educational levels and across all races. In 1992 the American Association of University Women ("AAUW") published a report entitled *How Schools Shortchange Girls*. The report found a range of differential treatment, performance expectations, and biases affecting curriculum, testing, and overall educational experiences. Despite small and declining differences in math achievement test scores, high school girls take less rigorous math classes. Schools offer inadequate information about teenage pregnancy, intimate violence, and eating disorders, health concerns that affect predominantly adolescent girls. Girls receive fewer scholarships than boys who have equal or slightly lower grades when those scholarships are based on SAT scores.[21]

In public primary and secondary schools, teachers interact more with boys, call on them 80 percent more often than girls, and offer them greater feedback. Education professors Myra and David Sadker note, "Whether male comments are insightful or irrelevant, teachers respond to them. However, when girls call out, there is a fascinating occurrence: Suddenly the teacher remembers the rule about raising your hand before you talk. And then the girl, who is usually not as assertive as the male students, is deftly and swiftly put back in her place."[22] Research in 2004 confirms the earlier findings: boys still speak nine times more than girls and are encouraged to dominate the "language space."[23]

The attention boys receive is both positive and negative. Teachers reprimand boys between eight and ten times as often as girls. The Wellesley College Center for Research on Women notes that "[w]hen both girls and boys are misbehaving equally, boys still receive more frequent discipline."[24] Boys, particularly minority race boys, are more likely than girls to repeat grades, drop out, flunk out, be suspended or expelled, and be assigned to special-education classes. Nationwide, two-thirds of students in special-education classes for learning, developmental, and behavioral difficulties are boys, and black males account for a disproportionate share of those placements.

Reviews of school textbooks reveal overrepresentation of the experiences of males. For example, science books often contain little narrative about the contributions of female scientists, or women's successes are isolated in "greatest hits" sections, such as a list titled "Ten Women Achievers in Science."[25]

Girls receive better grades and obtain higher class ranks from elementary school through college. A national study compared grade point averages of male and female high school students taking the ACT in 1992: the overall GPA for girls was 3.00, while for boys it was 2.89. In areas other than math and science, high school girls obtain more academic honors; they also surpass boys in making the honor roll, obtaining high class ranks, receiving writing awards, and being elected as class representatives. Nationally, sex differences on standardized achievement tests are very small. A 1997 National Assessment of Educational Progress comparison of male and female scores at the end of high school on a five-hundred-point scale in various subject matter areas showed males with a 5 point advantage in mathematics and an 8 point advantage in science; females scored 15 points higher in reading and 17 points higher in writing.[26]

The evidence is overwhelming that teachers—even those who believe they are being gender-neutral—treat boys and girls differently. Teachers may have lower performance expectations for boys in reading and writing and for girls in math and science. They address girls with fewer comments and ask less challenging questions of them. On the other hand, teachers tend to reward students they perceive as working harder with better grades, and "they often evaluate girls as harder workers."[27] In short, well-meaning teachers may discriminate, in different ways, against both boys and girls in classroom interactions. These prejudices and enforced gender role expectations result in the current situation where "[g]irls make up 57 percent of straight-A students; boys make up 57 percent of high school dropouts."[28] Discrimination against boys has received less attention than that against girls, perhaps because it has not translated into economic disadvantages in the workplace.

The disparities persist in higher education. More than 58 percent of all college undergraduates are women, but men earn 54 percent of doctorate degrees. When race is considered, the inequalities become particularly pronounced. The percentages of white male and female college students are close to equal (49 percent are male, 51 percent are female), but "[a]mong African-American students, 63 percent are female and only 37 percent are male. Among Hispanic college students, 55 percent are female and 45 percent male."[29]

The glass ceiling present in other occupations limits women's progress in academia as well. Although women constitute 38 percent of all faculty, they remain concentrated in lower-ranked, lower-prestige, and non-tenure-track positions: "Women make up 46 percent of assistant professors, 38 percent of associate professors, and 23 percent of full professors."[30] In the nation's top fifty engineering and science universities, women constitute 12.1 percent of chemistry faculty, 10.5 percent of chemical engineering faculty, 8.3 percent of math faculty, and 6.5 percent of electrical engineering faculty. Minority race female faculty are virtually nonexistent: "With the exception of one Black 'full' professor in astronomy, there are no female Black or Native American 'full' professors in the physical science or engineering disciplines surveyed."[31] The numbers alone do not tell the full story of occupational segregation by sex and race. Good evidence exists that female professors at all levels and minority race professors of both sexes perform much more of the committee work, service work, and student contact hours than their male and white peers. These inequities also translate into gendered wage inequalities. Across all institutions and ranks, women earn 80 percent of the salaries of their male counterparts.[32]

One indication of why these situations persist can be found in the firestorm prompted by comments of President Lawrence Summers of Harvard University in early 2005. At an academic conference Summers offered three possible explainations for the lack of female pro-

fessors in the sciences, in the order of his estimation of their likeli-
hood: women's inability or unwillingness to work the necessary long
hours; innate gender differences that make women less capable in
math and science; and socialized differences in interest in math and
science.[33] He did mention, but thoroughly discounts as unlikely, the
possibility that discrimination might be occurring in hiring or reten-
tion of female faculty in these areas.

Summers then told a story about his own attempts at gender-neutral parenting by playing with his twin two-and-a-half-year-old
daughters and giving them some trucks. They gave the trucks person-
alities, calling one the "daddy truck" and another the "baby truck."
While the point of the anecdote is unclear—maybe to suggest that girls
prefer family-building over mechanics—Summers seemed to be trying
to document that women lack natural abilities and inclinations in the
sciences. Although he later apologized for the remarks, Summers
claimed he made them "in the spirit of academic inquiry" to challenge
views that gender is socially constructed. Amid the subsequent criticisms and calls for his resignation, commentators began to look at the
promotional opportunities for women at Harvard. Since Summers's
appointment to the presidency in 2001 and his comments four years
later, the percentage of tenure offers to female arts and sciences faculty
at Harvard steadily declined from 37 percent to 11 percent.[34]

B. Single-Sex Education

Beginning in the early 1990s, one response to the differential treatment of boys and girls in the classroom was the introduction of public single-sex schools and classes. Some studies from the 1970s and
1980s seemed to indicate that girls in single-sex environments performed better academically and developed greater self-esteem than
girls in coeducational schools. Proponents of single-sex education argued that boys and girls learn differently and that the presence of the
opposite sex in the classroom is distracting. With respect to single-sex
education, feminists divide along ideological fault lines similar to the
equal treatment–special treatment views in earlier debates about pregnancy accommodation: some urge an assimilationist view that has its
roots in equality theory, while others advocate separatism based on
the distinct needs of girls.

The state of New York launched the Young Women's Leadership School in East Harlem in 1996. California opened pilot all-boys and all-girls academies in six districts in 1997. Middle schools across the country began to experiment with single-sex classes, such as Math PLUS (Power Learning for Underrepresented Students), originally intended for "math-phobic" girls, but later, under threat of legal challenge, opened to boys as well. The number of public single-sex schools and classes in the United States has increased dramatically since the mid-1990s, when only three schools provided any single-sex classes.[35] In 2004, 34 public schools nationwide were single-sex, while 113 other public schools offered some single-sex classes. In 2002 Congress passed the No Child Left Behind Act, which specifically makes available $450 million in federal funds for experiments in education, such as single-sex schools and classes. That provision was coauthored by Democratic senator Hillary Rodham Clinton and Republican senator Kay Bailey Hutchison, both alumnae of all-women's colleges.

Critics, such as the NOW, the National Education Association, the Feminist Majority Foundation, and the ACLU, respond that "'segregation breeds inequality.'"[36] While concerned about unequal treatment between male and female students, they argue that single-sex education is the wrong response. For some feminists, it was no small irony that in the fiftieth anniversary year of *Brown v. Board of Education,* school districts were endorsing segregation in the form of single-sex schools and classes.

1. The constitutional backdrop: equal protection

Decisions from the Supreme Court and lower federal courts over the past quarter of a century offer no clear guidance on the constitutionality of single-sex education in its current forms: voluntary single-sex classes or schools with parallel programs for the other sex equipped with substantially equal resources. Some of the early decisions appeared before modern equal protection law developed. The more modern education cases, while important, tend to concern what today might be called the "easy cases," situations in which segregation or other unequal treatment clearly disadvantaged females in relation to males.

The earliest federal decision was *Kirstein v. University of Virginia* in 1970, where a Virginia federal district court found the male-only

University of Virginia at Charlottesville in violation of the Fourteenth Amendment. The court decided the case without benefit of any special standards, but it noted the "relatively new idea that there must be no discrimination by sex in offering educational opportunity."[37] That same year, a South Carolina federal district court upheld the all-women admission policy of Winthrop College. The court in that case, *Williams v. McNair,* found that while the trend of education was toward coeducation, single-sex education received support from a long "history and tradition" and thus was not "wholly wanting in reason." The *Williams* court explicitly approved the legislature's construction of separate educational institutions for women and men, reflecting their traditional social roles: men could attend the state's all-male military school, the Citadel, while Winthrop "was designed as a school for young ladies," offering "courses thought to be specially helpful to female students," such as "sewing, dressmaking, millinery, art, needlework, cooking, housekeeping and such other industrial arts as may be suitable to their sex"[38] The value of *Williams* as precedent may be limited not only by the court's use of the lightest standard of constitutional review, but also by the court's reasoning about the usefulness of channeling women into traditionally female job categories.

Philadelphia maintained single-sex male and female academies that became the subject of litigation in both 1976 and 1984. The school district had constructed two sex-segregated senior high schools for academically gifted students: Philadelphia High School for Girls and Central High School for boys. In the earlier case, *Vorchheimer v. School District of Philadelphia,* the federal district court upheld the challenge of a female student, Susan Vorchheimer, seeking admission to the all-male school. The court focused on evidence of educational inequalities between the two schools—disparities in resources, educational offerings, and prestige. The court rejected the school board's justification that in creating the separate academies, it was trying to protect girls from the adverse effects of coeducation: "[I]f coeducation is detrimental to girls, all the public schools should be sex-segregated; if it is not, then there is no 'fair and substantial' relationship between sex-segregation and the educational goals of the School Board."[39]

The appellate court in *Vorchheimer* reversed, ruling that despite the resource differences, "the educational opportunities offered to girls and boys are essentially equal." Crucial to the appellate court was that the practice of sex-segregated instruction was a "time honored educational alternative" with "a long history of "world-wide acceptance." The court stressed that the plaintiff was offered the choice of an opportunity to enroll in a single-sex high school, that choice was "voluntary, not mandatory," and it was the same choice available to boys.[40] In dissent, Judge John Gibbons chided the majority's cramped definition of Susan Vorchheimer's choice as "voluntary":

> It was "voluntary," but only in the same sense that Mr. Plessy voluntarily chose to ride the train in Louisiana. The train Vorchheimer wants to ride is that of a rigorous academic program among her intellectual peers. Philadelphia, like the state of Louisiana in 1896, offers the service but only if Vorchheimer is willing to submit to segregation. Her choice, like Plessy's, is to submit to that segregation or refrain from availing herself of the service.[41]

The Philadelphia schools remained segregated by sex until a second challenge ended in the 1984 decision in *Newberg v. Board of Public Education*. The second time around, given changes in Supreme Court doctrine, a Pennsylvania court found the sex-based exclusion of female students from Central High violated the Fourteenth Amendment.[42]

In the years between these two decisions the Supreme Court decided to use a higher "intermediate" scrutiny for gender classifications, which it then applied in *Mississippi University for Women v. Hogan* in 1982. At issue in *Hogan* was the School of Nursing's women-only admission policy. Although the *Hogan* Court expressly declined to determine whether single-sex education itself was unconstitutional, it did hold that the all-female admissions policy could not operate as an affirmative-action program where the state had not proved any discrimination against admitting women into nursing.

No other nursing programs, coeducational or single-sex, were available in the vicinity to Joe Hogan. In that sense, *Hogan* was a formal equality case, concerned with resources being made available to one sex but not the other. But the *Hogan* Court mentioned antisubordination as well as antidiscrimination values. The majority in *Hogan* was concerned that decisions not be based on "fixed notions concerning the roles and abilities of males and females." A women-only nursing school reflected "archaic and stereotypic notions" that only women could be nurses. The Court further observed that the exclusion of males from one of the state's nursing schools "tends to perpetuate the stereotyped view of nursing as an exclusively women's job" and turns those assumptions into "a self-fulfilling prophecy."[43]

Parties continued to challenge the constitutionality of sex-segregated schools in the years after *Hogan*. For instance, in 1991 a Michigan federal district court in *Garrett v. Board of Education of the School District of Detroit* struck down a plan to open all-male academies with Afrocentric curricula for preschool through fifth grade. Justification for constructing the schools was the crisis facing African American males in unemployment, dropout, and homicide rates. Female students enrolled in the Detroit public schools argued that the schools unconstitutionally denied entry to at-risk girls.

Sex exclusivity was the constitutional problem in *Garrett*. First, the board failed to prove its assertion that coeducation would somehow contaminate boys: "The Board proffered no evidence that the presence of girls in the classroom bears a substantial relationship to the difficulties facing urban males." Second, the Detroit school board singled out African American males for special, remedial treatment to address educational disadvantages, but it paid little attention to African American girls, whom the educational system was also failing. While a school district that equally funded separate male and female academies might overcome the latter of these constitutional difficulties, the former would remain. Like the Supreme Court in *Hogan*, the *Garrett* court considered the social message implicit in the sex-exclusive curriculum, which "suggests a false dichotomy between the roles and responsibilities of boys and girls."[44]

Another single-sex education case reached the Supreme Court in 1996. *United States v. Virginia* concerned the opportunities for women to attend the public-supported all-male Virginia Military Institute ("VMI"). In 1990, after VMI refused a female high school applicant's admission, the Justice Department sued the school. Virginia defended the single-sex environment of "rigorous military training" as inappropriate for females and effective for males only in a sex-segregated environment.[45] This "adversative" training included spartan barracks living, a class system, mental stress, shaved heads, a stringently enforced honor code, a complete absence of privacy, upperclass hazing, and harsh physical training.

The federal district court found in favor of VMI, holding that the school actually added a "measure of diversity" to the educational system by providing this unique adversative training.[46] The Fourth Circuit Court of Appeals reversed, holding that while VMI's program of single-sex training was "justified by its institutional mission," Virginia failed to explain why it "offers the unique benefits of a VMI type of education to men and not to women."[47] It remanded the case to the district court for construction of a plan to remedy the equal protection violation. Virginia responded by creating a separate, parallel program for women, the Virginia Women's Institute for Leadership ("VWIL").

Located on the campus of nearby Mary Baldwin College, the VWIL program offered nothing similar to the rigors of VMI. A task force headed by the dean of Mary Baldwin determined that "a military model and, especially VMI's adversative method, would be wholly inappropriate for educating and training most women for leadership roles."[48] Instead, the VWIL program de-emphasized military education and used a cooperative method of education that reinforced self-esteem.

The admissions standards, financial resources, physical facilities, academic program, faculty qualifications, educational offerings, and curriculum at VWIL differed dramatically from those of VMI. Apart from participation in an ROTC program—the "largely ceremonial" Corps of Cadets—the women at VWIL would not experience a military education. VWIL students, whose entering SAT scores would average a full hundred points lower than those of VMI students, would not live in barracks, eat together, or wear uniforms. VWIL offered no bachelor of science or engineering degrees. Faculty at Mary Baldwin College held fewer Ph.D.'s (68 percent) than VMI's faculty (86 percent) and received substantially lower salaries. The initial $5.4 million endowment for VWIL, even when added to the $19 million endowment at Mary Baldwin, could not compare with the VMI's $131 million endowment. The physical facilities at Mary Baldwin contained "'two multi-purpose fields' and 'one gymnasium,'" while VMI offered "an NCAA competition level indoor track and field facility; a number of multi-purpose fields; baseball, soccer and lacrosse fields; an obstacle course; large boxing, wrestling and martial arts facilities; an 11-laps-to-the-mile indoor running course; an indoor pool; indoor and outdoor rifle ranges; and a football stadium." VWIL would lack the alumni network, history, reputation, and prestige of VMI. The district court upheld this plan, declaring that Virginia was not required "to provide a mirror image VMI for women."[49] The Fourth Circuit approved the VWIL program as "substantively comparable" to VMI.[50] The government petitioned the Supreme Court for certiorari.

The Supreme Court found VMI's male-only admission policy unconstitutional and held that the parallel program at VWIL was an inadequate remedy. Virginia failed to demonstrate an "exceedingly persuasive justification" for segregating students by sex for purposes of a military education. The decision to exclude women "rel[ied] on overbroad generalizations about the different talents, capacities, or preferences of males and females." Virginia's asserted policy of promoting educational diversity was an after-the-fact rationalization for historically affording unique educational benefits only to males. The Court noted that "however 'liberally' this plan serves the State's sons, it makes no provision whatsoever for her daughters."[51]

Justice Ginsburg's majority opinion, however, does not completely preclude single-sex education. The specific holding of the Court is that because VWIL was a "pale shadow" of VMI, Virginia failed to show "substantial equality in the separate educational opportunities." In fact, in a footnote, the majority left open the possibility of a state "evenhandedly" supporting "diverse educational opportunities."[52] The unresolved question after *United States v. Virginia* is whether a separate but truly equal VMI counterpart would have satisfied requirements.

2. The statutory backdrop: Title IX

In addition to the standards set by the Constitution's equal protection clause, single-sex education must also meet standards set by Congress and the U.S. Department of Education. Those standards follow from Title IX of the Education Amendments of 1972. Title IX bans sex discrimination in many aspects of American education. Or, as it states: "No person in the U.S. shall, on the basis of sex, be excluded from participation in, or denied the benefits of, or be subjected to discrimination under any educational program or activity receiving federal aid."[53] Recently the Supreme Court held that the statute's scope of protection applies not only to victims of discrimination, but also to "whistleblowers," teachers, and others who complain of discrimination against others.[54] While Title IX is often associated with athletics, its reach extends far beyond the soccer field. Consider that in 1972, when the act went into effect, only 9 percent of medical degrees and 7 percent of law degrees were earned by women; by 1994 those numbers had risen to 38 percent and 43 percent, respectively. As we will see later in this chapter, the laws against sexual harassment on campus are also anchored in this landmark legislation.

Part of the statute's influence relates to jurisdiction: while the equal protection clause regulates only government actors (in this context, public schools), Title IX applies to any public or private program that accepts federal aid, a much larger educational universe. Another aspect of Title IX's influence relates to its form. Constitutional protections, like those in the equal protection clause, are elaborated upon by courts, after a lawsuit has already defined and packaged the issue to be decided. The process is, by design, *singular* and *reactive*. In contrast, statutes can provide more comprehensive solutions by enlisting federal agencies to implement legislative objectives through detailed regulation. As a result, statutory solutions have the potential to be more *global* and *proactive* than constitutional solutions.

Another advantage, depending on what side you are on, is that statutory protections are more responsive to public debate. The issue of single-sex education in elementary and secondary schools illustrates the point. Since the adoption of Title IX, federal regulations discouraged school districts from experimenting with single-sex education. The regulations prohibit single-sex public schools unless a "comparable" public school is offered for students of the other gender.[55] The regulations also barred most single-sex programs *within* coeducational schools. Aside from specialized programs like choral groups, sex education, or physical education, coeducational public schools cannot segregate on the basis of sex unless separate girls' and boys' programs are "comparable" and are necessary to remedy the effects of past gender discrimination.[56] This standard is stricter than that of the equal protection clause, which appears to allow segregated programs to further "important objectives" unrelated to overcoming past discrimination.

But political winds have changed. Prompted by the No Child Left Behind Act, the Department of Education revised its Title IX regulations to promote more flexibility. Under the government's new proposed rules, public single-sex schools are permitted as long as students of the excluded sex are offered "substantially equal opportunities" at another single-sex *or* coeducational school. This would mean that a school district could establish a same-sex school for at-risk adolescent boys, so long as it provided its at-risk adolescent girls a coeducational or same-sex school with "substantially equal opportunities."

The revised regulations would also make it easier for coeducational schools to offer single-sex programs. They would permit single-sex programs as long as they were substantially related *either* to meeting particular educational needs of students *or* to providing "diversity of educational options." Same-sex programs within a coeducational school would no longer have to be "comparable" to programs offered to the opposite sex, but would instead be required to be "substantially equal," a term not clearly defined.[57] Thus a coeducational school could offer its girls an all-female Advanced Placement calculus course as long as it also provided its boys a coeducational or all-male course that was "substantially equal." Must that alternative course be an Advanced Placement course? Must it even be a calculus course? Questions like these will, no doubt, fall to the courts, as will the much broader question of whether these new regulations, as applied, meet the evolving standards of the equal protection clause.

3. The evidence concerning single-sex education

Both sides in this debate use educational research to defend their positions. Proponents of single-sex schools seized on the 1992 American Association of University Women study *How Schools Shortchange Girls: A Study of Major Findings on Girls and Education* to argue that the disadvantages girls experienced in coeducational classrooms required a single-sex remedy. But while the 1992 report seemed somewhat open to single-sex experiments, it stopped short of endorsing single-sex schools. By 1998, the AAUW had conducted a comprehensive review of several decades of research studies on single-sex classes and schools and issued a report specific to single-sex education. That report acknowledged the possibility that single-sex classes might offer advantages in certain subjects for some students, but concluded that "[t]here is no evidence that single-sex education in general 'works' or is 'better' than coeducation."[58]

A government report in 1993, based on research presented at a conference, found that "single-sex education provides educational benefits for some students."[59] The Department of Education's proposed change to Title IX's regulations to create more relaxed standards for justifying single-sex education is based in part on this thir-teen-year-old survey. It is a good example of how the choice of a study and the interpretation of it might lead to changes in law throughout the country.

The notion that single-sex education is "better" for girls receives little support from more recent studies in the sociology of education and those with careful methodological controls. Many of the claimed advantages of single-sex schools rest on studies from the 1970s com-paring women's colleges and coeducational colleges. Researchers re-viewed the data in these studies and documented that a significant proportion of the female achievers attended the Seven Sisters schools—Barnard, Bryn Mawr, Mount Holyoke, Radcliffe, Smith, Vassar, and Wellesley.[60] These were women who "came from privi-leged backgrounds, had tremendous resources, and . . . were going to succeed no matter where they went. Yet, these studies did not control for socio-economic status."[61]

Supporters of single-sex education herald the successes in contem-porary programs like the Young Women's Leadership School ("TYWLS") in New York. TYWLS, a small public high school whose budget is supplemented by private grant money, opened in East Harlem in the fall of 1996, with a seventh-grade class of fifty girls.[62] The school has nearly four hundred students in grades 7 through 12;[63] the students are predominantly racial minorities. The school reported high standardized test scores compared with citywide averages and proclaimed that 100 percent of the thirty-two seniors in its first grad-uating class received acceptance at four-year colleges.[64]

Even amid fairly good evidence of some performance differences relative to other schools in New York City, the key question—whether the results are attributable to the sex-exclusive nature of the school-ing—remains unanswered. The numbers are just tabulations, with no controls for other influential variables. For example, the entering class that graduated in 2001 originally contained fifty students.[65] Thus, it seems that eighteen of the original group were lost, which is a 36 per-cent attrition rate, roughly comparable to the attrition or transfer rate of other city schools.[66]

The reported success rate may be influenced in other, even less vis-ible, ways. The Leadership School is extremely selective: "For the 2002–3 year there were more than 550 applications for the 60 open-ings in the seventh grade and a waiting list of 1,200 for 3 ninth-grade slots."[67] Parental involvement is commanded and student performance demanded: "[A]ny girl who cannot or will not do the work will be asked to leave the school so a more deserving student can take her place."[68]

At TYWLS, the successes that supporters are attributing to sex segregation may be due instead to the infusion of economic resources (the Harlem school even provides tea and muffins in the morning for its students),[69] the self-selectivity of the students, the curriculum, tiny class sizes (originally, no more than ten students per class),[70] and academic counselors who meet with each student every single day.[71] Was it really the presence of boys in the classroom that had been impairing the academic performance of these girls who now attend TYWLS?

Female students in all-girl classes or schools certainly enjoy more participation opportunities in activities, since there is only one sex in the class or school. Anecdotal and self-reporting studies indicate somewhat higher measures of self-esteem and student satisfaction with the warmth or friendliness of an all-girl environment.[72] While single-sex classes may promote self-assurance in some girls, this does not translate into analytic or academic advantages. The American Association of University Women examined the findings of numerous studies and concluded: "Whereas girls perceive the classrooms in many cases to be superior, and may register gains in confidence, these benefits have not translated into measured improvements in achievement."[73] When studies control for student background differences (such as prior academic achievements, test scores, race, socioeconomic status, and educational aspirations), school selectivity, reputation, class sizes, curriculum, and resources, the results show no consistent advantages in educational quality in single-sex schools or classes. Indeed, once conflating variables are controlled, most studies show that performance differences between coeducational schools and single-sex schools entirely disappear.[74]

Some researchers have found that single-sex education may provide some advantages for minority race boys.[75] The general consensus, though, is that males do not flourish in single-sex environments. The majority of research suggests that boys are served best, academically and socially, in coeducational environments.[76] One significant drawback to all-male educational programs is that they may promote sexism. The all-male esprit de corps can create a "'hypermasculine ethos'": "It produces men who feel that they are superior to women, and it encourages racist and homophobic attitudes."[77] Observational studies of other all-male groups, such as sports teams and fraternities, suggest that when male identities take shape in a process that excludes women, masculinity becomes defined by misogyny and male supremacy.[78] Before its integration, students at the Citadel often referred to females as "pigs" and "sluts." Although the evidence is mixed, for both sexes, but particularly for boys, placement in sex-segregated classes is associated with the development of attitudes that favor traditional, even stereotypic, views of gender roles.[79]

This concern that segregation based on sex can reinforce gender stereotypes receives support from a study of the experimental California academies. In 1997, as a pilot project, California provided $5 million to institute twelve public single-sex academies, equal down to the number of pencils. A study sponsored by both the Ford Foundation and the Spencer Foundation evaluated the academies between 1998 and 2000, and researchers observed classes and interviewed more than three hundred students, parents, teachers, and administrators.[80] An important finding was that although the California administrators insisted on equal resources, assumptions about the different educational needs of boys and girls caused the educators to explicitly reinforce traditional gender stereotypes.[81] Teachers taught boys in regimented and competitive ways, reserving nurturing and cooperative techniques for girls. During a unit on frontier exploration, the boys' schools learned survival skills and the girls' schools learned how to quilt and sew.

Interestingly, media coverage of single-sex education is quite slanted. News reports provide little systematic information about studies regarding government-sponsored separatism or research regarding the benefits of integration. Newspaper articles reduce complex and nuanced studies of single-sex education to simplistic and favorable blurbs.[82] They report the latest trial run or episodic result at a single school and make glossy pronouncements about the general state of research. These experiments in single-sex schools or classes are reported simply as successes, with no consideration to other variables that might have affected the trial. Most people have little training in statistics; if they did, they might discount reports on an individual study or experience because it is unrepresentative. Work in the field of heuristics demonstrates that "people are overly influenced by single-case information."[83]

Articles in the popular media focus on human interest stories. This focus feeds the ways people like to receive information. In the "everybody loves a winner" tradition, newspaper and popular press articles report the success stories: reports of girls in single-sex classes and women in single-sex colleges who were satisfied with their experiences. Much of newspaper reporting is event based. Programs that do not work—single-sex schools that close, for example—tend to be non-events: they die quiet deaths. Compare the much-heralded opening of the California all-boys and all-girls academies with the absence of reports on the closing of all but two of the schools. Some newspaper articles fail to mention at all that any of the California pilot schools closed.[84] The popular media touting of celebrated single-sex experiments is at odds with the cumulative evidence emerging from studies in the sociology of education. If the lessons of prior single-sex research are any indication, once other variables are controlled, the effects attributable to sex exclusivity will likely disappear.

Ultimately resolution of the constitutionality of any program of sex-exclusive education may depend on the social science evidence supporting it. Those defending public single-sex programs will face a stringent burden of constitutional justification, since the constitutional test is whether the asserted educational benefits of single-sex schools and classes provide an "exceedingly persuasive justification" for state-sponsored segregation of the sexes.

C. Charter Schools and Vouchers

The renewed interest in single-sex education is part of a broader effort to shake up American education with new, or at least re-introduced, ideas. Two popular reforms, charter schools and tuition vouchers, could lend support to the single-sex movement by allowing for greater variety in publicly funded education. As with single-sex education, the law concerning charter schools and vouchers is of recent vintage and continues to evolve.

1. Charter schools

Charter schools are public schools founded on a contract, or "charter," with either a state agency or a local school board. The charter grants the school control over its operations and frees the school from the more complex state and local rules that other public schools must follow. This added flexibility aims to allow for a more agile and innovative style of management with the goal of increasing student performance. Charter schools have become very popular. As of 1999, more than 250,000 students attended charter schools, representing nearly 1 percent of all public school children in the twenty-seven states that operate such schools.[85]

Some activists believe the charter movement provides attractive opportunities for experiments in single-sex education. Currently, charter schools represent about one-fifth of public schools that offer single-sex programs.[86] But while a state law may free charter schools from many state and local regulations, charter schools are still bound by *federal* laws like Title IX and by state and federal constitutional protections against discrimination. Here is where the legal controversy lies.

Recall that Title IX's regulations have historically discouraged single-sex schools. We noted earlier that the Department of Education is revising the regulations to permit same-sex schools so long as school districts provide "substantially equal opportunities" to students of the excluded sex at another single-sex or coeducational school. Most charter schools, however, operate independently of state school districts. So when a charter school opens its doors to only girls or boys, it has no way of providing an equal opportunity to students of the opposite sex. The department's proposed regulations would exempt independent charter schools from the obligation to provide alternative opportunities of any kind.[87]

Critics of this rule argue that the government is now retreating even from "separate but equal," allowing children of one sex to profit from the charter movement without requiring that children of the opposite sex enjoy the same opportunity. Supporters of the rule argue that improvements in education require flexibility and experimentation. Besides, it should not be the job of a single school to provide a substantially equal alternative, but rather that of the state as a whole. Charter schools, the argument goes, should not be punished for the shortcomings of their host states.

As more single-sex charter schools open, the dispute will almost certainly land in the courts. One issue will be whether the language of Title IX actually allows (as the Department of Education believes) charter schools to exclude students on the basis of sex without providing a satisfactory alternative. The second issue will be whether the equal protection clause, as interpreted by decisions like *United States v. Virginia,* permits such an arrangement.

2. Vouchers

Another movement gaining steam in American education is tuition vouchers. In voucher programs, states provide financial assistance to families wishing to send their children to local private schools. Often the assistance is tied to the economic needs of the family and the quality of surrounding public schools. Voucher programs aim to provide private educational opportunities for families in poor school districts while forcing public schools to compete for students by raising educational quality. Currently, six states (Colorado, Florida, Maine, Ohio, Vermont, and Wisconsin) and the District of Columbia operate some kind of tuition voucher program; six states (Arizona, Florida, Illinois, Iowa, Minnesota, and Pennsylvania) offer either a tax credit or a deduction.[88]

Voucher programs are controversial because, among other reasons, the private schools that profit from such subsidies are not bound by the same antidiscrimination rules that bind public schools. The controversy is clearest in the case of religion. Since the large majority of American private schools have a religious affiliation, voucher programs divert tax dollars to pay for students to attend schools whose religious focus would not be allowed in the public system.

Voucher programs present a similar tension where gender is concerned. Although single-sex schools exist in the public school system, they are much more prevalent, and less restricted, in the private sector. This means that voucher programs could encourage students to attend single-sex schools in even greater numbers and without the protective limits of the equal protection clause. Is private discrimination more tolerable than public discrimination? If so, does private discrimination become less tolerable when it is publicly subsidized? These questions loop back to the public-private distinction, so important in feminist theory, which attempts to draw a line between permissible acts of private choice and impermissible acts of institutionalized discrimination.

As a constitutional matter, the Supreme Court appears to have chosen the side of permissible private choice where vouchers are concerned. In 2002, in *Zelman v. Simmons-Harris*,[89] the Court upheld Ohio's tuition program against charges that it unduly advanced religious interests. The Court reasoned that Ohio's program did not endorse religion because it was the family, and not the state, that ultimately decided whether a child would attend a religious school. While the case was decided under the religious freedom clauses of the First Amendment, the logic of *Zelman* appears to protect states from challenges under the equal protection clause as well, since families, and not the state, will ultimately decide whether to use state vouchers to support private single-sex education.

D. Athletics and Title IX

Chances are you have not gotten this far in our examination of education and Title IX without asking, Where's the sports? While Title IX has wielded enormous impact on American education as a whole, for most people the law is synonymous with sports and recreation, celebrated everywhere, from the girls' track meet to the "Title Nine" sportswear catalog. Title IX may be the first federal law to have achieved true pop status. What other statute has inspired a line of sports bras and capri pants?

By requiring schools to offer equal athletic opportunities to girls and women, Title IX has nurtured a new generation of student-athletes and challenged traditional stereotypes of female strength and endurance. The law has also sparked resource battles within athletic programs and raised questions about how equality between the sexes should be defined.

1. The importance of school athletics

Athletics nourishes both human relationships and individual autonomy, two concerns of feminist theory. Through sports, players learn to excel within a community, whether through collaboration on a team or competition among individual rivals. Sports teach many of life's social lessons: how to sacrifice personal desire for collective gain, how to support colleagues and respect adversaries, how to perform gracefully under public scrutiny, how to take risks, how to win, and how to lose.

Sports are also about channeling the psychological and physical powers of the individual. Being an athlete requires a focused awareness of one's body and mind, an "ownership," if you like, of the self. For this reason, feminists see great potential for the role of sports in feminism. On the track, beneath the hoop, or in the pool, female athletes are vigorously reclaiming their bodies for themselves.

Playing sports benefits women and girls in many ways. A study sponsored by the Women's Sports Foundation found that adolescent female athletes have lower rates of sexual activity and pregnancy.[90] Student athletes have higher grades, are less likely to drop out, and achieve higher graduation rates than their nonathletic peers.[91] Athletes learn important life skills, including an ability to work with a team, to perform under pressure, to set goals, and to take criticism. In addition, "playing sports helps young women develop self-confidence, perseverance, dedication and the 'competitive edge.'"[92]

The health benefits of regular rigorous physical exercise are extensive. Sports participation decreases a young woman's chance of developing heart disease, osteoporosis, and other health-related problems. Women who participate in sports significantly reduce their risk of developing breast cancer. Increased fitness levels can contribute to better posture, the reduction of back pain, and the development of adequate strength and flexibility, qualities that allow girls to participate in vocational and recreational activities.[93] Sports bring psychological benefits, too: young women who play sports exhibit higher self-esteem, lower incidence of depression, and a more positive body image.

Title IX's mandate of equality in sports is especially important for minority women and girls. Minority female athletes experience higher levels of self-esteem, are more likely to participate in extracurricular activities, and are more likely to become leaders in their communities than minority girls who do not play sports.[94] They are also 15 percent more likely to graduate from college.[95] Significantly, minority girls are more likely to participate in sports through their schools than through private organizations, making access through education particularly important.[96]

2. Empirical evidence: the good, the bad, and the ugly

Researchers have accumulated an impressive amount of statistical evidence documenting the recent progress of girls and women in sports. Title IX has significantly moved the ball forward. Before the act took effect, women represented only 2 percent of college athletes.[97] By 2001, women accounted for 43 percent of college athletes.[98] In absolute terms, the number of female athletes jumped from 32,000 to 150,000,[99] an increase of nearly 500 percent. At the high school level, the story is similarly impressive. Girls represented just 7 percent of high school athletes before Title IX.[100] By 2001 that figure had risen to nearly 42 percent.[101] In absolute terms, the number of girls playing high school sports rocketed from 300,000 to nearly 2.8 million,[102] an increase of more than 800 percent. The athletic participation of men and boys during this period also increased, although by modest amounts.[103]

In response to trends like these, law professor Catharine MacKinnon allows a rare victory lap:

> Women's income relative to men's has barely moved; occupational segregation remains stubbornly in place for most women; women and their children remain poor after divorce; sexual harassment, although now resisted by law, is as common as it was before it was made illegal. But women's everyday athletic reality has changed.[104]

But much work remains. In colleges with Division I programs (the most competitive division), women represent 53 percent of the student body but enjoy only 41 percent of the participation opportunities.[105] In addition, according to the National Women's Law Center, women's Division I programs receive only "43% of the total athletic scholarship dollars, 32% of recruiting dollars, and 36% of operating budgets."[106] Although no national data exist for elementary and secondary schools, anecdotal evidence suggests similar inequalities exist between girls' and boys' interscholastic sports programs.[107]

Ironically, while Title IX has dramatically expanded opportunities for female athletes, it appears to have diminished the opportunities for female administrators and coaches. After the enactment of Title IX, most college sports departments merged their men's and women's units into a single department; many female administrators were edged out. The new prestige (and money) that Title IX brought to women's sports also encourages more male coaches to compete against female coaches for leadership roles in top women's sports programs. Today women hold only 34 percent of policymaking positions in intercollegiate female sports.[108] As for coaching, the proportion of female university coaches has declined from 90 percent, before Title IX, to less than 50 percent in 2001.[109] The proportion of women coaching men's teams has not risen at all, effectively capped for three decades at 2 percent.[110] Prospects are particularly dour for women of color. A survey of Division I schools based on 1999 data found that African American women held 1.9 percent of head coaching positions in women's athletics, while occupying only 1.4 percent of administrative positions.[111] There is little information about the roles played by women of color in the leadership of college athletics.

Law professor Deborah Brake fears this backward trend has caused women's sports to take an ugly turn. Addressing a concern of dominance theorists, she argues the lack of female coaches and administrators is transforming women's athletic programs into yet another "arena where men exert control over women." She writes:

> Female athletes may be more vulnerable to abuse of the disparate power inherent in the coach-athlete relationship when they are coached by men. The sexual abuse of female athletes by male coaches is gaining increasing recognition as a widespread problem in girls' and women's sports. . . . When male coaches and administrators abuse their power over female athletes, it has the potential to transform athletics from a physically and psychologically liberating activity to one that exacerbates women's relative powerlessness in relation to men.[112]

3. Complying with Title IX

Title IX of the Education Amendments of 1972, which prohibits sex discrimination in educational programs that receive federal funds, does not specifically mention sports. But because athletics are considered part of a school's educational mission, Title IX's ban on discrimination applies. In 1979 the Office for Civil Rights ("OCR"), which is now a part of the U.S. Department of Education, issued a framework for Title IX compliance in college-level sports. That framework, called the Intercollegiate Athletics Policy Interpretation, remains in effect today. The interpretation identifies three areas of compliance: (1) athletic financial assistance; (2) "other program areas" (including equipment, training facilities, medical resources, tutoring, and recruitment services); and (3) meeting the interests and abilities of male and female students.[113]

A. THE "INTERESTS AND ABILITIES" THREE-STEP

The last compliance requirement—meeting the interests and abilities of male and female students—has prompted several lawsuits. Under OCR's policy interpretation, a university's athletic program will meet the "interests and abilities" test if it satisfies *one* of the following conditions: (1) sports opportunities are provided to women and men in numbers "substantially proportionate" to their respective enrollments; (2) where opportunities are not "substantially proportionate," the university shows "a history and continuing practice of program expansion" to develop the interests and abilities of the underrepresented sex; or (3) where opportunities are not "substantially proportionate" and where no history and practice of program expansion exists, the university shows that "the interests and abilities" of the underrepresented sex have been "fully and effectively accommodated."[114]

Most schools challenged in private lawsuits seek to establish compliance under the third standard.[115] But what does it mean to say that women's interests in athletics are "fully and effectively accommodated"? As illustrated in a case against Brown University, the answer depends on how you view the role of law.

B. COHEN V. BROWN UNIVERSITY

In the 1990s, a group of female students at Brown University brought a class action against their school, alleging its athletic policies violated Title IX. Their complaint focused on Brown's decision to cut costs by demoting its women's gymnastics and volleyball teams from university-funded varsity programs to donor-funded varsity programs. As part of the decision, Brown similarly demoted the status of two men's teams: water polo and golf. Even so, the plaintiffs argued the treatment was not evenhanded because at the time of Brown's decision, "[male] students at Brown already enjoyed the benefits of a disproportionately large share of both the university resources allocated to athletics and the intercollegiate participation opportunities afforded to student athletes."[116]

Specifically, the trial court found that, in 1993–94,

> Brown's varsity program—including both university- and donor-funded sports—afforded over 200 more positions for men than for women . . . [representing] a 13.01% disparity between female participation in intercollegiate athletics and female student enrollment, and that "[a]lthough the number of varsity sports offered to men are equal, the selection of sports offered to each gender generates far more individual positions for male athletes than for female athletes."[117]

The trial court then found Brown in violation of OCR's three-part "interests and abilities" test. Considering the first prong, the university's own figures showed it did not provide sports opportunities to men and women in numbers "substantially proportionate" to their respective enrollments. Regarding the second prong, the trial court found that Brown's willingness to demote women's programs, even as it demoted men's programs, could not be construed as "program expansion" for women. Finally, the trial court held that Brown failed the third prong because it had not "fully and effectively accommodated" the "interests and abilities" of female students.

Brown appealed the decision, mainly challenging the last point. In its view, the university was fully accommodating women's interest in athletics *as it existed*. The gender imbalance, it argued, was not a product of discrimination, but rather of female students' comparative lack of interest in sports. To require numeric balance independent of student interest would amount to, in the university's view, an affirmative-action-style "quota" system.

The appellate court was unconvinced. First, the court doubted that women's interest in sports was lacking—the demoted volleyball and gymnastics teams were in fact, popular with women. Second, and more important, it held that even if female demand for sports was lower than male demand, that fact alone did not justify a slimmer athletic program. The court wrote:

> Interest and ability [in sports] rarely develop in a vacuum; they evolve as a function of opportunity and experience. The [OCR's] Policy Interpretation recognizes that women's lower rate of participation in athlet-

ics reflects women's historical lack of opportunities to participate in sports. . . . [T]here exists the danger that, rather than providing a true measure of women's interest in sports, statistical evidence purporting to reflect women's interest instead provides only a measure of the very discrimination that is and has been the basis for women's lack of opportunity to participate in sports.[118]

The court's reasoning reflects a dynamic conception of law that refuses to accept the world as it is. According to this view, courts need not defer to the individual preferences of women and men as they exist; courts can use the power of law to reshape them. (Contrast this proactive view with the one offered in *EEOC v. Sears Roebuck & Co.*, discussed previously in **Chapter 4.**) The *Cohen* decision exemplifies what we might call the *Field of Dreams* approach to women's sports programs: "If you build it, they will come." It also placed greater emphasis on the "substantially proportionate" provision of the three-part test (prong one) by making the "effective accommodation" provision (prong three) harder to satisfy.

But the question of how to interpret the three-part test is not over. In 2005 the Department of Education issued a set of internal guidelines that appears at odds with the *Cohen* decision. Those guidelines make it easier for universities to demonstrate "effective accommodation" by allowing them to use student e-mail surveys to show that the female demand for athletics is being met. Some critics worry that e-mail surveys might not reflect the full extent of women's interest in sports. Under the guidelines, for instance, a student's failure to respond to the survey can be counted as a lack of interest in sports.[119]

But the guidelines suggest a deeper philosophical shift that undermines the *Field of Dreams* rationale. *Cohen* held that even assuming current female demand had been met, the universities might still bear an obligation to *increase* female demand until the ratio of women to men on the field looks more like the ratio of women to men on campus. The 2005 guidelines reject that view. Instead, they suggest that mere "statistical evidence" of student satisfaction—this time drawn from e-mail surveys—might represent effective accommodation after all, making gender ratios less relevant. Despite all this, the Department of Education insists it has not changed Title IX's compliance test in any way.[120]

c. "Boys against the girls"

Bringing a college sports program into compliance with Title IX often requires a shifting of resources to make the athletic opportunities offered for women "significantly proportionate" to those offered for men. That can mean increasing the offerings available to women, decreasing the offerings available to men, or both. Balancing men's and women's programs against each other sometimes degenerates into a childlike contest of "boys against the girls." After Brown University was held to be in violation of Title IX, its first remedial proposal sought to cut as many as 213 men's varsity positions so as to reduce the men's program to the size of the women's.[121] This proposal later gave way to one that both increased women's offerings and decreased men's offerings.

Most federal court jurisdictions agree that schools may comply with Title IX either by ratcheting up women's programs or by leveling down men's programs. In *Neal v. Board of Trustees of the California State Universities*,[122] the Ninth Circuit Court of Appeals specifically upheld a remedial plan, proposed by California State University, Bakersfield, that expanded the size of existing women's teams while limiting the size of existing men's teams. Some schools have gone further, actually cutting men's teams to make resources available for new women's teams. Because balance is measured by the overall number of athletes, new programs are likely to favor sports requiring large teams. For this reason some less traditional sports like women's rowing (nine athletes to a boat!) are growing dramatically. As one *New York Times* reporter observed wryly, "[W]omen are getting scholarships in sports they have never tried, perhaps never even heard of."[123]

Critics of Title IX charge that the statute's emphasis on gender ratios is clobbering men's sports. In an effort to equalize sports offerings for men and women, they argue, many schools have thrown nonrevenue sports like men's track and men's wrestling onto the chopping block. Indeed, since 1970, universities have cut more than 350 men's sports teams, including 45 track teams.[124] Balancing gender justice on the backs of male athletes is not only unfair, say these critics, but, in the long term, politically counterproductive.

Defenders of Title IX respond that such fears are overblown. While some men's teams have bitten the dust, that story is not representative. According to the General Accounting Office, 72 percent of universities that added women's teams from 1992 to 2000 did so without eliminating men's teams. Besides, sports opportunities for men, overall, have slightly increased since Title IX's passage.[125] If there is a villain in this piece, it is not women's rowing, this argument goes, but men's football, whose mammoth rosters of one hundred or more players make gender balancing extremely difficult. If colleges were willing to place reasonable limits on the size of their football teams, defenders say, they would not have to abolish nonrevenue men's teams to make room for women's sports.

Whichever side you take, Title IX has undeniably changed the role of women and girls in American sports. We end our discussion of athletics with the inspiring words of Judge Cynthia Holcomb Hall of the Ninth Circuit Court of Appeals, who, in *Neal v. Board of Trustees*, attributed to Title IX an even global significance.

[In the summer of 1999] 90,185 enthusiastic fans crowded into Pasadena's historic Rose Bowl for the finals of the Women's World Cup soccer match. An estimated 40 million television viewers also tuned in to watch a thrilling battle between the American and Chinese teams. The match ended when American defender Brandi Chastain fired the ball past Chinese goalkeeper Gao Hong, breaking a 4-4 shootout tie. The victory sparked a national celebration and a realization by many that women's sports could be just as exciting, competitive, and lucrative as men's sports. And the victorious athletes understood as well as anyone the connection between a [then] 27-year-old statute and tangible progress in women's athletics.[126]

E. Sexual Harassment in Schools

A young woman in the eighth grade is writing out her last will and testament. She leaves her stuffed animals to her mother and her record collection to her best friends. Life seems unbearable because the school day has become a living hell. The boys have been incessantly taunting her about the size of her breasts to the point where she cannot face them again at school. She would walk to school and, all of a sudden, she would hear the word "moo" bellowing out from a group of boys. This behavior occurred before school, after school, between classes, during classes, and at lunchtime. Her mother complained but the school refused to take any action. The school board's response: "boys will be boys."[127]

A 1993 survey of 1,600 eighth through eleventh graders conducted by the American Association of University Women ("AAUW") revealed that 85 percent of girls and 76 percent of boys reported that they had experienced "unwanted and unwelcome sexual behavior that interfere[d]" with their lives.[128] This definition included both physical harassment (being touched, grabbed, fondled, and pinched, or being subjected to bra snapping, skirt flipping, sexual assault, or even attempted rape) and nonphysical harassment (such as sexual comments, taunts, gestures, jokes, graffiti and rumors). The vast majority of this harassment comes from student peers. A follow-up study by the AAUW in 2001 of more than two thousand high school students found somewhat greater awareness of sexual harassment policies by students, but still found that 79 percent of boys and 83 percent of girls experienced sexual harassment at some point during high school, with 58 percent of the students having been subjected to physical harassment.[129] Over a quarter of the students reported being harassed "often." In a different study, four out of ten girls indicated they suffered some form of harassment every day.[130] For about a third of the girls, the harassment was so severe that they dreaded going to school.

Gay, lesbian, bisexual, and transgendered students experience even more virulent harassment. The Gay, Lesbian and Straight Education Network conducted a national survey of lesbian, gay, bisexual, and transgendered students, which showed that 84 percent of the respondents heard antigay remarks at school "frequently or often," 31 percent had "missed at least one entire day of school in the past month because they felt unsafe based on sexual orientation," 84 percent reported being verbally harassed, 31 percent physically harassed, and 21 percent physically assaulted because of their sexual orientation.[131] A National Mental Health Association study found that "more than half of teens surveyed said classmates use terms such as 'fag' and 'dyke' on a daily basis."[132]

One of the most astonishing sets of statistics about the rampant harassment and bullying is how rarely teachers intervene. The vast majority of harassment, both physical and nonphysical, occurs in classrooms and hallways. Yet whether teachers are afraid to confront perpetrators or fail to recognize the damage caused by sexual taunts or homophobic remarks, few intercede: "A study by the Massachusetts Department of Education found that gay students hear homophobic comments more than 25 times a day—and faculty intervene only about 3 percent of the time."[133]

Title IX prohibits sexual harassment in educational settings and establishes standards of liability for violators. The law of sexual harassment in education draws heavily upon Title VII's handling of sexual harassment in the workplace, a topic examined previously in **Chapter 4.** In 1992 the U.S. Supreme Court first held that a student sexually harassed by a teacher could sue a school district for damages under Title IX if the student informed school authorities, and the school acted with "deliberate indifference" in failing to stop the harassment.[134] Seven years later, the Supreme Court recognized a similar cause of action for *peer* sexual harassment under Title IX. In that case, *Davis v. Monroe County Board of Education,*[135] a fifth grader in a Georgia elementary school, LaShonda Davis, was grabbed, fondled, and repeatedly subjected to sexually explicit comments by a classmate over a five-month period. Her harasser, G.F., tried to touch her breasts and genital area. During a gym class, G.F. placed a doorstop in his pants to simulate an erection and acted suggestively toward LaShonda. At other times, he rubbed against her and said, "I want to feel your boobs" and "I want to go to bed with you." LaShonda told G.F. to stop, and she reported all these incidents to her teachers and her mother. Once LaShonda and several other girls asked a teacher if they could go to the principal to report G.F.'s behavior. The teacher replied, "If [the principal] wants you, he'll call you." LaShonda's mother called the school and spoke with the principal, who said, "I guess I'll have to threaten him a little bit harder." After LaShonda had endured the harassment for months, her grades dropped and she wrote a suicide note. Finally, her parents filed a criminal complaint and a civil suit against the school district for failing to protect her from this sexual harassment. G.F. ultimately pled guilty to sexual battery in juvenile court.

Five years later, the case reached the U.S. Supreme Court. The Court held that schools districts could be held liable for peer sexual harassment, but only if school officials knew about it, were "deliberately indifferent" to it, and the harassment was so "severe, pervasive, and objectively offensive that it effectively bars the victim's access to an educational opportunity or benefit."

These standards for school liability for teacher-on-student and student-on-student harassment are proving extraordinarily difficult for plaintiffs to meet. Since the Davis decision, federal courts have evaluated a number of school sexual harassment cases. Their holdings make clear how formidable the standards are. In some cases, courts find that the school did not have sufficient notice of the conduct—if, say, the teacher who observed the inappropriate conduct was not one who held the power to discipline students[136]—or that the conduct was not severe or pervasive. In other cases, courts deem schools' weak efforts to discipline harassers as not being clearly unreasonable or amounting to deliberate indifference. For example, in *Wills v. Brown University*,[137] when a student sought a professor's help with difficulties in his course, he pulled her onto his lap and fondled her breasts. Although the school issued a written reprimand about the incident to the professor, within three months it renewed his teaching contract for a year and gave him a raise. He was dismissed the following year after six other female students reported similar sexual assaults. The court determined that a single episode of harassment, even if severe, was not sufficiently pervasive to deprive the victim of educational opportunities. The court also found that while "[v]iewed in retrospect, Brown's procedures left much to be desired," the university's "reasonably firm reprimand" did not amount to deliberate indifference.

Title IX regulations require schools to develop sexual harassment policies and complaint procedures.[138] A challenge, particularly for elementary schools, is the difficulty of developing age-appropriate sexual harassment policies and training. Not all teasing is harassment; not all harassment is sexual. When Jonathan Prevette, a six-year-old boy in North Carolina, kissed a female classmate on the cheek, the case made national headlines. The media had a field day and reported that he was "suspended" for a "sex crime." Jonathan's mother went on the talk show circuit, CNN, *The Today Show,* and NBC News—and this seems to be where the sexual harassment label was applied. The parents threatened to sue unless the school issued an apology.

Conservative groups seized on the case as an example of "political correctness" and "feminist fanaticism."[139] In actuality, the principal sensibly talked to Jonathan about inappropriate touching and gave Jonathan an in-school suspension by making him miss the class ice cream party. Sadly, parents and the media may seize on cases like Jonathan Prevette's as ways of discounting what is an epidemic of much more extreme harassing behaviors. This misinformation and ridiculing of sexual harassment laws can cause people to overlook the delicacy and yet utmost importance of teaching young girls and boys the differences between good and bad touching.

F. *Questions for Discussion*

1. What is the harm of allowing several thousand of the nation's almost fifty million public school students to be educated in experimental single-sex schools and classes? Does the argument that the single-sex alternative is "diverse"—in the sense of providing an alternative (single-sex or coed)—have anything to do with the constitutional idea of diversity, which seeks to promote student bodies with a range of racial, ethnic, social, or economic backgrounds? Is it possible to imagine a sex-segregated program that would not reinforce traditional notions of separate spheres for males and females?

2. Where sports are concerned, Title IX is particularly tolerant of the separate-can-be-equal philosophy. The act's regulations specifically allow schools to operate separate teams for males and females "where selection for such teams is based upon competitive skill or the activity involved is a contact sport."[140] Defenders of the rule argue that if female students were given the chance to compete for places on male teams, few women or girls would make the cut. As a result, "mixed-sex" athletic squads—like the Massachusetts Institute of Technology ski team or Virginia State's golf team—are relatively rare. Should they be? What feminist legal theories might defend the operation of segregated sports teams? Equal treatment theory? Dominance theory? Cultural feminism? Postmodern feminism? Assuming that segregated teams have their place, should exceptional female athletes be allowed to jump from women's teams to men's teams if they are good enough?

SUGGESTED READINGS

AMERICAN ASSOCIATION OF UNIVERSITY WOMEN EDUCATIONAL FOUNDATION, GROWING SMART: WHAT'S WORKING FOR GIRLS IN SCHOOLS (1995).

Dianne Avery, *Institutional Myths, Historical Narratives and Social Science Evidence: Reading the "Record" in the Virginia Military Institute Case,* 5 S. CAL. REV. L. & WOMEN'S STUD. 189 (1996).

SUSAN K. CAHN, COMING ON STRONG: GENDER AND SEXUALITY IN TWENTIETH-CENTURY WOMEN'S SPORTS (1994).

ANNE FAUSTO-STERLING, MYTHS OF GENDER: BIOLOGICAL THEORIES ABOUT WOMEN AND MEN (2d ed. 1992).

ELEANOR E. MACCOBY, THE TWO SEXES: GROWING UP APART, COMING TO-GETHER (1998).

Denise C. Morgan, *Anti-Subordination Analysis After* United States v. Virginia: *Evaluating the Constitutionality of K–12 Single-Sex Public Schools,* 1999 U. CHI. LEGAL F. 381.

National Organization for Women Legal Defense and Education Fund, *Public Education Programs for African-American Males: Legal Issues Raised by Proposals for Single-Sex Public Schools* (working draft), 21 N.Y.U. REV. LAW & SOC. CHANGE 725 (1994–95).

MARIAH BURTON NELSON, THE STRONGER WOMEN GET, THE MORE MEN LOVE FOOTBALL: SEXISM AND THE AMERICAN CULTURE OF SPORTS (1994).

Suzanne Sangree, *Title IX and the Contact Sports Exemption,* 32 CONN. L. REV. 381 (2000).

BARBARA M. SOLOMON, IN THE COMPANY OF EDUCATED WOMEN: A HISTORY OF WOMEN AND HIGHER EDUCATION IN AMERICA (1985).

PHILIPPA STRUM, WOMEN IN THE BARRACKS: THE VMI CASE AND EQUAL RIGHTS (2002).

Symposium, *Gender and Sports: Setting a Course for College Athletics,* 3 DUKE J. GENDER L. & POL'Y 1 (1996)

Valorie K. Vojdik, *Girls' Schools After VMI: Do They Make the Grade?,* 4 DUKE J. GENDER L. & POL'Y 69 (1997).

NOTES

1. DAVID TYACK & ELISABETH HANSOT, LEARNING TOGETHER: A HISTORY OF COEDUCATION IN AMERICAN PUBLIC SCHOOLS 49, 5, 10, 14, 24 (1990).

2. Susan McGee Bailey & Patricia B. Campbell, *Gender Equity: The Unexamined Basis of School Reform,* 4 STAN. L. & POL'Y REV. 73, 75 (1992–93).

3. 2 THOMAS WOODY, A HISTORY OF WOMEN'S EDUCATION IN THE UNITED STATES 228 (1929).

4. TYACK & HANSOT, *supra* note 1, at 78.

5. *Id.* at 79.

6. *Id.* at 83–84.

7. Ronald Chen & Jon Hanson, *Categorically Biased: The Influence of Knowledge Structures on Law and Legal Theory,* 77 S. CAL. L. REV. 1106, 1116 (2004).

8. Leslie Miller-Bernal, *Coeducation: An Uneven Progression, in* GOING COED: WOMEN'S EXPERIENCES IN FORMERLY MEN'S COLLEGES AND UNIVERSITIES, 1950–2000 1, 4 (Leslie Miller-Bernal & Susan L. Poulson eds. 2004).

9. Deborah L. Rhode, *Association and Assimilation,* 81 NW. U. L. REV. 106, 129–30 (1986).

10. Jill Elaine Hasday, *The Principle and Practice of Women's "Full-Citizenship": A Case Study of Sex-Segregated Public Education,* 101 MICH. L. REV. 755, 805–8 (2002).

11. Cynthia Fuchs Epstein, *The Myths and Justifications of Sex Segregation in Higher Education: VMI and the Citadel,* 4 DUKE J. GENDER L. & POL'Y 101, 118 n.150 (1997).

12. Gerard N. Burrow & Nora L. Burgess, *The Evolution of Women as Physicians and Surgeons,* 71 ANNALS THORACIC SURGERY S27, S27–S28 (2001).

13. Council on Graduate Medical Education, Women in Medicine, Fifth Report, http://www.cogme.gov/rpt5_3.htm (last visited Sept. 9, 2005).

14. American Medical Association, Women Physicians Congress, *Table 1— Physicians by Gender (Excludes Students),* 2004, *Table 8—Medical School Faculty Distribution of U.S. Medical School Faculty by Gender and Rank, 2003,* May 2003, http://www.ama-assn.org/ama/pub/category/12919.html.

15. Deborah L. Rhode, *Perspectives on Professional Women,* 40 STAN. L. REV. 1163, 1173–74 (1988).

16. Katharine T. Bartlett, *Women in the Legal Profession: The Good News and the Bad,* 1997, http://gos.sbc.edu/b/bartlett.html.

17. Mary J. Mullarkey, *Two Harvard Women: 1965 to Today,* 27 HARV. WOMEN'S L.J. 367, 370–71 (2004).

18. Ruth Bader Ginsburg, *Introduction to Women and the Law: Facing the Millennium,* 32 IND. L. REV. 1161, 1162 (1999).

19. Deborah Rhode, *Midcourse Corrections: Women in Legal Education,* 53 J. LEGAL EDUC. 475, 475 (2003).

20. LANI GUINIER ET AL., BECOMING GENTLEMEN: WOMEN, LAW SCHOOL, AND INSTITUTIONAL CHANGE (1997).

21. AMERICAN ASSOCIATION OF UNIVERSITY WOMEN, HOW SCHOOLS SHORTCHANGE GIRLS (1992) *available at* http://www.aauw.org/research/hssg.pdf.

22. MYRA SADKER & DAVID SADKER, FAILING AT FAIRNESS: HOW AMERICA'S SCHOOLS CHEAT GIRLS 43 (1994).

23. Allyson Jule, Gender, Participation and Silence in the Language Classroom: Sh-Shushing the Girls (2004).

24. Jeff Jacoby, *"Alarming Facts" About Boys, Girls,* Boston Globe, Feb. 6, 1996, Op-Ed, at 15.

25. Karen Zittleman & David Sadker, *Teacher Education Textbooks: The Unfinished Gender Revolution* (2002–03), http://www.sadker.org/textbooks .htm.

26. Judith S. Kleinfeld, *The Myth That Schools Shortchange Girls: Social Science in the Service of Deception* (1998), http://www.uaf.edu/northern/schools/ myth.html.

27. Robert T. Brennan et al., *The Relative Equitability of High-Stakes Testing Versus Teacher-Assigned Grades: An Analysis of the Massachusetts Comprehensive Assessment System (MCAS),* 71 Harv. Educ. Rev. 173 (2001).

28. Cathy Young, *Where the Boys Are,* 32 Reason, Feb. 1, 2001, *available at* http://www.sonoma.edu/users/f/filp/ed420/boysare.htm.

29. Dina S. Gomez, *Gender Wars,* 20 NEA Today, Oct. 1, 2001, at 31.

30. John W. Curtis, American Association of University Professors, *Faculty Salary and Faculty Distribution Fact Sheet, 2003–04,* at http://www.aaup.org/re-search/sal&distribution.htm.

31. Donna J. Nelson, *A National Analysis of Diversity in Science and Engineering Faculties at Research Universities* (Jan. 6, 2005) at 2, 6 http://chem-info.chem.ou.edu/~djn/diversity/briefings/Diversity%20Report%20Final.pdf.

32. Curtis, *supra* note 30.

33. Lawrence H. Summers, *Remarks at NBER Conference on Diversifying the Science and Engineering Workforce,* Jan. 14, 2005, http://www.president .harvard.edu/speeches/2005/nber.html.

34. Rebecca Winters, *Harvard's Crimson Face,* Time, Jan. 31, 2005, at 52.

35. National Association for Single-Sex Public Education, *Single-Sex Public Schools in the United States,* http://www.singlesexschools.org/schools.html (last visited Oct. 1, 2004).

36. Mark O'Keefe, *Single-Sex School Debate Rekindled,* Chi. Trib., Oct. 13, 2002, at 9A (quoting Terry O'Neill, membership vice president NOW).

37. 309 F. Supp. 184, 186 (E.D. Va. 1970).

38. 316 F. Supp. 134, 137, 136 n.3 (D.S.C. 1970), *aff'd mem.,* 401 U.S. 951 (1971).

39. 400 F. Supp. 326, 342 (E.D. Pa. 1975), *vacated by,* 532 F.2d 880 (3d Cir. 1976), *aff'd mem. by an equally divided Court,* 430 U.S. 703 (1977).

40. 532 F.2d at 881, 882, 886.

41. *Id.* at 889 (Gibbons, J., dissenting).

42. 478 A. 2d 1352 (Pa. Super. Ct. 1984).

43. 458 U.S. 718, 724–25, 729–30 (1982).

44. 775 F. Supp. 1004, 1007 (E.D. Mich. 1991).

45. 766 F. Supp. 1407, 1413 (W.D. Va. 1991).

46. 766 F. Supp. at 1415.

47. 976 F.2d at 898.

48. 852 F. Supp. 471, 476 (W.D. Va 1994).

49. 518 U.S. 515, 527, 528 (1996).

50. United States v. Virginia, 44 F. 3d 1229, 1237 (4th Cir. 1995).

51. 518 U.S. at 546, 533, 540.

52. *Id.* at 553–54, 533 n.7.

53. 20 U.S.C. § 1681(a) (2001).

54. Jackson v. Birmingham Bd. of Educ., 125 S. Ct. 1497 (2005).

55. 34 C.F.R. § 106.35(b) (2003).

56. 34 C.F.R. § 106.34 (2003).

57. U.S. Dep't of Education, Nondiscrimination on the Basis of Sex in Educational Programs or Activities Receiving Federal Financial Assistance; Proposed Rules, 69 Fed. Reg. 11276, 11278–79 (proposed Mar. 9, 2004).

58. AMERICAN ASSOCIATION OF UNIVERSITY WOMEN, SEPARATED BY SEX: A CRITICAL LOOK AT SINGLE-SEX EDUCATION FOR GIRLS 2 (1998) [hereinafter SEPARATED BY SEX].

59. *See* U.S. Dep't of Education, Nondiscrimination on the Basis of Sex in Educational Programs or Activities Receiving Federal Financial Assistance; Proposed Rules, 69 Fed. Reg. 11276, 11276 n.3 (proposed Mar. 9, 2004).

60. *See* Joy K. Rice & Annette Hemmings, *Women's Colleges and Women Achievers: An Update*, 13 SIGNS 546, 555 (1988).

61. Beth Willinger, *Single Gender Education and the Constitution*, 40 LOY. L. REV. 253, 268 (1994).

62. *Girls Only?*, CHRISTIAN SCI. MONITOR, Sept. 5, 1996, at 20.

63. Tanyanika Samuels, *Women's Foundation Reveals Grant Recipients*, KAN. CITY STAR, Dec. 4, 2002, *available at* 2002 WL 101928308.

64. Nick Chiles, *Going First Class*, NEWSDAY, June 27, 2001, at A3.

65. ROSEMARY C. SALOMONE, SAME, DIFFERENT, EQUAL: RETHINKING SINGLE-SEX SCHOOLING 13 (2003).

66. Karen Stabiner, *The Pros and Cons of Single-Sex Schools*, MILWAUKEE J. & SENTINEL, May 20, 2002, at 11A.

67. SALOMONE, *supra* note 65, at 21.

68. Ellie McGrath, *Separate but Better? An Exploration of Single-Sex Education That Misses the Mark*, CHI. TRIB., Nov. 24, 2002, at 1.

69. *See* Jacques Steinberg, *All-Girls School Opens to Muffins and Media*, N.Y. TIMES, Sept. 5, 1996, at B6.

70. Robyn E. Blumner, *Single-Sex Education Won't Help Students in the Real World*, ST. PETERSBURG TIMES, May 26, 2002, at 6D.

71. SALOMONE, *supra* note 65, at 21.

72. ALEXANDER W. ASTIN, WHAT MATTERS IN COLLEGE?: FOUR CRITICAL YEARS REVISITED 324 (1993).

73. Pamela Haag, *Single-Sex Education in Grades K–12: What Does the Research Tell Us?,* in SEPARATED BY SEX, *supra* note 58, at 13, 22.

74. Nancy Levit, *Separating Equals: Educational Research and the Long-Term Consequences of Sex Segregation,* 67 GEO. WASH. L. REV. 451, 472–505 (1999). See also Valerie E. Lee, *Is Single-Sex Secondary Schooling a Solution to the Problem of Gender Inequity?* in SEPARATED BY SEX, *supra* note 58, at 41, 43.

75. Sociology professor Cornelius Riordan suggests that minority race sex segregation for economically disadvantaged students—segregation essentially by race and sex and class—may be academically beneficial. *See* Cornelius Riordan, *Single-Gender Schools: Outcomes for African and Hispanic Americans,* 10 RES. SOC. EDUC. & SOCIALIZATION 177, 192–202 (1994). Riordan's 1990 studies, however, were conducted in Catholic and private schools, which are environments with aspects, from religious constraints to rigid discipline to economic advantages, that make them unrepresentative of public education.

76. *See, e.g.,* Lee, *supra* note 74, at 41, 43.

77. Willinger, *supra* note 61, at 270.

78. PEGGY REEVES SANDAY, FRATERNITY GANG RAPE: SEX, BROTHERHOOD, AND PRIVILEGE ON CAMPUS 154–92 (1990).

79. *See, e.g.,* Margaret L. Signorella et al., *Single-Sex Versus Mixed-Sex Classes and Gender Schemata in Children and Adolescents: A Longitudinal Comparison,* 20 PSYCHOL. WOMEN Q. 599, 599, 606 (1996).

80. Amanda Datnow, Lea Hubbard, & Elisabeth Woody, *Is Single Gender Schooling Viable in the Public Sector? Lessons from California's Pilot Program,* May 20, 2001, http://www.oise.utoronto.ca/depts/tps/adatnow/final.pdf.

81. Amanda Datnow, *Single-Sex Schooling: Critique of Report Relies on "Disturbing Overgeneralization,"* EDUC. WK., Oct. 17, 2001, at 36, *available at* 2001 WL 12047039.

82. *See, e.g.,* Walter Sidney, *Solving Coed Conundrum,* DENVER POST, June 13, 2003, at B7.

83. Julian V. Roberts & Anthony N. Doob, *News Media Influences on Public Views of Sentencing,* 14 LAW & HUM. BEHAV. 451, 453 (1990).

84. *See* Marc Fisher, *One Gender Schools Would Offer Flexibility,* CONTRA COSTA TIMES (Walnut Creek, CA), May 19, 2002, *available at* 2002 WL 21118930.

85. Office of Educational Research and Improvement, U.S. Dep't of Education, National Study of Charter Schools: Fourth-Year Report 1 (2000), http://www.ed.gov/pubs/charter4thyear/index.html.

86. *See* Brighter Choice Charter Schools, Single-Sex Public Schools in the U.S. 1 (Mar. 2004), http://www.brighterchoice.org/single_sex.htm.

87. *See* Proposed Rulemaking Notice, 69 Fed. Reg. 11,276, 11,282 (Mar. 9, 2004).

88. Krista Kafer, Progress on School Choice in the States, Heritage Foundation, July 10, 2003, http://www.heritage.org/Research/Education/bg1639.cfm.

89. 536 U.S. 639 (2002).

90. Don Sabo et al., Her Life Depends on It: Sport, Physical Activity and the Health and Well-Being of American Girls 20–21 (2004), *available at* http://www.womenssportsfoundation.org/binary-data/WSF_ARTICLE/pdf_file/990.pdf.

91. National Federation of State High School Associations, The Case for High School Activities, http://www.nfhs.org/case.html (last visited Sept. 12, 2005).

92. National Women's Law Center, Title IX and Women's Athletic Opportunity: A Nation's Promise Yet to Be Fulfilled 3 (May 2002).

93. The President's Counsel on Physical Fitness and Sports Report, Physical Activity & Sports in the Lives of Girls (Spring 1997).

94. The Women's Sports Foundation, Minorities in Sports: The Effect of Varsity Sports Participation on the Social, Educational and Career Mobility of Minority Students 4 (Aug. 15, 1989).

95. Jerry Crowe, *Graduation Rates Fall for Most Players, Colleges*, L.A. Times, Nov. 21, 2000, at D6.

96. *See* Women's Sports Foundation, The Wilson Report: Moms, Dads, Daughters and Sports 5 (June 7, 1988).

97. Feminist Majority Foundation, Gender Equity in Athletics and Sports, http://www.feminist.org/sports/titleIXfactsheet.asp (last visited Sept. 12, 2005).

98. *Id.*

99. *Id.*

100. National Coalition for Women and Girls in Education, Title IX at 30: Report Card on Gender Equity 14 (June 2002), *available at* http://www.ncwge.org.

101. *Id.* at 15.

102. *Id.*

103. *Id.*

104. Catharine MacKinnon, Sex Equality 365 (2000).

105. National Women's Law Center, *supra* note 92, at 2.

106. *Id.*

107. *Id.* at 16.

108. Deborah Brake, *The Struggle for Sex Equality in Sport and the Theory Behind Title IX*, 34 U. Mich. J.L. Reform 13, 90–91 (2000–01) (citing Vivian Acosta & Linda Jean Carpenter, Women in Intercollegiate Sport: A Longitudinal Study—Twenty Three Year Update 1977–2000, at 9 (2000)).

109. National Women's Law Center, *supra* note 92, at 17.

110. *Id.*

111. Scott M. Reid, *For Black Women, A Coaching Void,* ORANGE COUNTY REG., Dec. 20, 1999, at D1.

112. Brake, *supra* note 108, at 90–91.

113. 44 Fed. Reg. 71413 (1979).

114. U.S. DEP'T OF EDUCATION, CLARIFICATION OF INTERCOLLEGIATE ATHLETICS POLICY GUIDANCE: THE THREE-PART TEST (Jan. 16, 1996), available at http://www.ed.gov/about/offices/list/ocr/docs/clarific.html#two.

115. Roy Whitehead et al., *Gender Equity in Athletics: Should We Adopt a Non-Discriminatory Model?*, 30 U. TOL. L. REV. 223, 225 (1999).

116. Cohen v. Brown Univ., 101 F.3d 155, 163 (1st Cir. 1996), *cert. denied,* 520 U.S. 1186 (1997).

117. *Id.* at 163–64 (quoting Cohen v. Brown Univ., 879 F. Supp. 185, 189 (D.R.I. 1995)).

118. *Id.* at 179.

119. Tamar Lewin, *U.S. Rule on Women's Sports May Ease College Compliance,* N.Y. TIMES, Mar. 23, 2005, at A15.

120. *Id.* (quoting James F. Manning, assistant secretary of education for civil rights, as saying, "There is no change in [Title IX compliance] policy").

121. MACKINNON, *supra* note 104, at 384.

122. 198 F.3d 763 (1999).

123. Juliet Macur, *Never Rowed? Take a Free Ride,* N.Y. TIMES, May 28, 2004, at D1.

124. Adam Buckley Cohen, *Under the Axe: Is Title IX Killing Men's Collegiate Track?*, RUNNING TIMES 24, 26 (Nov. 2003).

125. *The Politics of Equity in College Sports,* 13 WOMEN HIGHER EDUC. 7, 7 (Feb. 1, 2004).

126. *Neal,* 198 F.3d at 773.

127. Monica L. Sherer, Comment, *No Longer Just Child's Play: School Liability Under Title IX for Peer Sexual Harassment,* 141 U. PA. L. REV. 2119, 2120 (1993).

128. AMERICAN ASSOCIATION OF UNIVERSITY WOMEN EDUCATIONAL FOUNDATION, HOSTILE HALLWAYS: THE AAUW SURVEY ON SEXUAL HARASSMENT IN AMERICA'S SCHOOLS 7 (1993).

129. AMERICAN ASSOCIATION OF UNIVERSITY WOMEN EDUCATIONAL FOUNDATION, HOSTILE HALLWAYS: BULLYING, TEASING, AND SEXUAL HARASSMENT IN SCHOOL (2001), *available at* http://www.aauw.org/research/girls_education/hostile.cfm.

130. NAN STEIN ET AL., SECRETS IN PUBLIC: SEXUAL HARASSMENT IN OUR SCHOOLS 2–3 (Center for Research on Women Working Paper No. 256, Mar. 1993).

131. Gay, Lesbian and Straight Education Network, *The 2001 National*

School Climate Survey: Lesbian, Gay, Bisexual and Transgender Students and Their Experiences in Schools 2 (2001), http://www.glsen.org/binary-data/GLSEN_ARTICLES/pdf_file/1029.pdf.

132. Robert Tomsho, *Schools' Efforts to Protect Gays Face Opposition,* WALL ST. J., Feb. 20, 2003, at B1.

133. Mary Pasciak, *School Alliance Against Gay Harassment; Posts a Message of Tolerance for All,* BUFFALO NEWS, Feb. 22, 2003, at B1.

134. Gebser v. Lago Vista Indep. Sch. Dist., 524 U.S. 274 (1998); Franklin v. Gwinnett County Pub. Sch., 503 U.S. 60 (1992).

135. 526 U.S. 629 (1999).

136. Reese v. Jefferson Sch. Dist. No. 14J, 208 F.3d 736 (9th Cir. 2000).

137. 184 F.3d 20 (1st Cir. 1999).

138. U.S. Dep't of Education, Office of Civil Rights, *Sexual Harassment: It's Not Academic, available at* http://www.ed.gov/about/offices/list/ocr/docs/ocrshpam.html (last visited Sept. 12, 2005).

139. Deborah L. Rhode, *You Must Remember This . . . ,* NAT'L L.J., Oct. 28, 1996, at A28.

140. 34 C.F.R. § 106.41(b) (1995).

6

Gender and the Body

No woman can call herself free who does not own and control her own body. No woman can call herself free until she can choose consciously whether she will or will not be a mother. . . . She who earns her own living gains a sort of freedom . . . but . . . it is of little account beside the untrammeled choice of mating or not mating, of being a mother or not being a mother.   Margaret Sanger[1]

Women's childbearing ability is the most dramatic physiological difference between the sexes. Yet women's ability to control their reproductive lives is about much more than whether they choose to have children. Reproductive liberty is connected to all other aspects of women's equality—the ability to hold a job, obtain an education, participate in sports, or escape gender-based violence from spouses, from partners, or at clinics.

Many nations view women principally as mothers. A long-standing historical assumption holds that the state has a legitimate interest in regulating sexual and reproductive behavior. State and federal policies promote childbearing by limiting or discouraging sex education, contraceptive availability, and abortion services. Some states place limits on surrogacy contracts. Others have tried to ban or restrict pornography. All these activities are tied to issues of sexual and reproductive liberty. As we will see, even feminists do not always speak with one voice on these issues.

A. Abortion

Until the middle of the nineteenth century, most states permitted abortions. In the late 1840s, the American Medical Association began to express opposition to abortion because it posed dangers to women and because its availability might cause a woman to "'overlook[] the duties imposed on her by the marriage contract.'"[2] About this time, states started to enact laws criminalizing abortion. One of the driving forces behind laws prohibiting abortion in this era was a racist concern about declining birthrates among upper-middle-class white women and comparatively high rates of births to women of color. In 1873 Congress passed the Comstock Act, which made it a federal crime to mail or distribute across state lines any article (including information) that would prevent contraception or promote abortion. Approximately half the states passed their own versions of the Comstock laws. By the turn of the twentieth century all states had laws prohibiting abortion except when necessary to save the woman's life.

In the middle to late 1950s, population control groups, human rights organizations, and Planned Parenthood began to urge changes in restrictive abortion laws. In 1959 the American Law Institute ("ALI"), a group of lawyers, judges, and scholars dedicated to legal clarification and reform, proposed revisions to the Model Penal Code that would allow abortions if necessary to preserve the physical or mental health of the mother, if the pregnancy resulted from rape or incest, or if the fetus was severely defective. In 1967 Colorado revised its statutes in accordance with the ALI's suggestions, and a dozen other states followed suit.

By 1973, when *Roe v. Wade* was decided, thirteen states had adopted some variation of the ALI's Model Penal Code, thirty states permitted abortions only to save the mother's life, two more permitted abortions to preserve the mother's life or health, one allowed abortion to save the mother's life or if the pregnancy resulted from rape, and four others allowed abortions until the twenty-fourth week of pregnancy.

1. Abortion and the Constitution

In *Roe v. Wade,* the Court considered whether a state could prohibit a woman from terminating her pregnancy. The Supreme Court accepted review of a case challenging a Texas law criminalizing the acts of doctors who provided abortions, which had an exception for saving the life but not preserving the health of the mother. Because philosophers, doctors, and theologians could not arrive at consensus about when life begins, the Court avoided the question whether life

begins at conception. Instead, the decision in *Roe* attempted to rec-
oncile the uncertainties by balancing competing interests. Justice
Harry Blackmun wrote the decision for a seven-member majority in
Roe, holding that the fundamental right of privacy was "broad
enough to encompass a woman's decision whether or not to terminate
her pregnancy."[3] That right is not absolute, but must be balanced
against important state interests in regulating to protect potential life,
maternal health, and the integrity of medical practice. Justice Blackmun developed a trimester framework to determine when a state
could regulate a woman's decision whether to have an abortion.

During the first trimester, "the abortion decision and its effectua-
tion must be left to the medical judgment of the woman's attending
physician." (Although the actual language in *Roe* seemed to relegate
the pregnant woman to the status of a bystander—because the statute
threatened doctors who performed abortions, but not pregnant
women, with criminal prosecution—subsequent decisions have clarified that the decision rests with the woman and her doctor.) After the
first trimester, the state could create reasonable regulations related to
maternal health. At the end of the second trimester, approximately at
viability, the state's interest in protecting potential life became compelling, and the state could prohibit all abortions except when necessary to preserve the life or health of the woman.

The *Roe* decision framed abortion rights in terms of constitutional
privacy protections. Several groups of feminist legal theorists have cri-
tiqued the use of privacy analysis as a foundation for reproductive
rights. Grounding abortion rights on privacy doctrine reinforces the
idea of private choice and endorses an ideology feminists have long
criticized—the public-private dichotomy. If reproductive rights must
belong to the private realm to avoid state interference, it follows that
the state does not have to support these private choices with public
monies. Indeed, that was the holding in two Supreme Court cases,
Maher v. Roe in 1977 and *Harris v. McRae* in 1980—that the state
does not have to fund either nontherapeutic or medically necessary
abortions for women who cannot otherwise afford to have them.[4]
Catharine MacKinnon explains that "the doctrine of privacy has become the triumph of the state's abdication of women in the name of
freedom and self-determination."[5] It makes the state unaccountable
for disadvantages shouldered by women as a group.

Privacy doctrine is unhelpful if women do not have basic equality rights—in economic resources, employability, or the ability to make choices unfettered by gender norms and expectations. "The language of privacy implies that women are choosers against a background of a number of realistic, attractive alternatives. Pregnant women who consider abortion are not often so situated. The concepts of privacy, liberty and choice are at odds with the sense of choicelessness women seeking abortion actually feel."[6]

If the privacy rationale is unsatisfactory, constitutional equal protection analysis has traditionally been unavailable, because women and men are not similarly situated with respect to pregnancy. It is also difficult to meet the constitutional requirement that any pregnancy-based discrimination is intentional in the sense of a purpose to harm women. Language in later abortion rights cases recognizes that "[a] State's restrictions on a woman's right to terminate her pregnancy also implicate constitutional guarantees of gender equality,"[7] but favorable Supreme Court abortion decisions have not been grounded on equal protection theory.

Sixteen years after *Roe*, in *Webster v. Reproductive Health Services*,[8] the Supreme Court replaced *Roe*'s trimester framework with a viability line for deciding when the interest in potential life prevails over the woman's right to decide whether to terminate her pregnancy. Cases after *Roe* have centered on government attempts to influence women's decisions or to regulate abortion procedures so severely that the regulations impede the right of choice. In 1992, in *Planned Parenthood of Southeastern Pennsylvania v. Casey,* the Court examined a Pennsylvania law restricting abortion by imposing a twenty-four-hour waiting period and mandatory counseling and requiring spousal notification. Numerous amicus briefs, including one filed by the first Bush administration, urged reversal of *Roe*—a result that would have left it up to the states whether to criminalize abortions. A majority of the Court declined to reverse *Roe*. The *Casey* Court stated that adherence to precedent and concern for the Court's legitimacy required it to uphold *Roe* absent a "most convincing justification" for reversal.

In *Casey* the Supreme Court reaffirmed the central holding of *Roe* but retreated from *Roe* in two important respects. The Court rejected the trimester system because it was "a rigid prohibition on all previability regulation" and it "undervalues the state's interest in the potential life within the woman," an interest that the *Casey* Court found exists throughout pregnancy. It also held that a state regulation is unconstitutional only if it creates an "undue burden" on the woman's right to choose. An "undue burden" is a regulation that "has the purpose or effect of placing a substantial obstacle in the path of a woman seeking an abortion of a nonviable fetus."[9] Under this standard, the Court struck down Pennsylvania's requirement that women notify their husbands before terminating their pregnancies because it unduly burdened the rights of women, particularly if they were subject to domestic violence.

The Court, though, upheld the provisions that required women to have abortion counseling and to wait twenty-four hours after the initial consultation before undergoing the abortion procedure. The Court determined that even though the waiting period would require two visits to a doctor, which for some women would be "particularly burdensome," it did not impose a substantial obstacle and was "a reasonable measure to implement the State's interest in protecting the life of the unborn."[10] The Court also held it constitutionally permissible for a state to compel counseling that would inform the woman of the risks of the abortion procedure and alternatives to abortion. (One provision upheld in *Casey* also required abortion providers to show women pictures of developing fetuses to discourage them from having abortions.) Equality theorists pointed out that the mandatory counseling and required waiting period implied women were not capable of independently making one of the most important decisions of their lives without being told by the state to "go home and sleep on it."[11]

Twenty-eight states compel women seeking abortion to receive counseling that informs women of risks associated with abortions and alternatives to it. Twenty-two states also require a waiting period (usually twenty-four hours) between the counseling and performance of the abortion.[12]

A number of decisions since *Roe* and *Casey* have tested the contours of permissible state regulations of the abortion decision. Courts have held, for example, that states can require either one- or two-parent consent or notification as long as they provide an alternative judicial proceeding, whereby an unemancipated minor could avoid notifying her parents by proving to a court that she is sufficiently mature and informed to make her own decision.[13] Thirty-four states thus have enforceable laws requiring young women to prove they have no-tified or obtained consent from one or both parents or have received approval from a judge.[14] Commentators and courts have recognized that judicial bypass proceedings can be more emotionally traumatic to teenagers than the abortion procedure itself.

Other decisions upheld various procedural restrictions on the per-formance of abortions. Although women's identities must remain con-fidential, states can require the collection of specific medical informa-tion from women, including their age, marital status, and number of prior pregnancies and abortions. States can also insist that facilities performing abortions meet certain record-keeping requirements, such as identifying the physician who performed the abortion, the referring agency, the gestational age and weight of aborted fetuses, and any medical complications, since these requirements relate to maternal health. To uphold the state interest in protecting viable fetuses, it is constitutional to require that a second physician be present for abor-tions performed after viability, that second-trimester abortions be per-formed only in hospitals, and that a pathology examination of tissue occur for every abortion performed.[15] A state can prohibit public em-ployees and public hospitals from performing abortions.[16] The Court, however, has struck down as onerous or invasive reporting require-ments that exceeded state health-related interests, such as the "method of payment [and] the woman's personal history."[17]

In the past decade, one strategy of those opposed to abortions has been to disrupt access to abortion services by imposing unnecessary, costly, and increasingly burdensome conditions on abortion providers. These Targeted Regulation of Abortion Provider ("TRAP") laws inflict strict maintenance, record-keeping, building, landscaping, employment, and housekeeping rules on facilities and physicians who perform abortions. These rules are not imposed on any other compa-rable medical practices.

South Carolina, for example, passed twenty-seven pages of licens-ing regulations applicable only to abortion clinics, defined as facilities that perform any second-trimester or more than five first-trimester abortions per month. These detailed regulations, enforceable through a series of fines, establish requirements of inspections, housekeeping, in-service job training for employees, emergency drug kit inventories, an "approved platform" for holding garbage containers to avoid over-turning by animals, and extensive medical record keeping and reports.

The law also permits health department inspectors to make photocopies of patient records but does not impose any requirement of confidentiality regarding the patient's records on the health department, and it requires the testing of all patients for some sexually transmitted diseases, irrespective of whether the tests are medically necessary.

Some of these licensing provisions, such as the tuberculin skin tests or infection control procedures, would seem reasonable—except that they are not imposed on any physician's office other than those providing abortions. The federal district court evaluating the constitutionality of the South Carolina TRAP laws found that many of the regulations—such as the laws minutely regulating the airflow, requiring a disaster preparedness plan, specifying appropriate interior glazing materials, and insisting on certain landscaping and weed control outside the facility—"border on the absurd."[18] The court held that the regulations, in elevating costs and imposing medically unnecessary requirements on providers and patients, created an undue burden on women seeking first-trimester abortions. The court noted that, at a minimum, the TRAP scheme would raise the cost of an abortion between $30 and $300, or result in a complete elimination of services, depending on the area of the state. The regulations also violated the physician's rights of equal protection under the state and federal constitutions because they were not even rationally related to a legitimate state purpose.

The Fourth Circuit Court of Appeals reversed, holding that South Carolina could single out abortion clinics for regulations it deemed related to protecting the health of abortion patients. The appellate court also determined that the "incidental effect" of driving up the cost of abortion services did not create an undue burden on a woman's decision whether to have an abortion. In a brief requesting Supreme Court review of the Fourth Circuit's holding, the Center for Reproductive Rights argued, "Under the guise of protecting maternal health, these regulations actually threaten women's health by significantly hindering their access to safe, legal abortions. These regulations also subject abortion to unique levels of government intrusion and oversight, making it virtually impossible for physicians to provide abortions in their offices as part of their medical practice, and relegating abortions to separate facilities designed for more complex surgery."[19] The Supreme Court denied the petition for certiorari.

Other cases regarding TRAP laws are percolating in the federal district and appellate courts, with mixed results.[20] Currently, thirty-three states enforce TRAP laws, nineteen of which apply their schemes to abortions during the first trimester.[21]

Impeding access to abortion services through a heavy regulatory overlay is only one of the issues regarding availability. In 2003 approximately 1.3 million women had abortions, down from 1.6 million in 1990.[22] The vast majority of abortions—88 percent—are performed in the first trimester, 96 percent before the sixteenth week. Women who wait the longer amount of time typically "are young, poor or both: teens in denial about what's happening to their bodies, women trapped in abusive situations, rural women without transportation, women who spend the first trimester chasing the money to pay for the procedure even as delay drives up the price."[23] Nearly 90 percent of all counties in the United States have no abortion providers.[24]

2. Legislation and political strategies

The right-to-life movement did not begin to emerge as an organized force in the United States until 1970, when New York became the first state in the nation to explicitly legalize abortion. *Roe v. Wade,* three years later, galvanized abortion opponents. The pro-life movement began to chip away at *Roe* in the courts, challenged the legality of public funding, and attempted to place various restrictions on the procedure, the majority of which met with success. It lobbied successfully against pro-choice political candidates in the early 1970s. By the 1980s, it had begun concerted fund-raising and networking campaigns.

Joseph Scheidler founded the Pro-Life Action League in 1980; Randall Terry founded Operation Rescue in 1988. During the late 1980s, these and other organizations created an umbrella group of organizations and activists, the Pro-Life Action Network ("PLAN"), a coalition that holds yearly conventions, coordinates protests, and has the objective of shutting down abortion clinics.[25] The Roman Catholic Church, with fifty million members in this country alone, chastised its adherents who supported "murder."[26] The United States Conference of Catholic Bishops, the National Right to Life Committee, and other pro-life groups support letting each state decide whether to criminalize abortion. These groups believe that abortion should be illegal except for cases of rape or incest or to save the mother's life or health. The pro-life movement is now extremely well organized and superbly funded.[27]

In 2003 alone, antiabortion forces introduced in state legislatures more than six hundred bills targeted toward restricting abortion access and availability. These included measures that would obtain state funds for "crisis pregnancy" or "abortion alternative" centers through the sale of "Choose Life" license plates, limit funding for family planning and abortion clinics, enact longer waiting periods, require "informed consent" or biased counseling of patients with the provision of inaccurate information regarding such things as alleged links between abortion and breast cancer, mandate greater parental involvement in minors' abortion decisions, and impose TRAP schemes.[28]

The American public is ambivalent about abortion. While most polls of public attitudes indicate that about two-thirds of people in this country support a woman's right to obtain an abortion during the first trimester, about three-fourths approve of laws requiring twenty-four-hour waiting periods and parental notification, and 88 percent "support[] laws requiring doctors to inform women of alternatives to abortion."[29]

A. THE "PARTIAL BIRTH" ABORTION CONTROVERSY

A good example of a legal restriction that originated as a political stratagem is the controversy that began in the early 1990s over "partial birth abortions." The term is not one recognized in medical texts, but was coined by abortion opponents.[30] It refers to a rarely used procedure known in the medical literature as intact dilation and extraction ("D&X"). To keep the fetus intact during the procedure, the physician dilates the cervix and collapses the fetal skull prior to vaginally delivering the stillborn fetus.[31] It is a method used only after the fourth month of pregnancy, and then typically in rare cases of fetal abnormality, such as hydrocephalus, when the use of instruments in the uterus and the risks of sharp bone fragments present dangers to the woman's health. Of the abortions performed in the country after twenty-one weeks (about 1 percent of all abortions), the D&X procedure is utilized in only about 1 percent of those—so it is used in approximately one out of ten thousand abortions.[32] Right-to-life advocates have seized on graphic images of the D&X procedure to depict gruesome killings of partially born fetuses.

Legislatures in thirty states have passed statutes banning partial birth abortions. The Nebraska law, which made its way to the Supreme Court, is representative of other states that did not mention the medical term D&X, but instead prohibited partial birth abortions, defined as "an abortion procedure in which the person performing the abortion partially delivers vaginally a living unborn child before killing the unborn child and completing the delivery." In 1999, in *Stenberg v. Carhart,* on a 5-4 vote, the Supreme Court invalidated Nebraska's law because it placed an undue burden on a woman's right to choose, since the vagueness of its definitional language might cover a number of other abortion procedures. The statute also lacked an exception for situations where the D&X procedure was necessary to preserve the woman's health.

In 2003 Congress passed and President Bush signed into law the Partial Birth Abortion Ban Act,[33] a statute similar to the Nebraska law found unconstitutional in *Carhart,* and notable as the first federal ban on abortion. In June 2004 a federal district judge in California who heard the testimony of numerous expert medical witnesses found the law unconstitutional. The court found that the language of the statute was vague and so broad that it encompassed steps physicians often take during previability abortions, and it did not contain a required exception for maternal health. The opinion recognized that the tactic of trying to regulate partial birth abortions was in part political theater: "Congress' grossly misleading and inaccurate language, comparing the procedure to the 'killing of a newborn infant,' appears to have been intentional."[34]

The public health impact of safe, legal abortions cannot be overstated. In 1970, almost 25 percent of the abortions in the United States were performed at or after thirteen weeks of gestation, compared with 10 percent a decade later. The availability of nonsurgical abortions (like RU-486, discussed in the next section) likely will reduce even further the gestational age at which they are performed. Legal abortions have also sharply reduced morbidity and mortality rates: "Today, legal abortion is less likely than an injection of penicillin to cause death. . . . *Roe v. Wade* transformed abortion from an unsafe, clandestine procedure to one performed under safe medical conditions."[35]

B. RU-486

First created in 1980 by a French drug company, RU-486 is a nonsurgical form of abortion. RU-486 (now being marketed as Mifeprex) is a series of two different drugs given in pill form. The first drug, mifepristone, blocks the reception of progesterone that is needed for pregnancies to continue and prevents the uterus from forming a lining in which a fertilized egg can implant. The second drug, misoprostol, given during a second doctor's visit three days later, causes the embryo to be expelled. Mifeprex must be used within forty-nine days from the woman's last menstrual period. RU-486 is 96 to 97 percent effective in terminating pregnancies.[36]

RU-486 was first marketed in France in 1989. President George H. W. Bush banned its importation into the United States the same year, and President Clinton lifted that ban four years later. Despite the experiences of more than one million women in twenty countries with RU-486, the Food and Drug Administration ("FDA") tested the drug and conducted clinical trials on American women for almost eight more years before finally approving it in the fall of 2000.

Supporters of procreative choice heralded RU-486 as a drug that would revolutionize the politics of the abortion debate. As a less invasive, nonsurgical procedure, RU-486 can be ingested at home or in a doctor's office. It permits abortions immediately upon learning of a pregnancy, rather than requiring women to wait until the seventh week of pregnancy, which is the earliest time surgical abortions are performed. Most important, it permits women to avoid pressures from pro-life activists, "since protesters wouldn't know where to set up a picket line if abortion became part of mainstream family practice."[37]

Nonsurgical abortions account for only about 6 percent of abortions in this country. The low usage rate seems attributable to several factors, including the slightly higher cost of mifepristone compared with surgical abortion, the need for three physician visits, and the cramping and bleeding the drug causes that may last several days.

c. ANTIABORTION VIOLENCE AND CLINIC ACCESS

Other political strategies used by some in the right-to-life movement seek to make abortion impossible even if legal. Since the 1980s, antiabortion demonstrators have used tactics of intimidation and sensationalism to disrupt clinics and frighten women: picketing outside clinics with dead fetuses in jars; blocking clinic entrances; sending hate mail; making harassing phone calls; using bullhorns to scream at women who enter clinics; sending bogus anthrax mailings to clinics, and bombing and setting fire to them in the night; and following, harassing, and assaulting abortion service providers and clinic workers. Letters sent by "units of the army of God" claimed responsibility for some of the bombings. In the years between 1977 and 1994, opponents committed seventeen hundred acts of violence against abortion providers; in 1993 alone, clinic employees experienced seventy-eight death threats.[38] Some of the clinics that were bombed, burned, and picketed and whose workers received death threats simply shut down.

Some extremists then began to assassinate doctors who performed abortions. A gunman fatally shot Dr. David Gunn during a demonstration outside the clinic where he worked in Pensacola, Florida. Other attackers shot Dr. George Tiller in the arm as he left his clinic in Wichita, Kansas.

In response to this escalating violence, Congress passed the Freedom of Access to Clinic Entrances Act ("FACE") in 1994. The statute prohibits the use of "force or threat of force or . . . physical obstruction" to intimidate or prevent access to reproductive health services.[39] For a first conviction, it provided fines of up to $100,000 and one year's imprisonment.

Through high-visibility prosecutions, FACE did diminish some of the more severe clinic violence. Since its enactment, murders, attempted murders, death threats, stalkings, clinic blockades, and bombings have decreased—however, incidents of disruption, including trespassing, picketing, spreading photographs and videotapes of patients, and harassing calls and e-mails, have increased.[40]

FACE was used in a novel Internet harassment case. The American Coalition of Life Activists created a Web site called the Nuremburg Files. The site dripped with blood and contained "Wanted" posters of abortion providers, accusing them of "crimes against humanity." The site had the names, pictures, home addresses, car license plate numbers, and family details of hundreds of doctors and abortion clinic staff. Several physicians were murdered after they were identified on the site. Within hours after the murder of one physician, Dr. Bernard Slepian, his name was crossed out.

A jury determined that the Web site was essentially a hit list that violated FACE and awarded $109 million in actual and punitive damages to the plaintiff doctors and clinics and prohibited further publication of the information. A panel of the Ninth Circuit reversed the jury verdict because the First Amendment allowed speech that was not itself a "direct threat." The Ninth Circuit Court of Appeals, sitting en banc, reinstated the verdict, holding that the posters created an intimidating threat of force under FACE, since "a 'wanted'-type poster would likely be interpreted as a threat of death or serious bodily harm by a doctor in the reproductive health services community who was identified on one, given the previous pattern of 'wanted' posters identifying a specific physician, followed by that physician's murder."[41] The Supreme Court refused to hear the case, letting the Ninth Circuit ruling stand. As of this writing, the content of the Web site is still available on the Internet: the hit list was picked up and mirrored on another Web site that is not within the jurisdiction of the United States.

Courts have upheld the constitutionality of FACE against First Amendment challenges, since it is a content-neutral statute that regulates conduct that is not constitutionally protected. Picketers can still engage in protected speech activities with peaceful demonstrations and nonthreatening "sidewalk counseling." One new tactic is that militant antiabortionists are posting on the Internet photographs, license plates, and names of women entering abortion clinics, labeling them "homicidal mothers" and exposing them to violence.

D. Fathers' Rights

The U.S. Supreme Court has struck laws requiring a husband's consent for abortion and laws requiring spousal notification.[42] State courts have held that a father's offer to pay for an abortion will not allow him to later avoid the statutory duty to pay child support.[43] Fathers have filed restraining orders to prevent women from having abortions, and while some lower courts have issued injunctions, these have been reversed on appeal because they conflict with the women's constitutional rights.[44] The decisions seem fairly uniform that fathers have no decision-making ability in abortion cases.

3. Reproductive rights and feminist legal theories

A. TENSIONS OF CULTURAL FEMINISM

Most Western feminists have recognized the importance of reproductive rights in social and economic realms, whether those rights are viewed as a means of attaining economic and political equality, promoting autonomy, or avoiding subordination. One tension, however, has been between the alleged dangers and utility of cultural feminism to reproductive choice. Some cultural feminists argue that it is precisely because women have such a deep capacity for connection and caring that society should trust their independent and morally responsible decision making regarding abortion.[45] Other theorists have expressed concern that concepts of cultural feminism can be turned against the idea of autonomy underlying the right of choice.[46] One example where this may have occurred is *Hodgson v. Minnesota,* where four justices specifically endorsed a statute requiring two-parent notification regarding a minor's abortion decision, because it represented a legitimate state interest in trying to promote "the parent-child relationship by giving all parents the opportunity to participate in the care and nurture of their children."[47] Another example is the practice of some organizations such as Feminists for Life who have used the arguments of cultural feminism—that women have the interest and obligation to protect their unborn children (and that the availability of abortion is a domineering regime that encourages mothers to kill their babies)—to oppose the right of choice. In most legal cases, though, feminists endorsing various theories have been allied regarding the outcome in favor of expanded reproductive liberty.

B. WOMEN'S STORIES AND REPRODUCTIVE RIGHTS

Feminist legal theorists point out that women's voices have long been ignored in lawmaking. A strategy of feminist methodology to respond to this silence has been to find ways to incorporate women's experiences into law. An example of the point is the approach of the National Abortion Rights Action League ("NARAL Pro Choice America") to submit as an amicus brief in major Supreme Court abortion litigation letters and stories from women who have had abortions, both legal and illegal. Known as the "Voices Brief," the document was intended to convey what the abstract right of choice means in the reality of women's lives.[48] The storytelling technique in this brief was based on the idea that "moral convictions are changed experientially or empathically, not through argument."[49] It was an effort to have women speak directly to a Court composed of seven older men and two older women to show that abortion decisions are not made frivolously or easily and to illuminate the many circumstances in which abortion is a justifiable choice.

The Supreme Court has never cited the Voices Brief. However, some evidence indicates that these or other stories may have prompted some empathetic insights among some of the justices. In *Planned Parenthood of Southeastern Pennsylvania v. Casey,* for example, when the Court held unconstitutional the spousal notification provisions in Pennsylvania's abortion law, the plurality discussed the prevalence of domestic violence and recognized that married women who have suffered spousal abuse may have good reasons to not inform their husbands about their pregnancies.[50]

Another story in the abortion debate—that of the woman who was the plaintiff in *Roe v. Wade*—has drawn the media spotlight. Jane Roe was a pseudonym for Norma McCorvey, a twenty-one-year-old high school dropout and carnival barker who, in 1970, was seeking an abortion to end her third unplanned pregnancy. Linda Coffee and Sarah Weddington, two lawyers promoting abortion reform, were seeking a test case for the Texas abortion law.

In 1980, McCorvey revealed her identity and became a pro-choice activist, although she writes that she felt used by the pro-choice camp. She did not realize that her case would be used in *Roe* to represent women in a class-action lawsuit, and she did not know what the word "plaintiff" meant and had to look it up in a dictionary. She had thought the lawyers would lead her to an abortion provider, and she did not understand that by the time her case was decided it would be too late for her to have an abortion. McCorvey had the baby and gave it up for adoption.

Fifteen years later, she converted to Christianity, switched to the pro-life camp, and began to work for Operation Rescue.[51] In testimony before the Senate Judiciary Committee on a partial birth abortion ban, McCorvey said, "I am dedicated to spending the rest of my life undoing the law that bears my name."[52] Thirty years after *Roe* was decided, McCorvey, sponsored by the conservative Texas Justice Foundation, filed a lawsuit asking a federal district court in Texas to reconsider and reverse *Roe v. Wade.* In September 2004, a three-judge panel of the federal appeals court found that her attempt to revisit the issue was moot because the statutes at issue in *Roe* have since been repealed.[53]

c. MULTICULTURAL PERSPECTIVES

Abortion policies of various countries are influenced by complex social and geopolitical factors, including a country's history with genocide (as in the case of Germany, where the German Penal Code provides that abortion is always unlawful, but the offense is not punishable during the first twelve weeks of pregnancy); the prevalence of rape (as in South Africa, where abortion is available on demand); population control issues (as in China, where abortion has been available under all circumstances since 1979); political instability (which may result in coerced abortions to maintain racial or ethnic dominance); predominant religion (such as Islamic countries where religious teachings condemn abortion and the laws make it a crime); medical sophistication and health risks; and access to providers. Western feminists have been accused of imperialism when they argue for reproductive liberties as matters of universal international human rights.[54]

Should Western feminists be more sensitive to other voices and approaches—a stance that rejects universal ideas of right and wrong and embraces pluralism and tolerance of different cultural views? Or is the lack of reproductive liberties on a global scale—and the acceptance of it by large majorities of women in various nations around the world—a problem of false consciousness? Susan Moller Okin observes that "'we are not always enlightened about what is just by asking persons who seem to be suffering injustices what they want. Oppressed people have often internalized their oppression so well that they *have* no sense of what they are justly entitled to as human beings.'"[55] The two approaches as a matter of international policy seem to move in the direction of either cultural relativism (an acceptance of an individual culture's norms) or universalism (a uniform international policy based on standards set by more developed countries' norms). Is there any way to avoid that either-or choice?

d. PRO-LIFE FEMINISM

The view of several "feminists for life" organizations is that women have abortions not because they have choice, but because they lack choices—they do not have the education, the social support, or the economic resources to continue pregnancies. Feminists for Life of America points out that many early feminists such as Elizabeth Cady Stanton and Susan B. Anthony opposed abortion because they believed in the value of all human life, and they thought that the availability of abortion encouraged the exploitation of women.[56] Many of these organizations campaign for more expansive social programs such as higher minimum wages and family leave benefits, so that women can make choices to be mothers. Some of these groups also support bills such as the Unborn Victims of Violence Act, treating physical violence against a pregnant woman as separate crimes against both her and her unborn fetus.[57]

Some claim that "pro-life feminism" is an oxymoron and argue that women cannot have real equality unless they have control over their bodies. Pro-life feminists respond by drawing on principles of cultural feminism to argue that women, as nonviolent nurturers, should protect unborn children. Some make the more extreme argument that the availability of abortion works to oppress women because it allows "'society not to change the conditions which force women into abortions.'"[58] Pro-life feminists have formed temporary alliances with traditional feminist groups, such as Planned Parenthood, NOW, and NARAL, to contest welfare provisions that allow states to prevent women on welfare who have more children from receiving additional benefits for their care.

E. ANTIESSENTIALISM

Too often, reproductive rights are viewed exclusively as gender issues. The antiessentialist critique offers a reminder that considering matters of reproductive liberty as solely about gender (or about choice—that women should be able to choose what to do with their bodies)—essentializes the issues. Reproductive rights occur at the intersection of gender, age, race, and class. For poor women, and especially poor minors, the right of choice is meaningless without the ability to exercise it. If women cannot afford an abortion—and Supreme Court doctrine says the state does not have to pay for either nontherapeutic or medically necessary abortions—they cannot obtain one.

The antiessentialist critique continues by noting that reproductive freedom is affected by a host of factors. Race matters in myriad ways. Contraceptive use, for example, is distinctly related to race and socioeconomic circumstances. Studies show that lower economic class African American women have lower rates of contraceptive use and higher rates of unintended adolescent pregnancy.[59] Women of color also disproportionately suffer coerced sterilization, termination of parental rights, and prosecution for prenatal abuse or child endangerment among drug addicts who bear children.[60]

B. Contraception

Government has long tried to control reproductive choices, for a variety of reasons: to encourage procreation, to promote the "right" kind of people (read: white or wealthy or intelligent) having children, or to confine sex to marital relationships. In many reproductive decision-making cases, the state will assert that it has important interests— these range from ensuring that its citizens make informed decisions, to protecting the possibility of fetal life, to promoting procreation.

1. Contraceptive information

One of the earliest reproductive rights cases concerned the availability of contraceptives. In 1965, in *Griswold v. Connecticut*,[61] the Supreme Court found that a state statute banning the distribution and use of contraceptives intruded on marital privacy. Seven years later, the Court extended this right of privacy to contraceptive use by unmarried people.[62] In 1977 the Court held that a state could not ban the sale of over-the-counter contraceptives to minors under the age of sixteen, reasoning that even unmarried minors had a right to use contraceptives without parental consent.[63]

The more difficult issues with respect to birth control may not be the right to use it, but ability to afford it. In this country, approximately 33 million women use contraception, and about half of them need subsidies for their contraceptive services.[64] Since 1970, Title X of the Public Health Services Act[65] has provided federal funds for family-planning services (other than abortion) for 4.3 million low-income women each year, including 1.8 million women aged thirteen to nineteen.[66] Each dollar spent on contraceptive services saves about three dollars of public funds that would otherwise be needed for prenatal health care and medical care of newborns.[67] Although appropriations for Title X increased during the Clinton administration, they did not increase enough to keep pace with inflation. The second Bush administration has sought no increases for Title X since 2001 (choosing to fund abstinence-only sex education plans instead), and the real funding levels are now 60 percent lower than they were two decades ago.[68]

But accompanying public funding is government control of information and attempts to steer reproductive choices. A series of regulations issued by the Department of Health and Human Services during the Reagan and first Bush administrations created a global gag rule that prevented any facility, in this country or any other, that received U.S. federal funds from providing its patients with any information or referrals about abortion. These regulations were upheld by the Supreme Court, later suspended by executive order during the Clinton administration, and then reinstated in the first few hours after President George W. Bush's inauguration.[69] In each year from 2002 to 2004, President Bush has "unilaterally cancelled the entire U.S. contribution to the U.N. family-planning program (UNFPA)—an international agency that provides family planning and other reproductive health services (not including abortions) to the world's poorest women."[70]

In 1998 the House passed the Proposed Parental Notification Act,[71] which would have required clinics receiving public funds to notify parents before dispensing contraceptives to teenagers, but the bill was defeated in the Senate. The next year supporters reintroduced the bill, but withdrew it in exchange for a different bill that provided $50 million in funding for abstinence-only sex education. Confidentiality is assured at family-planning clinics receiving federal funds. In 2003 ten state legislatures considered bills that would require parental notification or consent for minors to receive contraception; only Texas passed its bill.[72]

A few school boards across the country have instituted condom distribution programs that make condoms available upon student request. Despite studies showing that condom distribution programs do not cause an escalation in sexual activity among teenagers,[73] parents successfully challenged one such plan in New York because it constituted the provision of health services without parental consent and lacked a parental opt-out provision. A Massachusetts court upheld a similar distribution program because it was a purely voluntary plan.[74]

2. Emergency contraception

Emergency contraceptives have been available for years in the form of oral contraceptives in higher doses. The challenge for many women has been access to the drugs. If a condom breaks on Friday night, getting a doctor's appointment and filling a prescription within the short three-day window in which emergency contraception is effective can be a problem.

In 2004 the FDA refused to allow over-the-counter sales of the emergency contraceptive aptly called Plan B, a morning-after pill that blocks ovulation and implantation if taken within seventy-two hours of intercourse. The FDA raised concerns about overuse and whether younger teenagers could use the product safely without a doctor's instructions. In five states (Alaska, California, Hawaii, New Mexico, and Washington), however, doctors have created collaborative agreements allowing pharmacists to dispense morning-after pills without a prescription. Reproductive rights groups claim that widespread availability of Plan B could reduce by half the more than three million unintended pregnancies in this country and thus significantly lessen the number of abortions. Antiabortion groups maintain that Plan B is actually an abortion drug because it may prevent the implantation of fertilized eggs and that ease of access to emergency contraception will increase unsafe sex.

3. Birth control costs and insurance coverage

Availability is not the only obstacle to obtaining contraception. The cost of birth control is a significant barrier to access: oral contraceptives cost approximately $540 per year, intrauterine devices ("IUDs") cost $400, and shots of Depo-Provera cost $380. Although more than two-thirds of all women have health insurance through employers, until recently most group plans did not include any coverage for contraception.[75] In 1993 only 28 percent of employer health plans included contraceptive devices. In 1998, when the erectile dysfunction drug Viagra was introduced in the United States, employment-related insurance policies covered more than half of the prescriptions for the drug.[76] Since 2001, three federal district courts have held that exclusion of prescription contraceptives from an employer's health insurance plan that covered other prescription drugs violated Title VII and the Pregnancy Discrimination Act. Even though the exclusions were framed in gender-neutral terms, as one of the courts recognized, "the law is no longer blind to the fact that only women can get pregnant, bear children, or use prescription contraception. The special or increased healthcare needs associated with a woman's unique sex-based characteristics must be met to the same extent, and on the same terms, as other healthcare needs."[77] Are the courts in these cases using an equal treatment approach that rejects employers treating women differently from men based on their childbearing capacity or a special treatment approach that responds to women's distinct physiology?

In 1998 the Federal Employees Health Benefits Plan approved contraceptive coverage for federal employees. By 2002, 86 percent of employer plans covered virtually all reversible contraceptive methods.[78] Congress, however, has failed to pass the Equity in Prescription Insurance and Contraceptive Coverage Act that would require all private health plans to cover the costs of contraceptives; nevertheless, twenty-two states have passed contraceptive equity laws that reach this result. Nearly half of all women still live in states that do not require equity in prescription contraceptive coverage.

C. Surrogacy

> A *mother is a mother still,/The holiest thing alive.*
>
> Samuel Coleridge Taylor[79]

> *We are two-legged wombs, that's all: sacred vessels, ambulatory chalices.*
>
> Margaret Atwood[80]

1. Surrogacy arrangements

Surrogacy, or contract pregnancy, describes "an arrangement to create a baby for transfer to others, including for compensation."[81] Surrogacy agreements of one kind or another have been around for thousands of years. Perhaps the best-known example involves the Old Testament couple Abraham and Sarah, who enlisted the services of Sarah's maid, Hagar, to perpetuate the husband's family line.[82] In the 1980s, the so-called *Baby M* case brought surrogacy law kicking and screaming into the modern world, as a New Jersey court struggled to assign custody between two couples, each claiming to be the lawful parents.[83]

Today's surrogacy arrangements usually take one of two forms. In the first, a contracting couple enlists another woman, called the "surrogate mother," to conceive, gestate, and give birth to a child who is then transferred to the contracting couple. The sperm is provided by the husband in the contracting couple, making him both the genetic and the legal father. The wife in the contracting couple, who has no genetic connection to the child, is considered the legal mother. The surrogate mother, who is meant to have no legal connection to the child, is the genetic mother (making the term "surrogate" somewhat of a misnomer). The second, less common, form of surrogacy involves in vitro fertilization. In this procedure, a zygote (a potential embryo) is formed in a laboratory process using ova and sperm provided by the contracting couple; the zygote is implanted into the uterus of a surrogate mother, who carries the fetus to term and, upon birth, transfers the resulting baby to the contracting couple. In this triangle, the contracting husband is the genetic and legal father. The contracting wife is the genetic and legal mother. The surrogate mother, sometimes called the "gestational mother," has no genetic or legal connection to the offspring.

These arrangements are almost always set down in written contracts and can be quite sophisticated, involving lawyers, placement agencies, and fertility clinics. In the typical surrogacy contract, the surrogate mother agrees to become impregnated, carry the fetus to term, and transfer all rights to the baby upon its birth. In exchange, the contracting couple agrees to pay all expenses and to compensate the surrogate mother for her gestational "services." (Because adoption laws forbid "baby selling," surrogacy contracts cannot require payment for the child itself.) Surrogacy contracts may also establish expectations regarding medical insurance, the surrogate's conduct during pregnancy (for instance, avoiding alcohol), and the terms under which the parties would consent to an abortion.

2. Freedom or slavery?

Advocates of surrogacy view such arrangements as empowering. For couples unable to bear children, surrogacy provides reproductive freedom, allowing them to have genetically related offspring. If we assume that couples so committed to starting a family have a good chance of becoming good parents, surrogacy may also be positive for the children involved (although there is not much research on this).

Most debates about surrogacy focus, instead, on the welfare of surrogate mothers, many of whom are limited in terms of income, career, and education.[84] Proponents argue that surrogate motherhood has the potential to empower such women by allowing them to use their reproductive capacity to help others or earn money. Law professor Lori Andrews reports that surrogate mothers she interviewed often spoke of "the tremendous psychic benefits they received from the feeling that they were helping someone meet a joyous life goal."[85] Many surrogate mothers, she writes, "viewed themselves as feminists who were exercising reproductive choice and demonstrating an ethic of care." For women whose economic power has been undercut by sexism and racism, surrogacy offers a way to transform procreative labor into a market asset.

Such arguments draw both from cultural feminism, which seeks to elevate the prestige of motherhood and childbirth, and from dominance theory, which emphasizes strength through economic power. The pro-surrogacy view also resembles the autonomy approach taken by abortion rights advocates: whether or not you like surrogacy, the ultimate choice should be left to the woman, not the state.

Critics view surrogacy in exactly the opposite terms, arguing that surrogacy contracts exploit women and compromise personal freedom. They note that while some surrogate mothers may see the experience as offering a gift, others feel exploited and objectified. ("I feel like a vehicle, just like a cow; it's their baby, it's his sperm.")[86] Some surrogate mothers experience significant emotional trauma when the time comes to give up the baby. As for economic empowerment, critics worry that surrogate mothers, who are often poorer and less sophisticated than the contracting couples, risk becoming an underclass of anonymous "rent-a-wombs" with few rights or legal protections. Summing up this side of the debate, law professor Margaret Jane Radin writes: "Entering the market by degrading oneself is not liberating under these circumstances [of economic need]. . . . Women have always both sold themselves and been degraded for it, so let's not do more of same."[87]

Like pro-surrogacy arguments, antisurrogacy arguments also draw from cultural feminism and dominance theory, suggesting the flexibility of feminist thinking. The concern about exploitation expresses a fear, shared by some cultural feminists, that the act of childbirth is de-meaned when sold as a service, like ironing shirts or scrubbing floors. The concern about an underclass follows from the possibility that an emerging "industry" of lawyers, doctors, and baby brokers will con-spire to keep surrogate mothers isolated and cheaply paid, thus de-feating their economic aspirations and increasing their oppression. In answer to claims that surrogate motherhood should remain a matter of individual choice, surrogacy skeptics respond that the "choice" to become a surrogate is less meaningful when the women choosing it have few economic options.

3. *In re Baby* M and *Johnson v. Calvert*

Courts have struggled in deciding how to regulate surrogacy arrange-ments. This is because until very recently, there were few written laws on the subject. Judges looked in their toolboxes only to find general doctrines about child custody or contract enforcement and abstract principles of fairness and freedom. They did the best they could, but their findings were usually fact-specific and hard to apply to the next case. Also, judicial analysis was often fragmented, focusing only on particular features of the surrogacy mosaic without appreciating the entire picture. We can see this phenomenon in two well-known cases, *In re Baby M*[88] and *Johnson v. Calvert*,[89] both of which required the assignment of parental rights within a surrogacy triangle.

In the *Baby M* case, William and Elizabeth Stern entered into a con-tract with Mary Beth Whitehead in which Whitehead agreed to be ar-tificially inseminated with William Stern's sperm, carry the resulting fetus to term, and transfer the child to the Whiteheads. In exchange, the Sterns paid Whitehead $10,000. Upon the birth of the child, Whitehead refused to give the baby up, and a lawsuit for possession of "Baby M" (for "Melissa") ensued. The court eventually sided with the Sterns, but not by enforcing the contract. Instead, it held that the surrogacy contract was invalid as against public policy. In its view, the surrogacy arrangement was simply a veiled attempt to sidestep the state of New Jersey's adoption laws, which prohibited the sale of chil-dren and allowed birth mothers an opportunity to change their minds within a reasonable period after the birth.

Without an enforceable contract, the dispute became a "child cus-tody" case, governed by the "best interests of the child" standard provided for in the state's family law provisions. After close factual analysis (in which the court questioned Whitehead's emotional stability), the court found that the child's best interests were served by living with the Sterns. William Stern was awarded primary custody of Baby M. Whitehead, the "natural" and "legal" mother of the child, was afforded rights of visitation.

Johnson v. Calvert approached a similar dispute in a very different way. In that case, Mark and Crispina Calvert entered a contract with Anna Johnson, in which Johnson agreed to become a gestational surrogate for the Calverts, who wished to produce a baby using their own genetic material through in vitro fertilization. During the pregnancy, the Calverts and Johnson fell into an argument over obligations in the contract and the payment of Johnson's fee ($10,000). Johnson threatened to keep the child if she was not paid on the terms she demanded. The Calverts later sued, asking the court to declare Crispina Calvert to be the child's legal mother. In response, Ann Johnson claimed that she, too, was the child's legal mother. The court summed up the perplexing situation this way: "[W]e are left with the undisputed evidence that Anna, not Crispina, gave birth to the child and that Crispina, not Anna, is genetically related to [the child]. . . . Yet for any child California law recognizes only one natural mother, despite advances in reproductive technology rendering a different outcome biologically possible."[90]

What to do? Resisting the temptation to stretch the law and declare the existence of *two* mothers (which the ACLU, as a "friend of the court," had urged), the court turned to traditional principles of contract law. Examining the parties' original intent, the court held that because the three had previously agreed that Crispina would be the only mother, Anna could not now claim to have it otherwise.

What is interesting about *Baby M* and *Johnson v. Calvert* is how single-mindedly they approach the underlying disputes. In *Baby M*, a complicated soap opera involving contractual promises, parental autonomy, and a mother's regret was resolved by way of a traditional family law standard—the "best interests of the child." In *Johnson v. Calvert*, a metaphysical struggle between genetic motherhood and gestational motherhood boiled down to the contents of a single contract. What about empowerment through reproduction, the prestige of motherhood, the evils of a surrogate underclass? While both opinions occasionally raised such issues, they steered away from any full examination. Perhaps the judges were insensitive to such queries. Perhaps they were waiting for the public, through the legislature, to weigh in. Whatever the reasons, courts have generally failed to bring much depth, uniformity, or predictability to this area of law.

4. Regulating surrogacy

Despite high-profile cases like *Baby M* and *Johnson v. Calvert,* the majority of states have no statutes or case law on surrogacy at all. This makes surrogacy arrangements a risk for everyone involved. Of the states that do regulate surrogacy, there is considerable diversity. After *Johnson v. Calvert,* California developed a reputation for being "surrogate friendly" and has attracted a number of lawyers and placement agencies specializing in such arrangements. A few states, including Nevada and Florida, have statutes defining surrogacy contracts as legal and enforceable as long as no compensation is involved (although expenses are reimbursable).[91] Other states, like Arizona, ban surrogacy in all forms.[92] Among those states that disapprove of surrogacy in some or all situations, most simply hold the contracts unenforceable, while a few allow for criminal prosecution against offending parties.[93]

D. *The Pornography Debate*

> *Men treat women as who they see women as being. Pornography constructs who that is.* Catharine A. MacKinnon[94]

In 1983 Andrea Dworkin and Catharine MacKinnon drafted a model antipornography ordinance that classified certain types of pornography as sex discrimination and a civil rights violation. Dworkin and MacKinnon argued that pornography injures both individual women and women as a group. They contended that pornography provides the impulses and is one of the instruments by which men dominate women.[95] Some pornography portrays women as submissive and deserving of sexual abuse or enjoying it. These depictions of women, they insisted, contribute to the subordination of women in other realms:

Pornography conditions its consumers to feel sexual excitement at the sight of women being abused, raped, tortured, and even murdered. Victims of sexual abuse report being made to act out what is depicted in pornographic pictures or films. Pornography is often used to intimidate and demean women at work as part of sexual harassment. Even when pornography is not used directly in sexual abuse or harassment, its message (which MacKinnon describes as "get her") can condition consumers to treat women as sexual objects.[96]

This construction of female sexuality reinforces male domination and female subordination—and it makes inequality erotic.

Soon afterwards, the city of Indianapolis, Indiana, adopted a version of the MacKinnon-Dworkin ordinance.The city defined pornography as "the graphic sexually explicit subordination of women [or men, children, or transsexuals], whether in pictures or in words," if it was combined with being "presented as sexual objects" who "enjoy pain or humiliation" or "experience sexual pleasure in being raped" or are "tied up or cut up or mutilated or bruised or physically hurt" or are "being penetrated by objects or animals" or "are presented in scenarios of degradation, injury, abasement, or torture" or "are presented as sexual objects for domination, conquest, violation, exploitation, possession, or use."[97] The law prohibited "trafficking" in pornography and created a cause of action for injunctive relief (a "cease and desist" order) and money damages against the maker or seller of the pornography on behalf of anyone who is forcibly exposed to pornography, coerced to participate in its creation, or attacked or assaulted "in a way that is directly caused by specific pornography." The Indianapolis ordinance was later struck down by a federal appellate court as a violation of free speech.

A city council in Minneapolis, Minnesota, passed a variation of the model ordinance, but the city's mayor vetoed it. Canada passed a somewhat different version of the statute, and the Canadian Supreme Court upheld the legislation, which banned depictions of explicit sex with violence or explicit sex that is degrading or dehumanizing, because the Court found that pornography harms women by treating them as inferior.[98]

The proposed ordinance prompted debate among feminists about whether the state should regulate pornography. While dominance theorists thought that pornography objectified women and violated women's autonomy, equal treatment theorists responded that women should have self-determination. The legal regulation of pornography, for equal treatment theorists, was protectionist, treating women as passive victims. The proposed ordinance, they claimed, implicitly promoted some of the worst stereotypes about both men and women: that all men are bad and that women need sheltering by the state.

Censorship opponents responded that the ordinances regulating pornography were both overinclusive and underinclusive. The porn-suppression strategy was overinclusive because it swept in gay and lesbian pornography, political statements, and various forms of artistic expression (like a photograph by Robert Mapplethorpe). It was underinclusive because it could not reach so many other cultural institutions that create subordinating images of women, such as television advertisements, Barbies, soap operas, the *Sports Illustrated* swimsuit edition, coaches' motivational terms for their players, and rap music lyrics. Nadine Strossen, an equal treatment theorist and former president of the ACLU, explains that free speech is the "strongest weapon for countering mysogynistic discrimination and violence, and censorship consistently has been a potent tool for curbing women's rights and interests. Freedom of sexually oriented expression is integrally connected with women's freedom."[99] Equal treatment theorists worried that censorship efforts would promote a conservative ideology, because they saw an unholy alliance forming between Catharine MacKinnon, Phyllis Schlafly, Attorney General Edwin Meese, and the Moral Majority. They pointed to cultural evidence showing that "women in cultures where sexuality and its imagery are suppressed are far more silenced in every way than women in cultures where sexual discourse, including porn, is uninhibited."[100]

Dominance theorists responded that current First Amendment law permits content regulation of numerous types of speech—such as threats, bribes, perjury, defamation, union-busting speech, obscenity, and fighting words—based on the harm they cause. The only difference, they argued, between pornography and those kinds of harmful speech that may be constitutionally restricted is that the public does not recognize pornography's damaging effects on women.

While none of the ordinances survived in this country, the pornography discussion itself was hugely educational. The debate could be seen in retrospect as a porn suppression versus free expression battle, since the ordinances were invalidated on First Amendment grounds.

A more nuanced view is that the debate and the controversy generated by that debate reached popular audiences and made people think about the ways gender is socially constructed. It raised consciousness by depicting in very concrete ways how social and cultural images and literature construct perceptions of women. In a somewhat ironic twist, the debate opened discussions about sexuality and about control over women's bodies.

E. Questions for Discussion

1. If women have the right to control their bodies, should that right extend up to the point of birth? If not, why not? On what principled basis would you make a distinction between abortions at two months and at eight months of pregnancy? Based on viability, which is emphasized by current constitutional doctrine? Based on the idea that in morally ambiguous situations, allowing extreme decisions is more likely to be morally wrong? Based on some other principle?

2. Imagine that you have been asked to advise a state legislature on a new law regulating surrogacy. What would you recommend? Would your law allow surrogacy at all? If so, under what circumstances? Would your law permit compensation? Would it make a distinction between traditional surrogacy and surrogacy that involves vitro fertilization? If your law sought to discourage surrogacy in some or all circumstances, how would it do so? Would it make such contracts unenforceable? Would it subject the parties to criminal penalties? What arguments could you make to justify your position to those who disagree?

SUGGESTED READINGS

DRUCILLA CORNELL, THE IMAGINARY DOMAIN: ABORTION, PORNOGRAPHY AND SEXUAL HARASSMENT (1995).

MARY ANN GLENDON, ABORTION AND DIVORCE IN WESTERN LAW (1987).

N.E.H. HULL & PETER CHARLES HOFFER, ROE V. WADE: THE ABORTION RIGHTS CONTROVERSY IN AMERICAN HISTORY (2001).

IN HARM'S WAY: THE PORNOGRAPHY CIVIL RIGHTS HEARING (Catharine A. MacKinnon & Andrea Dworkin eds. 1997).

KRISTIN LUKER, ABORTION AND THE POLITICS OF MOTHERHOOD (1984).

MOTHERS IN LAW: FEMINIST THEORY AND THE LEGAL REGULATION OF MOTHERHOOD (Martha A. Fineman & Isabel Karpin eds., 1995).

NEGOTIATING REPRODUCTIVE RIGHTS: WOMEN'S PERSPECTIVES ACROSS COUNTRIES AND CULTURES (Rosalind P. Petchesky & Karen Judd eds., 1998).

Charlotte Rutherford, *Reproductive Freedoms and African American Women*, 4 YALE J.L. & FEMINISM 255 (1992).

Dorothy E. Roberts, *The Genetic Tie*, 62 U. CHI. L. REV. 209 (1995).

LAURENCE TRIBE, ABORTION: THE CLASH OF ABSOLUTES (1990).

NOTES:

1. MARGARET SANGER, WOMAN AND THE NEW RACE 94–95 (1920).

2. Christopher P. Keleher, *Double Standards: The Suppression of Abortion Protesters' Rights of Free Speech*, 51 DEPAUL L. REV. 825, 834 (2002).

3. 410 U.S. 113, 153 (1973).

4. Harris v. McRae, 448 U.S. 297 (1980); Maher v. Roe, 432 U.S. 464 (1977).

5. Catharine A. MacKinnon, *Reflections on Sex Equality Under Law*, 100 YALE L.J. 1281, 1311 (1991).

6. Anita L. Allen, *The Proposed Equal Protection Fix for Abortion Law*, 18 HARV. J.L. & PUB. POL'Y 419, 438–39 (1995).

7. Planned Parenthood of Southeastern Pa. v. Casey, 505 U.S. 833, 928 (1992).

8. 492 U.S. 490 (1989).

9. 505 U.S. at 875, 877.

10. *Id.* at 886, 885.

11. Julie F. Kay, Note, *If Men Could Get Pregnant: An Equal Protection Model for Federal Funding of Abortion Under a National Health Care Plan*, 60 BROOK. L. REV. 349, 379 (1994).

12. Alan Guttmacher Institute, *State Policies in Brief, Mandatory Counseling and Waiting Periods for Abortion*, Sept. 1, 2004, http://www.guttmacher.org/statecenter/spibs/spib_MWPA.pdf.

13. Hodgson v. Minnesota, 497 U.S. 417 (1990).

14. Center for Reproductive Rights, http://www.reproductiverights.org/pub_fac_restrictions.html (last visited Sept. 22, 2004).

15. Planned Parenthood v. Ashcroft, 462 U.S. 476 (1983).

16. Webster v. Reproductive Health Servs., 492 U.S. 490, 522 (1989).

17. Thornburgh v. Am. Coll. of Obstetricians & Gynecologists, 476 U.S. 747, 766 (1986).

18. Greenville Women's Clinic v. Bryant, 66 F. Supp. 2d 691, 734, 735

(D.S.C. 1999), *rev'd,* 222 F.3d 157 (4th Cir. 2000), *cert. denied,* 531 U.S. 1191 (2001).

19. Center for Reproductive Rights, Petition for Certiorari in Greenville Women's Clinic v. Bryant, Nov. 17, 2000, http://www.crlp.org/pdf/SCTRAPcert-petition.pdf.

20. Women's Med. Ctr. of Northwest Houston v. Bell, 248 F.3d 411 (5th Cir. 2001) (finding that requiring a licensed abortion provider to ensure that its care enhanced the patient's "self-esteem and self-worth" was impermissibly vague); Tucson Woman's Clinic v. Eden, 371 F.3d 1173 (9th Cir. 2004), *aff'd in part, rev'd in part, remanded,* 379 F.3d 531 (9th Cir. 2004) (ruling that a provision allowing unlimited, warrantless searches of providers' offices violated the Fourth Amendment).

21. Center for Reproductive Rights, *Targeted Regulation of Abortion Providers: Avoiding the TRAP,* Apr. 2004, http://www.crlp.org/pub_fac_trap.html.

22. Planned Parenthood Federation of America, *Medical and Social Health Benefits Since Abortion Was Made Legal in the U.S.,* http://www.plannedparent-hood.org/library/ABORTION/HealthBenef.html (last visited June 21, 2004).

23. Katha Pollitt, *Down and Out in Texas,* NATION, May 10, 2004, at 9.

24. Kate Michelman, *Preserving Choice,* AM. PROSPECT, Oct. 1, 2003, at 21.

25. Fay Clayton & Sara N. Love, NOW v. Scheidler: *Protecting Women's Access to Reproductive Health Services,* 62 ALB. L. REV. 967, 974–76 (1999).

26. Note, *Safety Valve Closed: The Removal of Nonviolent Outlets for Dissent and the Onset of Anti-Abortion Violence,* 113 HARV. L. REV. 1210, 1215 (2000).

27. Planned Parenthood Federation of America, *supra* note 22. The Christian Coalition has an annual income of $27 million; Focus on the Family has an annual income of $126 million; the National Right to Life Committee has an annual income of $13.7 million.

28. National Abortion Federation, *2003 State Legislative Report,* http://www.prochoice.org/legal/legislation/2003statereport.pdf.

29. Cathy Young, *A Matter of Extremes,* BOSTON GLOBE, Jan. 27, 2003, at A11.

30. Partial Birth Abortion Ban: Hearing on H.R. 1833 Before the Senate Comm. on the Judiciary, 104th Cong. 104 (Nov. 17, 1995).

31. Stenberg v. Carhart, 530 U.S. 918, 926–27 (2000).

32. Ann MacLean Massie, *So-Called "Partial-Birth Abortion" Bans: Bad Medicine? Maybe. Bad Law? Definitely!,* 59 U. PITT. L. REV. 301, 317–18 (1998).

33. 18 U.S.C. § 1531 (2004).

34. Planned Parenthood Fed'n of Am. v. Ashcroft, 320 F. Supp. 2d 957, 1030 (N.D. Cal. 2004).

35. Willard Cates, Jr. et al., *The Public Health Impact of Legal Abortion: 30 Years Later,* 35 PERSP. ON SEXUAL & REPRODUCTIVE HEALTH (Jan./Feb. 2003), *available at* http://www.guttmacher.org/pubs/journals/3502503.html.

36. Planned Parenthood Fed'n of Am., *Mifepristone: Expanding Women's Options for Early Abortion,* http://www.plannedparenthood.org/library/ ABORTION/Mif_fact.html (last visited Sept. 22, 2004).

37. Nancy Gibbs, *The Pill Arrives,* TIME, Oct. 9, 2000, at 42.

38. MSNBC News, *Abortion Clinic Violence,* http://www.msnbc.com/modules/clinics/default.asp (last visited Sept. 22, 2004).

39. 18 U.S.C. § 248(a)(1) (1996).

40. National Abortion Federation, *NAF Violence and Disruption Statistics: Incidents of Violence and Disruption Against Abortion Providers in the US and Canada,* http://www.prochoice.org/Violence/Statistics/default.htm (last visited Sept. 22, 2004).

41. Planned Parenthood of the Columbia/Willamette, Inc., v. Am. Coalition of Life Activists, 41 F. Supp. 2d 1130 (D. Or. 1999), *rev'd,* 244 F.3d 1007 (9th Cir. 2001), *reinstated,* 290 F.3d 1058, 1063 (9th Cir. 2002) *on remand,* 300 F. Supp. 2d 1055 (D. Or. 2004) (upholding punitive damages award).

42. Planned Parenthood of Cent. Mo. v. Danforth, 428 U.S. 52 (1976).

43. People of Interest of S.P.B., 651 P.2d 1213 (Colo. 1982).

44. *See, e.g.,* Causeway Med. Suite v. Foster, 43 F. Supp. 2d 604 (E.D. La. 1999).

45. Robin L. West, *The Supreme Court 1989 Term, Foreword: Taking Freedom Seriously,* 104 HARV. L. REV. 43, 82–83 (1990).

46. Pamela S. Karlan & Daniel R. Ortiz, *In a Diffident Voice: Relational Feminism, Abortion Rights, and the Feminist Legal Agenda,* 87 Nw. U. L. REV. 858 (1993).

47. Hodgson, 497 U.S. at 484 (Kennedy, J., concurring in part and dissenting in part), cited in Karlan & Ortiz, *supra* note 46, at 882–83.

48. Brief of Amici Curiae Women Who Have Had Abortions, Webster v. Reproductive Health Services, 492 U.S. 490, 1989 WL 1115239 (1989) (No. 88-605). A similar brief, *Brief Amici Curiae of the National Council of Negro Women, Inc., et al., Webster v. Reproductive Health Serv.,* 492 U.S. 490, 1989 WL 1127686 (1989) (No. 88-605), accumulated data on the costs and availability of abortion to show that the right of choice is an illusion if the costs of abortion services are too high.

49. Robin L. West, *The Constitution of Reasons,* 92 MICH. L. REV. 1409, 1436 (1994).

50. 505 U.S. at 888–93.

51. NORMA MCCORVEY WITH ANDY MEISLER, I AM ROE: MY LIFE, ROE V. WADE, AND FREEDOM OF CHOICE (1994).

52. Cheryl Wetzstein, *Ex-"Jane Roe" Says Her Abortion Case Was Based on Lies,* WASH. TIMES, Jan. 22, 1998, at A7.

53. McCorvey v. Hill, 2003 WL 21554506 (N.D. Tex. July 8, 2003), *aff'd on other grounds,* 2004 WL 2035319 (5th Cir. 2004).

54. *See* Tracy E. Higgins, *Anti-Essentialism, Relativism, and Human Rights,* 19 HARV. WOMEN'S L.J. 89, 89 (1996).

55. *See id.* at 117 (quoting Susan M. Okin, *Gender Inequality and Cultural Differences,* 22 POL. THEORY 5, 19 (1994) (emphasis in original).

56. Feminists for Life, *Feminist History,* http://www.feministsforlife.org/text/history/foremoth.htm#sbanthony (last visited Sept. 22, 2004).

57. Scott Waldman, *Feminists for Life Lobby for Two Bills,* DEMOCRAT & CHRON., Mar. 21, 2004, at 3B.

58. Linda C. McClain, *Equality, Oppression, and Abortion: Women Who Oppose Abortion Rights in the Name of Feminism, in* FEMINIST NIGHTMARES: WOMEN AT ODDS: FEMINISM AND THE PROBLEM OF SISTERHOOD 159, 169 (Susan Ostrov Weisser & Jennifer Fleischner eds. 1994) (quoting testimony from the FFLA).

59. Ruth Colker, *An Equal Protection Analysis of United States Reproductive Health Policy: Gender, Race, Age and Class,* 1991 DUKE L.J. 324, 333.

60. *See* Dorothy E. Roberts, *Punishing Drug Addicts Who Have Babies: Women of Color, Equality and the Right of Privacy,* 104 HARV. L. REV. 1419 (1991).

61. 381 U.S. 479 (1965).

62. Eisenstadt v. Baird, 405 U.S. 438 (1972).

63. Carey v. Population Servs. Int'l, 431 U.S. 678 (1977).

64. Heather S. Dixon, *Pelvic Exam Prerequisite to Hormonal Contraceptives: Unjustified Infringement on Constitutional Rights, Government Coercion, and Bad Public Policy,* 27 HARV. WOMEN'S L.J. 177, 179 (2004).

65. Family Planning Services and Population Research Act of 1970, Pub. L. No. 91-572, 84 Stat. 1506 (codified at 42 U.S.C. §§ 300-300a-8 (1994)).

66. Alan Guttmacher Institute, *The Guttmacher Report, Title X: Three Decades of Accomplishment,* Feb. 2001, *available at* http://www.guttmacher.org/pubs/journals/gr040105.html.

67. Alan Guttmacher Institute, *Issues in Brief: Contraception Counts: State-by-State Information* 6 (1999), available at http://www.agi.usa.org/pubs/ib22.html.

68. Planned Parenthood Fed. of Amer., *A Planned Parenthood Report on the Bush Administration and Its Allies: The Assault on Birth Control and Family Planning Programs,* (Oct. 2003), *available at* http://www.plannedparenthood.org/library/birthcontrol/031030_birthcontrol_report.pdf#xml=http://plannedparenthood.org.master.com/texis/master/search/mysite.txt?q=title+x&order=r&id=3840507a38c4149b&cmd=xml.

69. Rust v. Sullivan, 500 U.S. 173 (1991); Title X "Gag Rule," 58 Fed. Reg. 7455 (Jan. 22, 1993).

70. National Abortion Rights Action League, *2003 Anti-Choice Federal Activity*, http://www.naral.org/yourstate/whodecides/trends/loader.cfm?url=/commonspot/security/getfile.cfm&PageID=10156.

71. H.R. 4721, 105th Cong. (1998).

72. National Abortion Rights Action League, *2003 Anti-choice and Pro-choice State Legislative Activity*, http://www.naral.org/yourstate/whodecides/trends/loader.cfm?url=/commonspot/security/getfile.cfm&PageID=10163.

73. Dore Hollander, *Sexual Behavior Is Safer When Students Can Get Their Condoms at Their Schools*, 35 PERSP. ON SEXUAL & REPROD. HEALTH 236 (Sept. 1, 2003).

74. Curtis v. Sch. Comm. of Falmouth, 652 N.E.2d 580 (Mass. 1995); Alfonso v. Fernandez, 606 N.Y.S.2d 259 (App. Div. 1993).

75. "Women of reproductive age today pay 68 percent more for their health care services than do men of the same age." *Planned Parenthood President Hails Effort in Congress to End Discrimination by Health Plans Against Women Seeking Contraception*, U.S. NEWSWIRE, July 15, 2003, *available at* 2003 WL 55660296.

76. Planned Parenthood, *Equity in Prescription Insurance and Contraceptive Coverage*, http://www.plannedparenthood.org/library/BIRTHCONTROL/EPICC_facts.html (last visited Sept. 22, 2004).

77. Erickson v. Bartell Drug Co., 141 F. Supp. 2d 1266, 1271 (W.D. Wa. 2001).

78. Adam Sonfield et al., *U.S. Insurance Coverage of Contraceptives and the Impact of Contraceptive Coverage Mandates, 2002*, 36 PERSP. ON SEXUAL & REPRODUCTIVE HEALTH 72 (Mar./Apr. 2004).

79. Samuel Coleridge Taylor, *The Three Graves, in* SAMUEL COLERIDGE TAYLOR: SELECTED POEMS 69, 72 (Richard Holmes ed. 1996).

80. MARGARET ATWOOD, THE HANDMAID'S TALE 176 (1985).

81. CATHARINE MACKINNON, SEX EQUALITY 1300 (2001).

82. Genesis 16:1-2. Other apparent surrogacy arrangements appear in Genesis 30:1-12, involving Jacob, his wives Rachel and Leah, and their maidservants.

83. *See* In re Baby M, 537 A.2d 1227 (N.J. 1988).

84. *See* MACKINNON, *supra* note 81, at 1305 n.38.

85. Lori B. Andrews, *Beyond Doctrinal Boundaries: A Legal Framework for Surrogate Motherhood*, 81 VA. L. REV. 2343, 2354 (1995).

86. HELENA RAGONÉ, SURROGATE MOTHERHOOD: CONCEPTION IN THE HEART 77 (1994) (quoting surrogate mother).

87. Margaret Jane Radin, *What, If Anything, Is Wrong with Baby Selling?*, 26 PAC. L.J. 135 (1995).

88. 537 A.2d 1227 (N.J. 1988).

89. 851 P.2d 776 (Cal. 1993).

90. *Id.* at 781.

91. Nev. Rev. Stat. § 126.045 (1999); Fla. Stat. ch. 742.13, 742.15, 742.16 (1997).

92. Ariz. Rev. Stat. Ann. § 25-218(A) (West 1991).

93. *See, e.g.,* La. Rev. Stat. Ann. § 9:2713 (West 1991) (unenforceable); Wash. Rev. Code Ann. § 26.26.250 (unenforceable and subject to criminal penalties).

94. Catherine A. MacKinnon, Feminism Unmodified: Discourses on Life and Law 148 (1987).

95. Andrea Dworkin, Pornography: Men Possessing Women 199–201 (1981); Catharine A. MacKinnon, Only Words 10–21 (1993).

96. Elaine Grant, *Only Words,* 20 N.Y.U. Rev. L. & Soc. Change 688, 689 (1993–94).

97. Indianapolis Code § 16-3(q), quoted in American Booksellers Ass'n v. Hudnut, 771 F.2d 323, 324 (7th Cir. 1985), *aff'd,* 475 U.S. 1001 (1986).

98. Regina v. Butler, [1992] 1 S.C.R. 452, 509–10 (Can.).

99. Nadine Strossen, Defending Pornography: Free Speech, Sex, and the Fight for Women's Rights 30 (1995).

100. Carlin Meyer, *Sex, Sin, and Women's Liberation: Against Porn-Suppression,* 72 Tex. L. Rev. 1097, 1193 (1994).

7

Marriage and Family

[W]hat freedom does any of us have to reimagine the terms of human association? Clare Dalton[1]

A. Marriage and Its Alternatives

1. Something old, something new

"Marriage has a long history," writes philosopher Susan Moller Okin, "and we live in its shadow."[2] In the early nineteenth century, under English common law, single women enjoyed the same rights as men to enter contracts, hold and manage property, and sue and be sued. But when a woman married, those rights transferred to her husband, according to the of doctrine of coverture (discussed briefly in **Chapter 1**). Under coverture, the husband acted as a kind of agent for his wife, exercising all legal power over her property and contractual rights with few restrictions. Legally speaking, marriage made man and woman one—and *he* was the one. Within the marriage, the law imposed certain duties upon husbands and wives. A husband was required to provide his wife (and children) some minimal level of financial support. A wife was expected to provide household services and to submit to her husband's discipline. Upon the death of a spouse, the common law provided the surviving spouse with an interest in some or all of the deceased's property. These interests—called "dower" for surviving wives and "curtesy" for surviving husbands—were generally more favorable toward husbands. In short, marriage laws of this era were extremely harsh toward women, treating them more as legal property than as legal persons. So common was this understanding that, in 1808, a Massachusetts court could observe, without irony, that "the condition of a slave resembled the connection of a wife with her husband, and of infant children with their father."[3]

In the second half of the nineteenth century, the tide slowly began to shift. Feminists successfully urged state legislatures to pass the Married Women's Property Acts, abolishing coverture and granting married women the same contract and property rights as unmarried women. While helpful, these acts fell short in significant ways. Because most wives lacked significant separate assets, the property protections were of little value to them. Some married women did earn wages, but the majority of states continued to allow husbands to retain control of such earnings. Later, most states also abolished dower and curtesy, replacing those doctrines with a more equitable system of spousal inheritance.

For most of the nation's history, no lawful marriage was possible between white and black Americans. That ended in 1948 when the Supreme Court of California invalidated such restrictions as unconstitutional.[4] In 1967 the U.S. Supreme Court followed suit, legalizing interracial marriage in all fifty states.[5] Soon afterward, states adopted "no-fault" divorce laws, which allowed women and men to dissolve their marriages unilaterally without having to allege adultery, abandonment, or other misconduct. Taken together, these reforms suggested a new concept of marriage based on equal treatment and individual choice. Couples could enter or dissolve marriages more easily than ever before. For the first time, husbands and wives could legally decide together who earns the wage, who manages the finances, or who incurs the debt. Often they both do.

Today, some fear that secular marriage has become too tolerant of choice, too "user-friendly." One proposed remedy is the "covenant marriage," now available in Arizona, Arkansas, and Louisiana. A state offering this arrangement allows couples planning to marry the option of designating their marriage as a covenant marriage. A couple choosing covenant marriage agrees to undergo premarital counseling and to make all reasonable efforts, including counseling, to preserve the marriage. Further, in contrast to a no-fault divorce, a spouse can only divorce upon a showing of abuse, adultery, abandonment, or other special circumstances. Supporters believe that covenant marriage laws help couples to see the value of their commitments to each other and stabilize their relationships. Some critics fear that covenant marriage laws seek to impose religious values on couples and make it too difficult for a spouse to leave a troubled or even dangerous relationship.

It may be too early to tell whether the covenant marriage movement will catch fire. Bills proposing covenant marriage have been submitted to legislatures in several states, including Iowa, Missouri, Texas, and Virginia. In Louisiana, the first state to offer covenant marriages, about 5 percent of marrying couples select the option.[6]

2. The pros and cons of tying the knot

Even a standard, noncovenant marriage imposes legal and social commitments on the people involved. In a culture so attached to the ideals of freedom and choice, it is worth asking why Americans get married at all. The answer, we suspect, is that by surrendering some level of personal choice and freedom, married people hope to capture greater rewards in other departments. At the most basic level, marriage allows couples to pool their talents, labor, and assets in ways that maximize economic welfare, and to obtain social recognition of their union. It provides a structure for people to care for each other in times of stress, and provides a context for romantic intimacy and companionship. Marriage often fosters a successful environment for child rearing. What is more, some studies suggest that married couples are just *happier* than nonmarried couples, although it is difficult to know why.[7]

In *Griswold v. Connecticut*, Justice William O. Douglas described matrimony in almost poetic terms: "Marriage is a coming together for better or worse, hopefully enduring, and intimate to the degree of being sacred. It is an association that promotes a way of life, not causes; a harmony of living, not political faiths; a bilateral loyalty, not commercial or social projects."[8] Surely none of these traits, from economic stability to "a harmony of living," is exclusive to marriage. But American law has always supposed that marriage is a source of social improvement and has therefore encouraged it. Today a twenty-year-old man or woman has about a 90 percent chance of marrying in his or her lifetime.[9]

Against this upbeat appraisal, many feminists note that, as an institution, marriage continues to prevent women from realizing an equal share of their full potential. Susan Okin, for instance, argues that marriage and family form "the pivot of a social system of gender that renders women vulnerable to dependency, exploitation, and abuse."[10] Such vulnerability stems from the expectation that women will be the primary caretakers of children, that they will rely on the economic support of their husbands, and that they will shoulder a greater proportion of household labor regardless of whether they also work outside the home. Marriage laws do not impose such expectations explicitly. But such power imbalances are extremely common because, as feminist legal theory holds, our laws concerning employment, education, and reproduction have weakened women's economic and social power. As we will see shortly, many feminists believe that the laws of divorce and child custody also expose women to special vulnerabilities.

3. Same-sex marriage

Many gay and lesbian couples favor marriage for the same reasons straight couples do: they hope to enhance loving companionships, pool resources, and provide stability for children. (About one-quarter of all same-sex couples have children in the home.)[11] In addition, gays and lesbians seek to benefit from the long list of legal and economic advantages available to married couples. Such advantages, which the married world often takes for granted, include spousal employment benefits, tax deductions for dependent spouses, workers' compensation payments upon death of a worker spouse, the right to sue for wrongful death of a spouse, property succession laws favoring a surviving spouse, the power to make medical decisions for an incapacitated spouse, eligibility for prisoner-family visitation programs, and family discounts for clubs and other recreational activities. Because same-sex households earn less than opposite-sex households,[12] the financial benefits of marriage may be especially important for same-sex couples.

Critics of same-sex marriage raise many interrelated concerns. Some believe that same-sex marriage violates important religious values and, therefore, should not be "endorsed" by the state. Some believe that same-sex marriage would "devalue" marriage for straight couples by making the institution less exclusive and more open to experimentation. Others fear the effect that such relationships could have on children. Still other critics focus on the procedural arguments. They believe that the decision to recognize same-sex marriage should be left to elected, representative bodies, like Congress or state legislatures, rather than judges.

In *Goodridge v. Department of Public Health,* the Massachusetts Supreme Court took up these issues, concluding that same-sex marriage must be allowed under the state constitution. In that case, gay and lesbian couples sued the Massachusetts Department of Public Health for refusing marriage licenses to same-sex couples. They argued that the state's policy violated state constitutional guarantees of personal liberty and equal protection. The state responded that restricting marriage to opposite-sex couples was justified by the government's interest in providing a "favorable setting for procreation" and "ensuring the optimal setting for childrearing."[13]

Applying a "rational basis" standard of scrutiny, the court rejected both justifications. The court found that while marriage might provide a setting for procreation, the hallmark of marriage was a "permanent commitment, not begetting children."[14] As for concerns over parenting, the court found no evidence that banning same-sex couples would increase the number of opposite-sex marriages, and noted that people in same-sex couples may be "excellent" parents. Because no convincing justification could be found for the marriage ban, the court ruled that same-sex couples had been "arbitrarily deprived of membership in one of our community's most rewarding and cherished institutions."[15]

The large majority of states have statutes banning same-sex marriage (and in some cases same-sex civil unions). Nearly twenty states have constitutional amendments barring same-sex marriage, although the legality of some is in question. Vermont, by statute, provides for same-sex civil unions, which offer same-sex couples many of the benefits enjoyed by married couples.[16] Outside the United States, same-sex marriages are legally recognized in Belgium, the Netherlands, and six Canadian provinces.

Some are worried that gay marriage will "spread" into other states when married same-sex couples visit or move to other states and then demand recognition as a married couple under the Constitution's Full Faith and Credit Clause. Whether an unwilling state could be legally compelled to recognize same-sex marriage is a matter of debate.[17] Nonetheless, the federal Defense of Marriage Act,[18] passed in 1996, seeks to protect states from same-sex "spillovers." In 2004 President George W. Bush called for an amendment to the U.S. Constitution that would ban same-sex marriage in all fifty states.

The campaign for same-sex marriage, with its emphasis on equal treatment, can be viewed as an extension of the women's rights struggles of the early 1970s and the civil rights struggles of the 1950s and 1960s. By emphasizing principles of equality, proponents highlight the similarities between same-sex and opposite-sex couples. Welcoming same-sex couples into the marriage tent should not threaten straights because both groups essentially want the same thing—security, family, and companionship. The implication is that gay and lesbian marriage would not change the institution very much, just as interracial marriage did not change the institution very much. This view resembles the perspective taken by equal treatment feminists in the early employment cases: women did not want to change the nature of any given job, they just wanted a chance to obtain it.

Some feminists, however, give same-sex marriage a more radical spin. Law professor Nan Hunter favors same-sex marriage on the grounds that it "could . . . destabilize the cultural meaning of marriage" by introducing "the possibility of marriage as a relationship between members of the same social status categories."[19] Because same-sex partners are less likely to adopt sex-based roles of dominance and submission, Hunter believes same-sex marriage might provide a more liberating vision for those in opposite-sex relationships. In contrast to the equal-treatment view, Hunter's argument suggests that same-sex marriage would, indeed, change the marital institution—in bold and creative ways.

4. Domestic partnerships

Some couples live together without being married. Their reasons are diverse. Some couples live together as a prelude to tying the knot. Others see it as a more permanent arrangement, chosen because of economic considerations, personal preferences, legal restrictions against same-sex marriage, or religious restrictions against remarrying. According to recent census data, more than five million unmarried couples live in the same household, with more than 85 percent representing couples of the opposite sex.[20] No descriptive term adequately captures the diversity of such relationships. "Cohabitants" is too broad; "significant others," is too vague; and "live-ins" is, well, *so* seventies. As Virginia Woolf once quipped, "The English language is much in need of new words."[21] We settle on the term "domestic partnership" to describe an unmarried couple sharing a household, of the same or opposite sex, with or without children.

In law, domestic partnerships raise two related questions. First, what rules should govern the duties and responsibilities *internally* between domestic partners? Second, what rules should govern the duties and responsibilities *externally* between the domestic partnership and outside third parties? The answers to both questions continue to evolve.

A. RULES BETWEEN DOMESTIC PARTNERS

When married partners pool their labor and property into a single household, the law provides a background set of duties and benefits between the parties, particularly upon dissolution of the marriage. But the law maintains a more "hands-off" approach to domestic partners. If Catherine and Heathcliff move in together, with Catherine earning a paycheck and Heathcliff cooking and cleaning, the law will not assume that either owes anything to the other when they break up three years from now. The law assumes that each is an equal and is operating independently of the other.

Often, of course, domestic partners combine households according to some explicit or implicit "understanding" of shared benefits and obligations. Catherine might have promised Heathcliff, beneath a full moon, that she would provide for his material needs in exchange for his giving up a career. In theory, "contracts" between domestic partners, whether explicit or implicit, are enforceable to some degree in most states. But unless an agreement can be established by reference to a document or other clear evidence, courts are reluctant to impose obligations on domestic partners that may not have been intended. This approach may honor the contract rights of the individual parties, but it also tends to disadvantage a party who is less sophisticated and financially weaker.

In an effort to protect parties in domestic relationships, the American Law Institute's ("ALI") *Principles of Family Dissolution*[22] recommends that upon identification as a "domestic partnership," unmarried couples should be governed by the same standards for allocating shared assets as would married couples. The document defines "domestic partners" as "two persons of the same or opposite sex, not married to one another, who for a significant period of time share a primary residence and a life together as a couple."[23] In determining whether such a relationship exists, courts are asked to consider, among other things, statements made by the parties, the intermingling of funds in bank accounts, and the assumption of parental functions over children, if any, in the household.[24] The institute's recommendations, which are not binding on courts, have stirred controversy among lawyers and policymakers. Neither traditional contract law nor the *Principles of Family Dissolution* affect the rules that govern the *external* relationship between a domestic partnership and outside third parties.

B. RULES BETWEEN A DOMESTIC COUPLE AND THIRD PARTIES

Newlyweds sometimes remark that what changes the most after the wedding is how they are treated by *other people*. Government and private organizations treat married couples differently, too, often offering benefits to one spouse that have value to the other. The federal government provides Social Security benefits to the nonemployed spouse of a wage earner. Private employers offer medical insurance plans and life insurance benefits to spouses of employees. Hospitals provide visitation rights to spouses of patients. Some of these benefits are now being offered on the same terms to domestic partnerships. In California, same-sex or opposite-sex couples can register as domestic partners, making them eligible for many benefits and protections, including hospital visitations, the right to sue for a partner's wrongful death, and the right to designate a partner as an insurance beneficiary. Similar programs are also offered in New Jersey, Maine, and about ten other states. More than 130 municipalities now also extend some form of benefits to domestic partners. Many private employers also extend benefits to their employees' domestic partners. Currently more than 160 companies in the Fortune 500 offer benefits to domestic partners.

B. Divorce and Its Economic Consequences

By now it is well-known that about 40 percent of all American marriages end in divorce.[25] Within that statistic, there exists diversity. Women with college degrees are less likely to divorce than women with less education.[26] Black women are more likely to divorce than white women.[27] Asian women divorce the least.[28] Almost no one enters a marriage believing that divorce is a possibility. Few people anticipate the dramatic emotional, social, and economic changes that divorce can bring.

1. The divorce revolution

Divorce was uncommon until the late nineteenth century. States then made it possible for couples to end their marriages for certain "fault-based" reasons—adultery, abandonment, and, eventually, drunkenness, nonsupport, and abuse. The trend reflected a developing expectation that marriage should promote individual satisfaction and happiness, in addition to the more utilitarian ends of maximizing assets and rearing children. Related to this idea was an expanding notion of personal liberty, which was used to justify giving couples slightly greater control over the terms of their relationships.

In 1969 California became the first state to adopt a "no-fault" divorce system, by which a party could unilaterally end a marriage without showing that anyone did anything wrong. Soon afterward, no-fault divorce reforms of one kind or another followed in every other state. After these changes, the national divorce rate soared, then eventually leveled out near the 50 percent rate, only recently dropping to near 40 percent. The change to no-fault divorce was fueled by many interests. Some no-fault advocates resented the old system because they believed it gave wives an unfair economic advantage over their husbands, who were statistically more likely to be deemed "at fault." Conversely, some feminists believed that no-fault divorce helped women by allowing them more power to escape an unhappy relationship. Others hoped the new system would streamline judicial proceedings by eliminating the need to air a couple's dirty laundry in open court.

2. Dividing property upon divorce

Mounting evidence suggests that divorce is not kind to women. According to the U.S. Census Bureau, "[M]arital disruption results in much poorer economic circumstances for women than for men."[29] Once recent study found that women experienced a 27 percent decline in their standard of living after divorce, while men experienced a 10 percent increase.[30] Separated and divorced women are more than twice as likely to live in poverty than are similarly situated men.[31]

What explains the disparity? Some social historians trace the problem to a decline in alimony awards. Alimony, which was typically based on a spouse's financial need, fell into disfavor in the 1980s as policymakers (some of them feminists) worried that such payments led female recipients into a pattern of financial dependency. But this explanation goes only so far, since alimony, even at its height, was mainly a phenomenon of the white middle and upper classes.

A more complete explanation involves property division. Today, most states direct courts to make an "equitable distribution" of property between the two spouses.[32] In addition to who owned the property originally, factors often considered include the length of the marriage, the age of the spouses, custodial responsibilities for children, and spousal "contributions" (money and household labor) to the marriage. The process is meant to replace a model of dependence and need with one of relative contribution, a victory for advocates of equal treatment. The idea is that marriage is a partnership, and that what you take out should be equal to what you put in. Yet, for a variety of reasons, when courts apply such criteria, their "equitable" property awards are not always equal. In many cases, women receive less than 50 percent of assets. A study commissioned by the Florida Supreme Court on gender bias found that when judges applied that state's equitable distribution laws, they awarded men between 65 and 75 percent of the marital property and women only 25 to 35 percent.[33]

To complicate matters, some feminists argue that even if women were awarded half of all marital property, they would still be at a financial disadvantage. This is because women are more likely to have deferred their educations and careers during marriage and more likely to have primary responsibility for the children after divorce. By examining women's lives within the marital context, law professor Martha Fineman argues that equal treatment must still be tempered with considerations of need:

> To emerge from a divorce in a position that even begins to put them on an economic par with their ex-husbands, many women need to receive more in property division than the strict equality concept . . . will allow. . . . Equal treatment in divorce . . . can only be fair if spouses have access to equal resources and have equivalent needs. Realistically, many women do not have such economic advantages.[34]

3. What about my law degree?

An additional problem is that not all things of value in a marriage are easily divided between divorcing spouses. This is particularly true in marriages between young adults, where a couple's largest assets are often not tangible items, but education and potential earning power. Consider the value of a law school degree. Suppose you are a young lawyer one year out of law school, now contemplating a divorce. While you studied full-time for three years in law school, your spouse worked two jobs to support the household and contribute to your tuition (the remainder of which was paid from marital savings). Assume the present value of your new degree (in terms of earning potential) is $1 million. The actual contribution in tuition dollars was $40,000. Upon divorce, should a court consider your degree as property subject to division? If so, how should it be valued and divided?

Courts approach such problems in different ways. For the most part, courts do not recognize professional degrees or licenses as being "property" subject to division. But courts in a few states will use their discretionary powers to reimburse a spouse for contributions made toward tuition and related expenses. In most states, then, your law degree is safe, although you might have to reimburse your ex-spouse for tuition.

In contrast to the general rule, the law of New York recognizes professional degrees as a bona fide asset subject to equitable division. In *O'Brien v. O'Brien,* the state's high court held that a husband's license to practice medicine was subject to division after his wife accompanied him to Guadalajara, Mexico, where he studied medicine and she worked to help pay his way. (He filed for divorce two months after receiving his license.) Perhaps most striking, the court rejected the husband's argument for a reimbursement of tuition and instead awarded his wife a share of the license's estimated present value, which at that time totaled nearly $500,000. Likening the wife's contribution to "a down payment on real estate or contribution to the purchase of securities," the court reasoned that the wife deserved more than a refund, but a return on her investment.[35] Similar issues of division and valuation occur in cases involving vested pensions and intangible business assets.

C. Child Custody

Until the late nineteenth century, fathers held rights to custody over children upon divorce, on the theory that offspring, like property, were within the husband's control. In the beginning of the twentieth century, states exhibited a preference toward the mother in a child's early years. This so-called tender years presumption derived from trends in psychological theory that emphasized the importance of a maternal connection in child rearing. As one indirect effect, this bright-line rule gave some divorcing mothers greater leverage in negotiating financial settlements, since they would not be intimidated by husbands who strategically threatened to "take the kids." But the "tender years" presumption was also discriminatory, and unfair to fathers negotiating in good faith.

In the 1970s, judges and legislatures adopted more gender-neutral standards associated with the "best interests of the child." The standard led to more case-by-case analysis of many factors, including past parenting practices, the quality of emotional bonds, household stability, and financial resources. But the emphasis on context made custody law less predictable and, to some observers, more arbitrary. Some feminists believed that the best interests test allowed predominantly male judges to favor fathers over mothers. In addition, the standard's lack of predictability led many risk-averse mothers to accept less generous property settlements in exchange for child custody. The result was that some women won custody of children without adequate finances to care for them. (Although child support, in theory, is designed to take care of this, support awards are often insufficient and, in many cases, hard to enforce.)

The 1980s saw the rise of two other gender-neutral standards, one presuming in favor of joint custody, the other in favor of the "primary caretaker." Parents with joint custody share responsibilities over legal decisions affecting the children, like choices regarding school, religious upbringing, and medical treatment. Children in this arrangement typically live primarily in one parent's home and regularly visit the other. The "primary caretaker" standard, used for a time in Minnesota and West Virginia, resembled the tender years presumption, but presumably without the sexism. The standard favors custody for the parent most involved in child care activities (the cooking, the laundry, the crosstown drives to violin lessons, and so on). The standard would apparently favor mothers over fathers, since, even in households with two wage-earning parents, mothers statistically take on more such tasks than do fathers. While no state uses a pure primary caretaker standard anymore, the concept is folded in to the ALI's suggestion that custody be apportioned proportionately to caregiving time invested during the marriage.[36]

The primary caretaker standard has been criticized by advocates on all sides. Advocates for men argue that emphasis on the primary caretaker disadvantages men who may be very good parents, but who have chosen a more traditional career path as economic provider. Some feminists argue that the standard, in practice, does not reward caretaking as much as it should. They point to instances where courts have awarded custody to fathers who have gone "above and beyond" the duties typical of most dads, but whose efforts still pale in comparison to those of the mother. Other feminists charge that the standard emphasizes caretaking too much and disadvantages mothers who take on ambitious outside careers.

All states allow joint custody arrangements, and almost half of them have statutory presumptions or preferences for it. Even in joint custody arrangements, though, typically one parent has primary physical custody. Only about 10 percent of custody decisions are made by judges. But in those contested cases, fathers obtain custody 70 percent of the time.[37] Given that the parties themselves work out custody arrangements in most cases, what factors explain why mothers wind up with custody an overwhelming percentage (by one estimate, 85 to 90 percent) of the time?[38]

D. *Questions for Discussion*

1. Imagine yourself in a conversation with your steady, unmarried partner (opposite or same-sex, it doesn't matter). Make the case that you should one day get married. How much of your argument depends on personal reasons? Social reasons? Legal reasons? How easy is it to tell the difference?

2. Some believe that law can help shape society by encouraging people to adapt their economic or social behavior. For women, the messages are often mixed. Rules of marital property division appear to suggest that wives should nurture their careers, work to-

ward financial autonomy, and beware of student-husbands. The standards of child custody, on the other hand, appear to reward women who have adopted more traditional roles of homemaker and caretaker. Should these laws be made more consistent? If most people do not expect to divorce anyway, how much influence can such laws actually have on current behavior?

3. Of the gender-neutral child custody standards discussed in this chapter, which is most likely to benefit mothers? Fathers? Children? In selecting a standard, whose needs should be paramount? If you say "the children" (and we suspect many of you will), is it possible to serve children without using a standard that visits unfairness upon one of the parents?

SUGGESTED READINGS

Mary Becker, *Maternal Feelings: Myth, Taboo, and Child Custody,* 1 S. CAL. REV. L. & WOMEN'S STUD. 133 (1992).

Martha M. Ertman, *Marriage as a Trade: Bridging the Private/Private Distinction,* 36 HARV. C.R.-C.L. L. REV. 79 (2001).

WILLIAM N. ESKRIDGE, JR., EQUALITY PRACTICE: CIVIL UNIONS AND THE FUTURE OF GAY RIGHTS (2001).

MARTHA ALBERTSON FINEMAN, THE AUTONOMY MYTH: A THEORY OF DEPENDENCY (2004).

MARY ANN GLENDON, THE TRANSFORMATION OF FAMILY LAW (1989).

Martha Minow, *"Forming Underneath Everything That Grows": Toward a History of Family Law,* 1985 WIS. L. REV. 819.

Twila L. Perry, *Alimony: Race, Privilege, and Dependency in the Search for Theory,* 82 GEO. L.J. 2481 (1994).

SAME SEX MARRIAGE: PRO AND CON: A READER (Andrew Sullivan ed., 1997).

JOHN WITTE, JR., FROM SACRAMENT TO CONTRACT: MARRIAGE, RELIGION, AND LAW IN THE WESTERN TRADITION (1997).

NOTES

1. *An Essay in the Deconstruction of Contract Law,* 94 YALE L.J. 997, 1109 (1985).

2. SUSAN MOLLER OKIN, JUSTICE, GENDER, AND THE FAMILY 140 (1989).

3. Winchendon v. Hatfield, 4 Mass. 123, 129 (1808).

4. Perez v. Lippold, 198 P.2d 17 (Cal. 1948).

5. Loving v. Virginia, 388 U.S. 1 (1967).

6. Katherine Shaw Spaht, *What's Become of Louisiana Covenant Marriage Through the Eyes of Social Scientists?*, 47 Loy. L. Rev. 709, 720–21 (2001).

7. Barbara Dafoe & David Popenoe, Should We Live Together? What Young Adults Need to Know About Cohabitation before Marriage 6 (2d ed. 2002) (citing studies), *available at* http://marriage.rutgers.edu.

8. 381 U.S. 479, 486 (1965).

9. *See* Rose M. Kreider & Jason M. Fields, U.S. Dep't of Commerce, Number, Timing, and Duration of Marriages and Divorces: 1996 at 17, Figure 4 (2001).

10. Okin, *supra* note 2, at 135–36.

11. Gary Gates & Jason Ost, The Gay and Lesbian Atlas 45 (2004).

12. *Id.* at 37, Figure 5.4 (comparing median household incomes).

13. 798 N.E.2d 941, 961 (Mass. 2003) (internal quotation marks omitted).

14. *Id.*

15. *Id.* at 949.

16. Vt. Stat. Ann. tit. 15 §§ 1201–7 (2004).

17. *See* Andrew Koppelman, The Gay Rights Question in Contemporary American Law 131 (2002) (arguing that states would not be so compelled).

18. 1 U.S.C. § 7 (2000); 28 U.S.C. § 1738C (2000),

19. Nan D. Hunter, *Marriage, Law, and Gender: A Feminist Inquiry,* 1 Law & Sexuality 9 (1991).

20. U.S. Census Bureau, Marital Status by Sex, Unmarried-Partner Households, and Grandparents as Caregivers: 2000, *available at* http://factfinder.census.gov/servlet/QTTable?_bm=y&-geo_id=01000US&-qr_name=DEC_2000_SF3_U_QTP18&-ds_name=DEC_2000_SF3_U&-_lang=en&-_sse=on.

21. Virginia Woolf, Three Guineas 80 (1938).

22. American Law Institute, Principles of the Law of Family Dissolution: Analysis and Recommendations (2002).

23. *Id.* at § 6.03(1).

24. *Id.* at § 6.03(7).

25. That figure used to be close to 50 percent but has dropped in recent years. National Center for Health Statistics, National Vital Statistics Reports, Births, Marriages, Divorces, and Deaths, vol. 52, no. 22 (U.S. Dep't of Health & Human Services: June 10, 2004), available at http://www.cdc.gov/nchs/data/nvsr/nvsr52/nvsr52_22.pdf.

26. Barbara Dafoe & David Popenoe, Ten Important Research Findings on Marriage and Choosing a Partner: Helpful Facts for Young Adults 1–2 (Nov. 2004), *available at* http://marriage.rutgers.edu.

27. Kreider & Fields, *supra* note 9, at 18, Figure 5 (2001).

28. *Id.*

29. KREIDER & FIELDS, *supra* note 9, at 14 (2001).

30. Richard R. Peterson, *A Re-evaluation of the Economic Consequences of Divorce*, 61 AM. SOC. REV. 528, 532 (1996).

31. *See* KREIDER & FIELDS, *supra* note 9, at 14 (2001).

32. While some differences exist between "community property" states and "separate property" states, both systems generally follow a principle of equitable distribution.

33. REPORT OF THE SUPREME COURT GENDER BIAS STUDY COMMISSION 59 (1990).

34. MARTHA A. FINEMAN, THE ILLUSION OF EQUALITY: THE RHETORIC AND REALITY OF DIVORCE REFORM 52 (1994).

35. 489 N.E.2d 712, 718 (N.Y. 1985)

36. AMERICAN LAW INSTITUTE, *supra* note 22, at § 2.09(1).

37. Nancy K. D. Lemon, *Statutes Creating Rebuttable Presumptions Against Custody to Batterers: How Effective Are They?*, 28 WM. MITCHELL L. REV. 601, 608 n.37 (2001).

38. Solangel Maldonado, *Beyond Economic Fatherhood: Encouraging Divorced Fathers to Parent*, 153 U. PA. L. REV. 921, 966 n.221, 986 n.326 (2005).

8

Sex and Violence

Nearly 5.3 million intimate partner victimizations occur each year among U.S. women ages 18 and older. This violence results in nearly 2 million injuries and 1,300 deaths.[1]

Black women are between two to three times more likely to be raped than White women. The profile of the most frequent rape victim in this country is a young woman, divorced or separated, poor, and Black.[2]

A survey commissioned by the Departments of Justice and Health and Human Services showed that "nearly 18 percent of American women were either raped or have been attempted rape victims at some point during their lives."[3]

Worldwide, at least one in three women and girls has been beaten or sexually abused in her lifetime.[4]

More than half of all rape prosecutions are dismissed before trial or result in acquittal. A rape case is twice as likely to be dismissed as a murder case. Nearly a quarter of convicted rapists never serve time in prison, and almost half of convicted rapists serve a year or less behind bars. A robber is 30 percent more likely to be convicted than a rapist.[5]

The extraordinary disjunction between the statistics on the frequency of violence against women, particularly intimate partner violence,[6] and the absence of criminal penalties is perhaps best understood in historical context. In early Anglo-American law, since women were considered property of their fathers or husbands, rape by a stranger was not a crime against a woman, but "'a property crime of man against man.'"[7] If an unmarried woman was raped, this diminished her future marital value; if a married woman was raped, this brought disgrace to her husband. Essentially, the woman was a bystander in the law of rape.

This notion of women as property also meant that men could never be guilty of raping their wives, since men could treat their possessions, or "chattel," in nearly any way they wanted. Indeed, the doctrine of "chastisement" allowed husbands to beat their wives—in "moderation"—to make them obey. Nineteenth-century feminists tried desperately to change these injustices. But the Married Women's Property Acts that conferred on women some rights—such as the rights to make contracts and own property—left the immunity for marital rape and the doctrine of chastisement untouched. Courts were not inclined to change things either. When feminists challenged the laws on chastisement during the Reconstruction era, judges invoked the public-private distinction, reasoning that "the legal system should not interfere in cases of wife beating, in order to protect the privacy of the marriage relationship and to promote domestic harmony."[8]

Not until a hundred years later, in the 1970s and 1980s, were second-wave feminists moderately successful in encouraging fewer than half of the state legislatures to reform rape laws by abolishing the absolute marital exemption. (Some states created limited exemptions, for example, by considering husbands and wives who did not live together as not married for purposes of the rape statute.) Even today more than half the states still retain some form of immunity for rape within marriage. "[T]wenty states grant marital immunity for sex with a wife who is incapacitated or unconscious and cannot consent. Fifteen states grant marital immunity for sexual offenses unless requirements such as prompt complaint, extra force, separation, or divorce are met."[9] While many jurisdictions now punish spousal rape, they make marital rape a lesser crime than nonmarital rape. To this day, the majority of states define marital violence as being less serious than the same violence occurring outside of marriage.

In the last twenty-five years, feminist legal theorists have analyzed intimate violence, including rape, from many perspectives. Cultural feminists used storytelling—women's accounts of their experiences with rape and intimate violence—to illustrate the criminal law's unequal treatment of rape victims. Dominance theorists studied rape as the paradigm example of male power, female submission, and coercion masquerading as consent. Building on this idea, dominance theorists suggested that even nonphysical acts of domination and psychological abuse should be recognized as violence. Formal-equality theorists insisted that the legal system treat domestic violence like other crimes. Critical race theorists viewed rape as an issue where racism and sexism intertwined. They showed how the rape experiences of women of color often differed from the rape experiences of white women. They also studied the experiences of the perpetrators and alleged perpetrators of sexual crimes, arguing that the law sometimes, perhaps even often, treated whites and people of color differently.[10]

Cumulatively, feminists showed how the public-private distinction shielded intimate violence from criminal sanction.[11] They redefined intimate violence not as a personal or family issue, but as a manifestation of a social system in which males dominate females through power and violence. They have raised consciousness about the prevalence, effects, and gendered nature of intimate violence and the cultural norms that shape current legal responses to it.

Before moving forward, we should note that approximately 15 percent of the victims of intimate violence are men, a statistic that includes violence perpetrated by both female partners and gay male partners.[12] Although we use female pronouns to refer to victims of intimate violence in this chapter, we do not mean to diminish the importance of intimate violence to male victims. The rape laws in all fifty states protect men as well as women against such assault, although one must acknowledge that same-sex rape is vastly underreported and probably underprosecuted. To make matters worse, the legal literature regarding sexual assault on male victims is minuscule.

A. Rape

1. The criminal law rules

Late at night, a woman is walking briskly through her college campus in the North End of Philadelphia. . . . She attempts to unlock the door of her apartment, and her worst nightmare materializes when she is surprised by the intrusion of an assailant. He tells her to take her clothes off. She is surprised, afraid, and unsure of what to do. In only a few precious seconds, she has to make a potentially life or death decision. He has made no threat, but she is afraid of what may happen if she does not obey. Reluctantly, she complies, out of fear. She does not verbally or physically resist his penetration, and the two have intercourse. The woman files a complaint alleging rape.[13]

Common law defined rape as "the carnal knowledge of a woman forcibly and against her will."[14] American states adopted this definition, and the laws of almost every jurisdiction today require these same three elements: intercourse, some kind of forcible compulsion, and nonconsent.

Most rape statutes currently require proof that the defendant used force or a credible threat of force beyond the penetration itself. As a result, the wording in some rape statutes means that certain types of coerced rapes are not prosecuted. In a case from 1990, the Montana Supreme Court upheld the dismissal of a rape charge by a high school student against her principal who threatened that she would not graduate unless she submitted to sexual intercourse with him.[15] The rape statute in existence at the time required that the offender compel the victim to "submit by force or by threat of imminent death, bodily injury, or kidnapping." The court refused to interpret the force element to include intimidation, fear, or coercion—and because the principal did not use force or any of the threats listed in the statute, he was not prosecuted for rape. While most rape statutes, including Montana's, have been revised to include coercing the woman to submit through duress, intimidation, or fear, most still require some type of forcible compulsion. This idea that rape requires force dates back to a rape case that reached the Supreme Court more than a hundred years ago, *Mills v. United States,* in which the Court held:

> The mere nonconsent of a female to intercourse where she is in possession of her natural, mental and physical powers, is not overcome by numbers or terrified by threats, or in such place and position that resistance would be useless, does not constitute the crime of rape on the part of the man who has connection with her under such circumstances. More force is necessary . . . to make out that element of that crime.[16]

Early interpretations of the force and lack of consent elements originally required a woman to offer the "utmost resistance." This meant that the prosecutor had "to prove beyond a reasonable doubt that the woman resisted her assailant to the utmost of her physical capacity to prove that an act of sexual intercourse was rape."[17] In a wave of rape law reforms during the 1970s and 1980s, most states replaced the requirement of "utmost" resistance with one of "reasonable" resistance. Over the next two decades many courts recognized that requiring women to physically resist might, in some circumstances, increase their risk of other injuries.[18] In a few decisions, judges acknowledged that some rape victims might be paralyzed with fear and unable to display physical resistance. In those jurisdictions, courts found that verbal resistance was enough. Yet even today a handful of states retain the reasonable resistance requirement to show forcible compulsion (and in other states with a forcible compulsion rule, although it is not a technical element, many courts still look to see if the woman physically resisted). In those states, verbal resistance—crying, begging, screaming, or simply saying "no"—is not enough to show nonconsent.

What makes "no" so difficult for some lawmakers to understand? Why is the criminal law shaped so that nonconsent plus penetration is insufficient? One explanation of why rape law allows men to infer that silence means consent is that because rape is a serious crime, men need to be clearly informed that their sexual advances are unwelcome. Another rests on now-outmoded courtship rituals in which men were expected to pursue sexual conduct and women to resist repeatedly until they reluctantly submitted. A third explanation for the requirement that women must prove force or threat of force sufficient to compel them to submit is simply distrust of the accuser: "Rape law has assumed that women lie about their nonconsent to sexual activity for various reasons, such as discovery of their activity by family or others, a desire to coerce the alleged attacker into marriage, and so on."[19] In fact, only a small number of states—eight at current count—have broadened the definition of rape to permit women to withdraw consent after intercourse has begun.[20]

2. Rape myths

These rape myths are familiar to us all—women mean "yes" when they say "no"; women are "asking for it" when they wear provocative clothes, go to bars alone, or simply walk down the street at night; only virgins can be raped; women are vengeful, bitter creatures "out to get men"; if a woman says "yes" once, there is no reason to believe her "no" the next time; women who "tease" men deserve to be raped; the majority of women who are raped are promiscuous or have bad reputations; a woman who goes to the home of a man on the first date im-

plies she is willing to have sex; women cry rape to cover up an illegiti-
mate pregnancy; a man is justified in forcing sex on a woman who
makes him sexually excited; a man is entitled to sex if he buys a
woman dinner; women derive pleasure from victimization.[21]

Myths about rape abound. Some of these myths excuse rape; others
minimize its seriousness or deny that the woman suffered harm; still
others question whether a rape even occurred at all.

Although these ideas are widespread and powerful, the fact is that
empirical evidence disproves them. The best estimates indicate that
the rates for false reports of rapes are comparable to false charge rates
for other crimes. The idea that rape victims are primarily women with
bad reputations is countered by both the statistics on acquaintance
and marital rape and studies showing that more than 80 percent of
women who were raped had "good reputations." Women do not "ask
for it": the National Commission on Crimes of Violence concluded
that "only 4 percent of reported rapes involve any precipitative behavior by the victim, consisting of as little as a gesture."[22]

Nevertheless, these unfounded stereotypes about rape have sifted
into societal attitudes and affect every level of the criminal justice system: women are reluctant to report rapes for fear that they will be
blamed; police fail to investigate complaints; prosecutors lack zeal for
filing cases; trials contain demeaning cross-examinations that focus
on the attire, behavior, and past sexual history of the complainant;
and unsympathetic juries focus on the woman's responsibility for the
situation. It is therefore unsurprising that data from national studies
conducted by the U.S. Department of Justice indicate that only "between 14% and 32% of all sexual assaults or rapes are ever reported
to the police."[23]

3. Special evidence requirements

Worst of all, the effects of such myths persist in the law itself. Under
the old common law, the idea that rape victims are untrustworthy and
are likely to falsely accuse men of this crime led courts to apply special rules of evidence for rape cases. Until the 1980s, many states held
that a defendant could not be convicted of rape based solely on the un-
corroborated testimony of the victim. This requirement meant the
prosecution would have to produce either witnesses (a rarity in rape

cases) or physical evidence to support a victim's testimony. The rule itself seems pointless because if a jury does not find the accuser's testimony credible beyond a reasonable doubt, the jury is instructed to acquit. Still, a handful of states retain the rule even today.

More than a dozen other jurisdictions still permit judges to give a "cautionary instruction" to the jury.[24] These instructions warn jurors that rape is a charge that is easily made and one that is hard to disprove even if the defendant is innocent and caution jurors therefore to scrutinize the complainant's testimony. One additional rule—now alive in only three states and only for sexual offenses by spouses—requires a "fresh complaint," typically barring prosecutions if the woman did not report the crime within just a few months.

Many of these special rules of evidence invite further scrutiny and humiliation of already vulnerable rape victims. The rules themselves were not widely questioned until the 1970s, timing that corresponded to an influx of women into the practice of law.[25]

In early common-law rape cases, defendants were permitted to undermine the credibility of their accusers by introducing evidence of the rape victim's promiscuity or even lack of prior chastity. By the early 1980s, Congress and nearly all state legislatures had passed "rape shield" laws to prevent defense lawyers from cross-examining rape victims about their previous sexual activities. Many state statutes do allow evidence of the victim's prior sexual behavior with the accused to show consent, or evidence of specific instances of sexual activity with someone else to show the source of semen, a disease, or pregnancy, or to show that someone else committed the alleged rape. The rape shield statutes have been helpful in preventing a "second assualt" on the victim at trial.

4. Public perceptions, media coverage, and legal theory

Although rape is an area in which feminists generally have had exceptional success in bringing about reforms—and even though most states have abandoned these antiquated evidentiary rules—a fundamental suspicion remains of women who assert charges of rape. Media reports both document and feed that public distrust. Television and newspaper accounts strongly influence societal attitudes about what constitutes rape. Yet that same press is slanted toward reports of lurid rapes, particularly vulnerable victims, or cases in which the accuser can be portrayed as a "slut." Recall the coverage given to the women who charged William Kennedy Smith and Kobe Bryant with rape and the focus on the *victims'* behaviors of barhopping, partying, and having affairs.

Despite the media's still merciless inquiries into accusers' backgrounds, the law regarding rape has come a long way since its origins, when rape was not even viewed as a crime against the woman. A number of types of feminist legal theory over several generations contributed to rape reform legislation. For instance, dominance theory connected the phenomenon of rape to male dominance in social, political, and economic realms and presented the stark social realities of rape in ways that called for more determined state interventions.

Equal treatment theory led reformers to insist that the legal system abolish discriminatory rape laws and treat rape as seriously as other crimes of violence. The equal treatment emphasis on individual autonomy and choice may have meant that these theorists were more concerned with assymetrical evidentiary rules and less concerned with challenging "traditional rape law's focus on female non-consent as the dividing line between sex and rape."[26] Although equal treatment and dominance theorists' views of rape differ—for the former, it is "a gender-neutral crime of violence"; for the latter, it is "a gender-specific sex crime"—both schools have been instrumental in focusing legislative attention on violence against women.[27] The narratives of rape victims, inspired by cultural feminism, helped raise awareness of the crime itself, as well as the ways almost all women fear being raped and alter their behaviors to avoid it—foregoing a run late at night, avoiding provocative clothing, or staying away from certain stores, bars, or parts of town.

While changes in rape law are considered a success of the feminist movement, empirical data indicate that the evidentiary reforms have not translated into significantly better reporting, arrest, indictment, or conviction rates. Statutory reforms have produced only a modest increase in reports and convictions, and only in some jurisdictions.[28] The requirement that the rape victim prove force or threat of force plus nonconsent remains the law. Even if resistance is not required as a technical legal element, prosecutors still think that jurors will not convict unless the woman resisted. Juries still believe myths and misconceptions about rapists and rape victims. Women are still discouraged from reporting rapes because they think—not without reason—

that despite rape shield laws, their conduct and actions will be closely scrutinized at trial.

5. Acquaintance rape

Men who use force to obtain sexual gratification from social partners may admit violating the rules of romance, but heatedly deny any criminal wrongdoing. Meanwhile female victims often blame themselves for provoking the man's conduct or putting themselves in a vulnerable position.[29]

Most people think of rape as a crime that is committed by malevolent strangers, yet seven out of ten victims of rape or sexual assault say that the perpetrator was a friend, acquaintance, or relative.[30] Although the law does not treat rape by acquaintances differently from rape by strangers, one study indicates that jurors are four times more likely to convict in stranger rape cases.[31] Underlying the reluctance to prosecute acquaintance rape cases and the difficulties obtaining convictions are social norms, beliefs, and attitudes that foster a presumption of consent, provocation, or entrapment.

While some feminists have tried to challenge prevailing cultural beliefs and combat rape myths, others have seemed to undermine reform efforts. In her controversial book, *The Morning After: Sex, Fear and Feminism on Campus,* Katie Roiphe claims that "rape crisis feminists" exaggerate the incidence of acquaintance rape, portraying women as victims, blurring the distinction between "bad" sex and acquaintance rape, and "reinforc[ing] traditional views about the fragility of the female body and will." Her conclusion is that "[t]here is a gray area in which someone's rape may be another person's bad night."[32] According to Roiphe and others, like Camille Paglia, Christina Hoff Sommers, and Naomi Wolf, women must bear responsibility for putting themselves in compromising situations and stop whining about being raped. In the words of Camille Paglia, "A girl who lets herself get dead drunk at a fraternity party is a fool. A girl who goes upstairs alone with a brother at a fraternity party is an idiot. Feminists call this 'blaming the victim.' I call it common sense."[33]

Their views coincide with mainstream public attitudes toward rape: "One of the most extensive studies of citizen perceptions of rape found that 66% of the polled population believed that women's behavior or appearance provokes rape and 34% believed that women should be held responsible for preventing their own rape."[34] Similarly, a telephone survey conducted in 1991 found that "38% of men and 37% of women believed that a woman is partly to blame for her own rape if she dresses seductively."[35]

These writers offer descriptions of feminism for the popular presses. Sommers and Paglia describe themselves as "equity" feminists; Wolf proposes a theory of "power feminism." All of them indict what they call "gender" or "victim" feminism. "Victim" feminists, according to some of these writers, emphasize inherent differences between the sexes, tell stories of women's disempowerment, create images of women as helpless, shirk responsibility, blame men, and do not enjoy sex.

The "equity" theory propounded by Paglia and Sommers bears little resemblance to equal treatment theory in law. In fact, these theories of feminism—some have described them as "faux" feminism or even antifeminism—are set up in opposition to academic feminism. Nonetheless, their hyperbolic criticisms of academic feminists as ideologues, propagandists, and elitists have captivated media attention. They offer a message—feminism "means being a victim, and it means being bitter and angry"—that some quarters want to hear.[36]

These somewhat extremist versions of gender relations have shaped public understandings of feminist theory. They have also influenced popular beliefs about specific issues, like whether the acquaintance rape crisis is real or manufactured by feminists. These popularized portrayals of acquaintance rape as something concocted by feminist theorists undermine efforts of various feminist organizations and theorists to make the public understand that rape by an acquaintance is rape. Even the term used—"date" rape—makes the crime seem somehow less serious than "real" rape.

But "equity" or "power" feminists should not be completely dismissed by other feminists because, in a way, they are both fighting for the same thing: sexual autonomy for women. The difference is that equity and power feminists think women can seize control over their sexuality without the help of legal reform by taking responsibility for their behavior. They can dress less provocatively, drink less at the fraternity house, and avoid the dark running trails. Academic feminists believe that sexual violence is a national, *public* problem and, therefore, beyond the scope of women's individual choices.

Even if a woman could shield herself from sexual assault by altering her behavior, academic feminists argue that she should not have to. Aren't dress, socializing, and recreation also part of a woman's autonomy?

B. Domestic Violence

He used to fine me if I said anything considered out of order. All these sort of weird things, trying to get control, power.

He almost burnt my work one time—three years of research and writing. . . .

Within a couple of weeks, he started snarling at me about the way I laid the breakfast table. It was something stupid like the marmalade on the wrong side of the table. . . . I got to the stage of wondering about everything, if I was going to get it right or wrong. . . .

He would say things like "It took all my self-control last night not to get the bread knife and come upstairs and knife you." I never knew how far he could go. I just knew that I was in fear for my life.

He always found something wrong with what I did, even if I did what he asked. No matter what it was. It was never the way he wanted it. I was either too fat, didn't cook the food right. . . . I think he wanted to hurt me. To hurt me in the sense . . . to make me feel like I was a nothing.

The physical stuff was bad though, but I think the silences were worse. They were psychological torture. You could never predict what would send him into one of these silences. Or how to get him out of them. These silences were the ultimate control.[37]

Domestic violence in particular is an area that highlights the interdisciplinary nature of feminist understanding. It also directly raises in doctrinal form whether gender neutrality (in the form of traditional "self-defense" rules) promotes equality. Psychologists who have studied battered women's experiences explain that the patterns of violence in battering relationships demonstrate that concepts of imminence (while the violence may not be immediately threatened, it could come again at any time), resistance, and reasonableness should be evaluated differently in situations of long-standing intimate violence.

1. Understanding abusive relationships: "Why didn't she just leave?"

Juries have difficulty comprehending why women stay in violent relationships. The truth is that many women do make efforts to leave by reporting the abuse, seeking shelter, obtaining restraining orders, or separating or filing for divorce from their abusers. Studies indicate that more than 70 percent of battered women leave their spouses or partners at some point.[38] District attorney Sarah Buel explains, "It is a myth that [battered women] do not leave. We generally leave many times before we are finally able to leave and stay away."[39]

Some stay because they are isolated and have no jobs skills, no shelters, no knowledge of their options, and no place to go. Some stay because they are illiterate or have substance abuse problems, or because they have previously been victims and have learned to blame themselves. They stay because their abusers have power and money, and they have no resources for a home or food or clothing; they stay because of guilt, gratitude for prior help, or despair; they stay because of family or religious pressures; they stay "for the sake of the children" or to avoid shame; they stay because they are terrified to leave—and this fear is rational. "It is estimated that a battered woman is 75 percent more likely to be murdered when she tries to flee or has fled, than when she stays."[40] They stay because they love their batterers and believe those batterers when they promise to change.

In the late 1970s, psychologist Lenore Walker interviewed fifteen hundred battered women and noticed patterns in their descriptions of the abusive relationships. She developed a theory about the dynamics of battering relationships, called "the "battered woman syndrome"— a constellation of characteristics shared by victims of domestic abuse. Walker's theory has two significant components: the "cycle of violence" and "learned helplessness." The cycle of violence describes the course of battering relationships over time. It begins with a "gradual tension-building" phase in which the batterer expresses dissatisfaction, exhibits controlling behavior, isolates the victim, and engages in verbal hostilities and small amounts of physical abuse—a slap, an arm grab, breaking furniture. The victim tries to diffuse the tension and placate her batterer. In the second phase, these incidents escalate and culminate in an acute battering episode. The third stage is the "loving-repentant" phase, a honeymoon period in which the batterer is contrite and extremely kind. He continually apologizes, begs for forgiveness, and promises to change. The victim hopes her partner will change, bonds with him again, and loses any resolve to leave. Then the caring behavior lapses, the tensions build again, and the cycle repeats.[41]

The second part of Walker's theory is learned helplessness, which assists in explaining why some women stay in abusive relationships. In developing the theory, Walker relied on Martin Seligman's research on caged dogs that were given electric shocks. When the dogs were repeatedly shocked and learned that they had no control, they became passive and did not escape, even when given the opportunity. Walker theorized that women subjected to continual abuse also learn to be helpless and stop trying to leave. They acquire survival skills within the relationship but develop an inability to see escape alternatives. Her later works characterize the syndrome as a type of post-traumatic stress disorder.[42]

A decade after Walker developed the concept of the battered woman syndrome, other researchers suggested that many women develop more complex coping mechanisms than just the paralysis of learned helplessness. Edward Gondolf and Ellen Fisher suggested an alternative hypothesis, the "survivor theory," which says that women do not learn passivity and helplessness, but actually make repeated and increasing attempts to seek help from friends and family, law enforcement, and social service agencies. When help-seeking fails—because the outside resources, such as available shelter space, are inadequate, or because the woman has children, is deeply committed to the relationship, has been conditioned by her background to accept abuse, or has no economic alternatives—the woman may return to her abuser.[43] While the survivor theory challenged the idea that battered women were helpless or dependent, the battered woman syndrome theory gained widespread acceptance in courts.

No single profile, of course—neither the battered woman syndrome nor the survivor theory—explains the situation of all battering relationships. While some consider the survivor theory to be a direct theoretical challenge to the battered woman syndrome, the latter is, in essence, a survival strategy. It is related to the Stockholm syndrome, the phenomenon in which prisoners of war, hostages, or kidnap victims develop strong emotional ties with their captors in large part to save their own lives.[44]

Statistically, relatively few battered women kill their abusers: several million women are battered each year; only an estimated eight hundred to twelve hundred of them kill the partners who are abusing them.[45] While killing an abuser may seem inconsistent with the idea of learned helplessness, women may believe they are powerless to stop the abuse in any other way and see no realistic alternatives. Research has indicated that when battered women kill, it is typically the case that the batterer has introduced some "lethality factor" into the abusive relationship—purchased a gun or started to perpetrate violence against children.[46] The next section explores the ways criminal defense lawyers have used the battered woman syndrome as a partial or complete defense for women who kill their batterers.

2. Battered women who kill their abusers

In the late 1970s, women who killed their abusers began to use the battered woman syndrome to support their claims of self-defense. If women are threatened with imminent death or serious bodily injury, they have a good self-defense claim anyway. If women kill in a non-confrontational situation (the stereotypical case—although exceedingly rare—is killing a sleeping husband), the syndrome is helpful in explaining why the woman believed that another attack on her was inevitable, although not immediate. The syndrome evidence worked legally to expand the scope of the imminence requirement of a self-defense claim; the cycle of violence theory explains that the woman reasonably believes that violence will come again at any time. By the mid-1990s, all states permitted expert testimony regarding the battered woman syndrome in at least some situations. Many courts allowed it even in confrontational circumstances that would satisfy the traditional self-defense rules, either to support the credibility of the woman or to explain to jurors why she did not leave the relationship.[47]

Some feminist legal theorists maintained that the idea of a "syndrome," or indeed any theory that focuses primarily on women's response to violence, stigmatizes battered women and makes it seem that they are maladjusted or suffering from pathology, are emotionally unstable, or are irrational and incapable of exercising self-control. This stigmatization can cause people to ignore the larger, more complex causes of violence, the varying individual experiences of battered women, and institutional indifference: "If one somehow sees the woman as psychologically impaired, the link between her individual victimization and a criminal justice system that has condoned violence against women is never made."[48] One aspect of these critiques, though, misses an important feature of both the "battered woman syndrome" and the survivor theory—that neither theory necessarily pathologizes the behavior of battered women: both view the women's responses as understandable mechanisms for coping with the abnormally dangerous situations in which they find themselves.

Other critics charged that the syndrome created an easily manipulated standard for female victims of domestic violence that, if accepted by courts, would spawn claims of "abuse excuse" by other interest groups. Critics worry that the defense is too subjective and that, if permitted in a homicide trial, women will literally get away with murder. Harvard law professor Alan Dershowitz argued that "the abuse excuse is a symptom of a general abdication of responsibility" that is dangerous in a democracy that relies on "personal accountability for choices and actions."[49] But in addition to personal accountability, law also respects context. This is why a man who kills his wife upon learning of her infidelity can seek a reduction in charge from murder to manslaughter on the grounds that he acted in a "heat of passion." (The law permits female perpetrators the same opportunity, but most such killings are perpetrated by men.) Should battered women not be given the same respect for context when they attack their batterers?

The evidence seems to belie the claim that admitting expert testimony regarding the syndrome causes jurors and judges to become unduly sympathetic toward a disadvantaged population. Social science studies indicate that using abuse as a mitigating defense is typically not a successful strategy for obtaining an acquittal or a reduced sentence. When battered women kill their abusers, they are rarely acquitted. Studies indicate that between 72 and 80 percent either are convicted or accept a plea bargain. Women who kill violate strong social taboos and receive extremely harsh sentences. Ironically, "[b]attered women who kill tend to receive even longer sentences" than nonbattered women, with one study finding that almost 84 percent of battered women who killed their partners "received sentences ranging from twenty-five years to life."[50] In fact, women who kill their abusers receive longer sentences than men who raise mitigation claims such as heat of passion when they kill their intimate partners.[51]

Ultimately, the battered woman syndrome may not have dramatically altered trial outcomes in the case of abused women who kill. But debates about the admissibility of the syndrome have played a large part in raising consciousness about the prevalence of intimate violence and the lives and experiences of its victims.

3. Intimate violence at the intersections of identity

Ling's husband had beaten her for eight years. One evening, he tried to pick a fight with Ling as she cleaned fish for dinner. She ignored him, which angered him. He tried to strike her with a chair and Ling used the fish knife to defend herself. Her husband kept lunging at her and cut himself on the knife. Ling ran to a nearby store to call the police. When the police arrived, her husband—who spoke English well—accused Ling of attacking him. Ling did not speak enough English to defend herself. The police, whom Ling had called to protect her, ended up arresting her instead.[52]

One of the myths about domestic violence is that it occurs predominantly or almost exclusively within particular racial groups or socioeconomic classes. Intimate violence occurs across all races, classes, ethnicities, sexual orientations, and religions, although some studies indicate that Latina, African American, Asian, Native-American, and immigrant women experience such violence at greater rates than white women.[53] One of the stark realities about domestic violence is that some populations have fewer community services available or face greater barriers in their attempts to obtain official intervention. A variety of groups have diverse experiences with domestic violence and different needs for services.

Language barriers, distrust of authorities, and fears of the legal system can deter reporting. Many immigrant women are reluctant to report domestic violence to authorities out of fear that they would be deported. Non-English speakers, migrant workers, or victims with disabilities may face specific obstacles in reporting. (Although it is true that in recent years, particularly in larger metropolitan areas, service providers recognize the need to have rapid access to multilingual staff and translators, the funding for multicultural services has not kept pace with the demand.) Traditional expectations in some cultures that demand the silent subservience of women make it hard for battered women to report the abuse and deprive those women of community support.[54] In traditional Navajo culture, for example, "peacemakers" who informally adjudicate claims of battering may try to restore harmony by encouraging women to remain in abusive relationships.[55]

Lesbians and gay men may be reluctant to report intimate violence to avoid disclosing their sexual orientation, or they may fear police hostility. If gay men or lesbians use physical force to defend themselves from their battering partners, police may assume that two men wrestling is a "fair fight" or think that two women struggling is a catfight or quarrel. If lesbians who are battered by their partners seek refuge at a shelter, their partners, who are also women, can gain access to them. In the United States, shelters for battered men are virtually nonexistent. Some victims of violence in dating relationships are unable to obtain orders of protection because they are not defined as "family members" under state statutes. In most states, gay and lesbian partners are not even eligible for protective orders.[56]

The experiences of domestic violence victims at the intersections of race, class, ethnicity, language, and sexual orientation may be among the clearest examples of the practical application of antiessentialist legal theory. The battered women's movement focused initially on women in heterosexual relationships. The very existence of abuse in same-sex relationships—and "estimates are that somewhere between twenty-five to thirty-three percent of gay, lesbian, transgender, and bisexual people suffer abuse at the hands of their intimate partners"[57]—calls into question one theory of intimate violence: that it is an expression of male domination of females. The experiences of intimate violence among people of different cultures, races, and sexual orientations raise questions not only whether domestic violence is a matter of gender or power, but even more fundamentally whether comprehensive theories can explain the phenomena of battering.

C. Legal Intervention

1. Police responses

Last night I heard the screaming
Loud voices behind the wall
Another sleepless night for me

It won't do no good to call
The police
Always come late
If they come at all.[58]

Good evidence exists that historically—and still today in many areas—police officers did not respond as rapidly to domestic violence calls or treat intimate violence situations as seriously as other violent crimes. Evidence presented during hearings on the Violence against Women Act in 1992 indicated that fewer than 5 percent of domestic violence calls to law enforcement agents in the District of Columbia resulted in arrests, and that police failed to arrest more than 85 percent of the time when the victim had significant visible injuries that the police could see.[59] The anemic response of law enforcement officials rested on a variety of reasons. Responding to domestic calls swallows more police time "than all other felonies combined."[60] Victims often do not cooperate in prosecutions, which makes officers feel that their efforts are an even greater waste of time.

Police also hesitate to answer domestic calls because police themselves are more likely to be injured or killed in responding to domestic abuse. An FBI report from 1998 found that response to disturbance (which could include domestic or stranger) calls accounted for almost one-third of assaults on police officers and one-tenth of police deaths.[61] But in large part police were reluctant to intervene in "domestic disturbances" because they considered this sort of violence a private, family matter and not even a real crime.

Law enforcement responses have racial, ethnic, and class components as well: police respond even less rapidly to domestic calls from communities of color than they do in predominantly white areas. Women of minority races face the additional problem of knowing that when they seek police protection, they are subjecting the abuser to a racially biased criminal justice system.[62] Thus women of color, especially those who live in poor neighborhoods, face the twin dilemmas of underpolicing and overaggressive policing with racialized effects.[63] The racial disparity in treatment of victims and perpetrators of intimate violence does not end with police responses. As just one example, "when black women are treated for domestic violence related injuries in inner-city hospitals, protocols for [suspected abuse] are 'rarely introduced or followed.'"[64]

In the middle to late 1980s, women began to file civil rights suits against police departments for giving lower priority to domestic violence calls or for failing to make arrests or enforce orders of protection. They could not sue simply for inadequate police protections, because the Supreme Court has held that the state does not have any general affirmative duty to protect its citizens from dangers that it did not create.[65] So many of these suits alleged that the police violated the equal protection rights of domestic violence victims by having a policy or custom of affording them less protection than they gave to victims of stranger violence.

The primary difficulty with an equal protection claim is the constitutional standard. To obtain intermediate scrutiny, plaintiffs must show that police intentionally treat domestic abuse claims less seriously because they intend to discriminate against women. If police departments simply treat the category of domestic violence offenses differently from nondomestic violence, the matter is reviewed under the rational basis test, because it is not intentional discrimination based on sex. Most courts either have invoked the rational basis test—in part because not all victims of domestic violence are women and in part because reasons other than gender (police injuries, victim noncooperation) exist for differential enforcement—or they have required specific proof of motivation to discriminate against women.[66] This means that even if such policies exist and have a disproportionate impact on women, they do not amount to unconstitutional sex discrimination.

These rulings subtly permit the public-private dichotomy regarding "domestic" situations to continue. Absent a specific intent to discriminate against women, police are free to relegate domestic cases to a lower response priority than any other felony. The law enforcement disparity cases also raise the problem of identifying when discrimination is, in fact, based on gender, but hidden by the use of domestic violence as a proxy for gender. Although the constitutional cases have usually been unsuccessful, the recognition of these inequalities in law enforcement response has prompted changes in police policies and training to provide consistent and serious responses to domestic violence calls.

2. Mandatory reporting, arrest, and prosecution policies

Reformers, pressing for the elimination of disparate treatment of domestic violence by the criminal justice system, sought the development of policies that took crimes of domestic violence seriously, removed police discretion, and sent messages to would-be batterers that these crimes would be prosecuted. In the mid-1980s some social science research indicated that police arrests had a strong deterrent effect on future episodes of intimate violence. U.S. Attorney General William French Smith recommended that police departments make misdemeanor arrests standard practice, and by 1986, one-third of all police departments in the country had made arrests in domestic violence situations their standard policy.[67]

Required state intervention policies have taken three primary forms: mandatory reporting, mandatory arrest, and mandatory prosecution (i.e., "no-drop") policies. Most states have mandatory reporting laws that typically compel medical or hospital personnel to report suspected intimate violence to law enforcement authorities. Mandatory arrest policies require police to arrest the offender any time they have probable cause to believe intimate violence has occurred, even if they did not witness the occurrence. The majority of jurisdictions have some form of mandatory or preferred arrest policies, either by state statute or by departmental policy. Two-thirds of district attorneys offices in urban areas have adopted no-drop policies, which means they usually will continue to prosecute even if the victim urges them to drop the charges.[68]

One question concerning mandatory arrest policies is simply whether they are actually increasing arrests. Police still have discretion to determine whether probable cause exists to believe a crime of domestic violence has occurred. Although the information is from the early to mid-1990s, one review of the data showed that despite mandatory arrest policies in three major metropolitan areas—Minneapolis, Phoenix, and New York City—the domestic violence arrest rates in those jurisdictions were, respectively, only 20 percent, 18 percent, and 7 percent.[69] Thus, even if specialized legal tools exist to criminalize battering, institutional practices change slowly.

Pro-arrest policies, however, had some unintended consequences, one of which was a disproportionate effect on racial minorities. People of color were arrested, prosecuted, and incarcerated "'more often than similarly situated whites in almost all counties studied.'"[70] During the early years of mandatory arrest laws, many police departments developed the practice of dual arrests, if both parties had any visible marks; the thought was that the primary perpetrator could be sorted out later back at the station. Thus, in many states, mandatory arrest policies resulted in a sharp increase in the number of women—and particularly minority race women—arrested for domestic violence: "In some areas a quarter or more of the domestic violence arrestees are women."[71] The practice of dual arrests can discourage battered women from calling for help. In the late 1990s, research revealed that while women might inflict defensive wounds or even initiate arguments early in the cycle of violence (so that beatings would be less severe), they were the primary perpetrators much less often than their male partners.[72] Now statutory or internal law enforcement directives in many jurisdictions call for police to decide who is the primary aggressor and arrest only that individual.

Policy reforms also targeted the low rates of prosecution and high dismissal rates of domestic violence offenses relative to other crimes of violence. In many domestic violence cases, victims refuse to testify. Victims are often uncooperative because they are threatened by their batterers. Traditionally, prosecutors would simply dismiss cases at the victim's request. Beginning in the early 1990s, prosecutors' offices in many jurisdictions adopted "no-drop" policies. The policies stemmed from good impulses: to aggressively pursue domestic violence cases and to treat them similarly to cases of stranger violence. A no-drop policy limits prosecutors' discretion to dismiss cases once charges are filed and commands prosecutors to pursue cases whether or not the victim wants to press charges. Prior to the adoption of no-drop policies, prosecutors dismissed between 50 and 80 percent of domestic violence cases; after the adoption of these mandatory prosecution policies, the rate of cases dismissed plummeted to between 10 and 34 percent.[73]

The aggressive prosecution policies adopted by different jurisdictions' domestic violence units vary in their content and the extent to which they compel victim participation:

> Pro-prosecution policies are often characterized as either "hard" or "soft" no-drop policies. Under "hard" policies, cases proceed regardless of the victim's wishes when there is enough evidence to go for-

ward. . . . The San Diego approach is to pursue every provable felony case, regardless of the victim's wishes. Under this city's hard no-drop policy, the prosecutor can request a continuance and a bench warrant when a victim fails to appear or cooperate if the case cannot be proved without her testimony.[74]

Anecdotal evidence indicates that most jurisdictions have "soft" policies, under which prosecutors do not compel victims to testify. Some of the softer policies require prosecutors to continue cases, using whatever evidence is available, such as a recording of a victim's 911 call or even the reliable testimony of a 911 operator to whom the victim spoke. A recent U.S. Supreme Court ruling that criminal defendants must have the opportunity to confront witnesses may mean that this evidence cannot be used in the case of a nonparticipating victim.[75] In jurisdictions with harder policies, mandatory prosecution may mean forced participation of the victim.

While most prosecutors use techniques of sympathy to encourage victim cooperation, some have used more coercive tactics, such as threatening the victim with prosecution or requiring the victim to come before a judge to explain her reasons for noncooperation. One study showed that 92 percent of prosecutors' offices issue subpoenas to compel victims to testify.[76] More than a few horror stories of forced participation have surfaced. One judge in Kentucky imposed fines of $100 and $200 on two different women who obtained protective orders against their batterers and then reestablished contact with them.[77] In 2005 a judge in a south-central Kansas town jailed a woman for several days for contempt of court when she refused to testify against the ex-boyfriend she had charged with raping her.[78]

Some theorists worry that no-drop policies will put victims at a greater risk of physical harm, while others charge that a batterer will have "less incentive to try to control or intimidate his victim once he realizes that she no longer controls the process."[79] A few studies indicate that mandatory intervention practices have increased prosecutions and even lowered rates of recidivism,[80] yet a number of theorists have urged caution in aggressive intervention until policymakers sort out the empirical evidence regarding the impact of these practices on victim safety.

Compulsory intervention policies raise a familiar tension for feminist legal theorists: the conflict between protecting women and permitting them autonomy. They limit the power of victims to make decisions about their own cases. Under a no-drop policy, the victim is stripped of the ability to choose whether to pursue a case after police are called (and the victim may not have been the one to place the call). One theorist made a strong version of the argument—that mandatory state intervention practices work their own kind of violence and that the dynamic set up by the state compelling victims to prosecute "comes dangerously close to mirroring the violence in the battering relationship."[81]

These mandatory intervention policies began to break down the public-private dichotomy in favor of state intervention in what had formerly been considered private matters. They prompted the recognition of domestic violence as a real crime—something deserving of prosecution. Yet these policies may counterpoise effective law enforcement solutions with the absence of women's autonomy to choose whether to pursue a case.

3. The Violence against Women Act

In 1994, after four years of hearings, President Clinton signed into law the landmark Violence against Women Act ("VAWA"), a federal statute intended to diminish violence against spouses and intimate partners.[82] VAWA, among other things, made domestic violence a federal crime for any perpetrator crossing state lines, increased the possible period of imprisonment for repeat domestic abuse offenders, and making civil protection orders issued in one state enforceable in any other state.[83]

One of the specific problems VAWA addressed was that of abused immigrant women, whose abusers often threatened them with deportation if they reported the abuse. The remedy contained in VAWA was a provision allowing battered immigrant spouses who are married to U.S. citizens or legal permanent residents, and who are of "good moral character," to self-petition for lawful permanent residence (rather than rely on an abusive spouse to sponsor them) or to request cancellation of their removal.[84]

The legislation also created a pool of federal funds for states to create shelters, prevention education, legal advocacy programs, and training programs for law enforcement officers, medical personnel, and judges about domestic violence and sexual assault.[85] It also created a twenty-four-hour toll-free national hotline for victims of domestic violence (1-800-799-SAFE), with specific help available for non-English speakers and the hearing-impaired.

Evidence exists that the incidence of domestic violence has declined, at least somewhat, in recent years, perhaps in response to the concerted efforts of various branches of the criminal justice system and domestic violence reformers.[86] One setback was a U.S. Supreme Court decision in 2000 holding unconstitutional one section of VAWA. In *United States v. Morrison,* the Supreme Court evaluated a civil remedy provision in VAWA that allowed victims of gender-motivated violence to sue their attackers in federal court.[87] The Court held that this provision violated the commerce clause because Congress did not have the power to protect victims of gender-based violence—a purely intrastate activity. Despite "four years of hearings" and a "mountain of data assembled by Congress . . . showing the effects of violence against women on interstate commerce,"[88] the Court held that "[g]ender-motivated crimes of violence are not, in any sense of the phrase, economic activity" and do not "substantially affect commerce."[89]

The Supreme Court's dismissive treatment of the mound of data assembled by Congress to demonstrate the impact on commerce from violence against women—the number of women affected; the time off from work; statistics on women fleeing violence, often between states; and the medical costs absorbed by states—was perhaps a greater symbolic than actual loss. Many victims of physical assault could still bring state tort suits, even if they did not have a federal remedy available. However, it is often the symbolic cultural messages about accountability that have had the most influence in diminishing violence against women.

D. Questions for Discussion

1. Many of the inequalities in the laws regarding rape and intimate violence reflect cultural norms. Reformers have attempted to challenge deeply entrenched social norms through changes in laws and policies. Take as just one example the Sexual Offense Prevention Policy adopted by Antioch College in 1990. It says that "[c]onsent

must be obtained verbally before there is any sexual contact or conduct," that "[s]ilence is never interpreted as consent," and that obtaining consent is an ongoing process during any sexual encounter: "If the level of sexual intimacy increases during an interaction (i.e., if two people move from kissing while fully clothed, which is one level, to undressing for direct physical contact, which is another level), the people involved need to express their clear verbal consent before moving to that new level."[90] The intent of the policy is to place on the person who wants to move to a different level of sexual intimacy the burden of obtaining a clear, verbal expression of consent from his or her partner. Although the Antioch policy was mocked by major news magazines and parodied in a *Saturday Night Live* skit, according to reporters who interviewed students about the policy's effects, "[p]eople are not having less sex, they are just talking about it."[91] Are perceptual gaps between men and women so vast that states should change their consent statutes along the lines of Antioch's policy to require explicit verbal consent or overt conduct indicating consent?[92]

At the other end of the spectrum is the question of whether American courts should permit defendants from other countries to raise "cultural defenses" to criminal charges. In one such case a California court allowed a Hmong man to introduce evidence that he reasonably believed the woman he was accused of raping consented to intercourse because her behavior fit with the traditional practices of bride capture. In another case, a Chinese immigrant admitted bludgeoning his wife with a hammer, but argued in defense that in his village, bludgeoning was the penalty for her infidelity. In the spirit of multicultural sensitivity, should courts permit the admission of relevant cultural evidence—or is this unacceptably prejudicial to victims or offensive to the policies underlying American criminal laws?[93]

2. Debates are occurring across a variety of disciplines about whether biological or sociocultural theories provide better explanations for the phenomenon of rape. At one end of the spectrum is a claim that rape is essentially a political act that institutionalizes subordination. Susan Brownmiller writes that rape is "nothing more or less than a conscious process of intimidation by which all men keep all women in a state of fear."[94] Intermediate positions suggest multiple

causes of sexual aggression and emphasize psychopathology, as well as social and cultural influences. At the other end of the continuum are theories of sociobiology. Camille Paglia, for example, argues that "[a]ggression and eroticism, in fact, are deeply intertwined. Hunt, pursuit, and capture are biologically programmed into male sexuality. Generation after generation, men must be educated, refined, and ethically persuaded away from their tendency toward anarchy and brutishness."[95]

In 2000, the biological camp received a boost with the publication of *A Natural History of Rape: Biological Bases of Sexual Coercion*. In their book, biology professor Randy Thornhill and anthropology instructor Craig T. Palmer draw on their observations about the mating of scorpion flies to construct an evolutionary view of rape. They offer two possible hypotheses: "[R]ape is either a 'specific adaptation' (that is, natural selection explicitly promoted the act) or a 'by-product of evolution' (there was no direct selection for rape; rather it is an accidental product of selection for, say, male promiscuity and aggression)."[96] The authors suggest that their theory could be used to reduce the incidence of rape if, before being allowed to obtain a driver's license, males must complete a course to learn how to restrain their sexual behaviors and females take a similar course to learn how to minimize their risks of being raped by not wearing revealing clothing or attending fraternity parties.[97]

Scientists immediately challenged the rape-as-evolutionary-adaptation hypothesis, noting that it does not account for oral or anal rape, rapes of men, rapes of children (29 percent of rape victims are under the age of eleven), mass genocidal rape of civilians during wartime, or rape of women outside of childbearing years. Academics from various disciplines argued instead that rape is a much more complex phenomenon than simply a product of evolution.[98] But even if the theory has some validity, does a biological explanation offer any argument for legal mitigation or perhaps reduced penalties? Even if the theory offers no legal excuse, is the biological view—or a slightly twisted interpretation of it, that rape is somehow natural—likely to sift into popular consciousness and perhaps influence juror behavior?

SUGGESTED READINGS

Kathryn Abrams, *Songs of Innocence and Experience: Dominance Feminism in the University*, 103 YALE L.J. 1533 (1994).

ALAS, POOR DARWIN: ARGUMENTS AGAINST EVOLUTIONARY PSYCHOLOGY (Hilary Rose & Steven Rose eds., 2002).

Alyson M. Cole, *"There Are No Victims in This Class": On Female Suffering and Anti-"Victim Feminism,"* 11 NWSA J. 72 (Mar. 22, 1999).

Anne M. Coughlin, *Excusing Women*, 82 CAL. L. REV. 1 (1994).

Alexander Detschelt, *Recognizing Domestic Violence Directed Towards Men: Overcoming Societal Perceptions, Conducting Accurate Studies, and Enacting Responsible Legislation*, 12 KAN. J.L. & PUB. POL'Y 249 (Winter 2003).

David Faigman & Amy Wright, *The Battered Woman Syndrome in the Age of Science*, 39 ARIZ. L. REV. 67 (1997).

Jill Elaine Hasday, *Contest and Consent: A Legal History of Marital Rape*, 88 CAL. L. REV. 1373 (2000).

RICHARD LEWONTIN, BIOLOGY AS IDEOLOGY: THE DOCTRINE OF DNA (1991).

Catharine A. MacKinnon, *Rape: On Coercion and Consent, in* TOWARD A FEMINIST THEORY OF THE STATE 171 (1989).

Martha R. Mahoney, *Legal Images of Battered Women: Redefining the Issue of Separation*, 90 MICH. L. REV. 1 (1991).

Leslye E. Orloff et al., *Battered Immigrant Women's Willingness to Call for Help and Police Response*, 13 UCLA WOMEN'S L.J. 43 (Fall/Winter 2003).

Ruthann Robson, *Lavender Bruises: Intra-lesbian Violence, Law and Lesbian Legal Theory*, 20 GOLDEN GATE U. L. REV. 567 (1990).

DIANA E. H. RUSSELL, RAPE IN MARRIAGE (1982).

ELIZABETH M. SCHNEIDER, BATTERED WOMEN AND FEMINIST LAWMAKING (2000).

Elizabeth A. Schneider, *Resistance to Equality*, 57 U. PITT. L. REV. 477 (1996).

STEPHEN J. SCHULHOFER, UNWANTED SEX: THE CULTURE OF INTIMIDATION AND THE FAILURE OF LAW (1998).

NOTES

1. National Center for Injury Prevention and Control, Centers for Disease Control, www.cdc.gov/ncipc/factsheets/ipvfacts.html (last visited Apr. 25, 2005).

2. Osa A. Benson, *The Intersection of Race, Sex, and Parental Status: Employment Discrimination Against Single Black Women with Children*, 4 HOW. SCROLL 37, 51 n.24 (1999).

3. Joe Heaney, *17.7 Million U.S. Women Report Rape or Assault*, BOSTON HERALD, Nov. 18, 1998, at 5.

4. *Staging a Revolution*, WILKES-BARRE TIMES LEADER, Feb. 18, 2004, *available at* 2004 WLNR 4255375.

5. MARY BECKER ET AL., FEMINIST JURISPRUDENCE: TAKING WOMEN SERIOUSLY 299 (2d ed. 2001) (quoting Michael Tackett, *Study Details Rape Victims' Obstacles*, CHI. TRIB., May 28, 1993, § 1, at 3).

6. Intimate partners include spouses, girlfriends/boyfriends, dating partners—past and present, straight and gay. Violence encompasses physical, sexual, and psychological force, or threats of these. *See* Centers for Disease Control, Intimate Partner Violence Surveillance, Aug. 5, 2004, http://www.cdc.gov/ncipc/pub-res/ipv_surveillance/05_UNIFORM_DEFINITIONS.htm.

7. Note, *To Have and to Hold: The Marital Rape Exemption and the Fourteenth Amendment*, 99 HARV. L. REV. 1255, 1256 (1986) (quoting 1 W. BLACKSTONE, COMMENTARIES *442).

8. Reva B. Siegel, *"The Rule of Love": Wife Beating as Prerogative and Privacy*, 105 YALE L.J. 2117, 2123, 2120 (1996).

9. Michelle J. Anderson, *Marital Immunity, Intimate Relationships, and Improper Inferences: A New Law on Sexual Offenses by Intimates*, 54 HASTINGS L.J. 1465, 1472 (2003).

10. *See, e.g.,* Kimberlé Crenshaw, *Mapping the Margins: Intersectionality, Identity Politics, and Violence Against Women of Color*, 43 STAN. L. REV. 1241, 1266 (1991) ("Historically, the dominant conceptualization of rape as quintessentially Black offender/white victim has left Black men subject to legal and extralegal violence.").

11. *See, e.g.,* Sally F. Goldfarb, *Violence Against Women and the Persistence of Privacy*, 61 OHIO ST. L.J. 1 (2000).

12. U.S. Dep't of Justice, Bureau of Justice Statistics, Intimate Partner Violence, May 2000, http://www.ojp.usdoj.gov/bjs/abstract/ipv.htm.

13. Joshua Mark Fried, *Forcing the Issue: An Analysis of the Various Standards of Forcible Compulsion in Rape*, 23 PEPP. L. REV. 1277, 1277 (1996).

14. 4 WILLIAM BLACKSTONE, COMMENTARIES ON THE LAWS OF ENGLAND 210.

15. State v. Thompson, 792 P.2d 1103 (Mont. 1990).

16. 164 U.S. 644, 648 (1897).

17. Michelle J. Anderson, *Reviving Resistance in Rape Law*, 1998 U. ILL. L. REV. 953, 962.

18. Fried, *supra* note 13, at 1292–94.

19. John Dwight Ingram, *Date Rape: It's Time for "No" to Really Mean "No,"* 21 AM. J. CRIM. L. 3, 12 (1993).

20. Matthew R. Lyon, Comment, *No Means No?: Withdrawal of Consent During Intercourse and the Continuing Evolution of the Definition of Rape*, 95 J. CRIM. L. & CRIMINOLOGY 277 (2004).

21. Morrison Torrey, *When Will We Be Believed? Rape Myths and the Idea of a Fair Trial in Rape Prosecutions,* 24 U.C. DAVIS L. REV. 1013, 1014–15 (1991).

22. *Id.* at 1026.

23. Dean G. Kilpatrick, National Violence Against Women Prevention Research Center, Rape and Sexual Assault, http://www.vawprevention.org/research/sa.shtml (last visited Mar. 4, 2005).

24. Michelle J. Anderson, *The Legacy of the Prompt Complaint Requirement, Corroboration Requirement, and Cautionary Instructions on Campus Sexual Assault,* 84 B.U. L. REV. 945, 976–77 (2004).

25. Beverly J. Ross, *Does Diversity in Legal Scholarship Make a Difference?: A Look at the Law of Rape,* 100 DICK. L. REV. 795, 846–47 (1996).

26. Christina E. Wells & Erin Elliott Motley, *Reinforcing the Myth of the Crazed Rapist: A Feminist Critique of Recent Rape Legislation,* 81 B.U. L. REV. 127, 152 (2001).

27. Kathleen Mahoney, *Theoretical Perspectives on Women's Human Rights and Strategies for Their Implementation,* 21 BROOK. J. INT'L L. 799, 821 (1996).

28. *See* David P. Bryden & Sonja Lengnick, *Rape in the Criminal Justice System,* 87 J. CRIM. L. & CRIMINOLOGY 1194 (1997).

29. Samuel H. Pillsbury, *Crimes Against the Heart: Recognizing the Wrongs of Forced Sex,* 35 LOY. L.A. L. REV. 845, 848 (2002).

30. Bureau of Justice Statistics, U.S. Dep't of Justice, Crime Characteristics (2003), http://www.ojp.usdoj.gov/bjs/cvict_c.htm (last visited Mar. 6, 2005).

31. SUSAN ESTRICH, REAL RAPE 4–5 (1987). *See also* Bryden & Lengnick, *supra* note 28, at 1263.

32. KATHERINE ROIPHE, THE MORNING AFTER: SEX, FEAR AND FEMINISM ON CAMPUS 79–81, 66, 54 (1993).

33. CAMILLE PAGLIA, SEX, ART AND AMERICAN CULTURE 51 (1992).

34. Katharine K. Baker, *Sex, Rape, and Shame,* 79 B.U. L. REV. 663, 683 (1999).

35. *Id.*

36. CHRISTINA HOFF SOMMERS, WHO STOLE FEMINISM? 4 (1994). *See also* NAOMI WOLF, FIRE WITH FIRE: THE FEMALE POWER AND HOW IT WILL CHANGE THE 21ST CENTURY (1993).

37. Deborah Tuerkheimer, *Recognizing and Remedying the Harm of Battering: A Call to Criminalize Domestic Violence,* 94 J. CRIM. L. & CRIMINOLOGY 959, 967 (2004).

38. EDWARD GONDOLF & ELLEN FISHER, BATTERED WOMEN AS SURVIVORS: AN ALTERNATIVE TO TREATING LEARNED HELPLESSNESS 92–93 (1988)

39. *Defending Our Lives* (Cambridge University Films 1993).

40. Sarah M. Buel, *Fifty Obstacles to Leaving, A.K.A., Why Abuse Victims Stay,* 28 COLO. LAW. 19, 19 (Oct. 1999).

41. Lenore E. A. Walker, The Battered Woman Syndrome (1984, 2d ed. 2000); Lenore E. A. Walker, The Battered Woman (1979).

42. Walker, The Battered Woman Syndrome, supra note 41, at 177.

43. Gondolf & Fisher, supra note 38.

44. Dee L. R. Graham & Edna Rawlings, Survivors of Terror: Battered Women, Hostages, and the Stockholm Syndrome, in Feminist Perspectives on Wife Abuse (Kerri Yllo & Michelle Bogard eds., 1988).

45. Joan L. Cordutsky, Note, True Equality for Battered Women: The Use of Self-Defense in Colorado, 70 Denv. U. L. Rev. 117, 118 n.8 (1992).

46. See, e.g., Janet A. Johnson et al., Death by Intimacy: Risk Factors for Domestic Violence, 20 Pace L. Rev. 263, 282–84 (2000).

47. Janet Parrish, Trend Analysis: Expert Testimony on Battering and Its Effects in Criminal Cases, 11 Wis. Women's L.J. 75 (1996).

48. Cheryl Hanna, No Right to Choose: Mandated Victim Participation in Domestic Violence Prosecutions, 109 Harv. L. Rev. 1849, 1879 (1996).

49. Alan M. Dershowitz, The Abuse Excuse and Other Cop-outs, Sob Stories, and Evasions of Responsibility 4, 321–41 (1994) (lumping the battered woman syndrome with, among other listed abuse excuses, the black rage defense, chronic lateness syndrome, football widow syndrome, the premenstrual stress syndrome defense, the Twinkie defense, and the UFO survivor syndrome).

50. Elizabeth Schneider, Battered Women & Feminist Lawmaking 280–81 (2000).

51. Sarah M. Teal, Domestic Violence: The Quest for Zero Tolerance in the United States and China: A Comparative Analysis of the Legal and Medical Aspects of Domestic Violence in the United States and China, 5 J. L. Society 313, 333 (2001).

52. Karin Wang, Comment, Battered Asian American Women: Community Responses from the Battered Women's Movement and the Asian American Community, 3 Asian L.J. 151, 162–63 (1996).

53. See Michelle Decasas, Protecting Hispanic Women: The Inadequacy of Domestic Violence Policy, 24 Chicano-Latino L. Rev. 56, 61 (2003) ("According to the 1996 Statistical Handbook of Violence in America . . . Hispanic women were domestic violence victims at a rate of 181 per 1,000 couples. In comparison, White women had a domestic violence rate of 117 per 1,000, and Black women had a rate of 166 per 1,000.").

54. See, e.g., Leah Riggins, Criminalizing Marital Rape in Indonesia, 24 B.C. Third World L.J. 421, 422 (2004) ("Indonesian law does not currently criminalize marital rape or domestic violence."); Manar Waheed, Note, Domestic Violence in Pakistan: The Tension Between Intervention and Sovereign Immunity in Human Rights Law, 29 Brook. J. Int'l L. 937, 942 (2004) ("[I]n Pakistan, the perpetrators of domestic violence go virtually unpunished. According to the

Pakistan Institute of Medical Sciences, over 90% of married women report being physically or sexually abused by their spouses.").

55. Donna Coker, *Enhancing Autonomy for Battered Women: Lessons from Navajo Peacemaking*, 47 UCLA L. REV. 1, 92–94, 103–4 (1999).

56. Kathleen Kingsbury, *Restraining Order Laws Fail to Protect Same Sex Victims*, Columbia News Serv., Mar. 1, 2004, http://www.jrn.columbia.edu/studentwork/cns/2004-03-01/572.asp.

57. Melody M. Crick, Comment, *Access Denied: The Problem of Abused Men in Washington*, 27 SEATTLE U. L. REV. 1035, 1045 (2004).

58. Tracy Chapman, *Behind the Wall*, TRACY CHAPMAN (SBK April Music, Inc. 1988).

59. Violence Against Women: Hearing Before the Subcommittee on Crime and Criminal Justice Before the House of Representatives, 102d Cong. 2d Sess. 98–100 (Feb. 6, 1992) (statement of Sandra Jean Sands, Office of General Counsel, Department of Health and Human Services).

60. Heather Fleniken Cochran, *Improving Prosecution of Battering Partners: Some Innovations in the Law of Evidence*, 7 TEX. J. WOMEN & L. 89, 95 n.39 (1997).

61. Federal Bureau of Investigation, Law Enforcement Officers Killed and Assaulted 1998, http://www.fbi.gov/ucr/killed/98killed.pdf, at 39, 79.

62. Lisa M. Martinson, *An Analysis of Racism and Resources for African-American Female Victims of Domestic Violence in Wisconsin*, 16 WIS. WOMEN'S L.J. 259, 272, 265–67 (2001).

63. Donna Coker, *Crime Control and Feminist Law Reform in Domestic Violence Law: A Critical Review*, 4 BUFF. CRIM. L. REV. 801, 852 (2001).

64. Linda L. Ammons, *Mules, Madonnas, Babies, Bathwater, Racial Imagery and Stereotypes: The African-American Woman and the Battered Woman Syndrome*, 1995 WIS. L. REV. 1003, 1019.

65. DeShaney v. Winnebago County Dep't. Soc. Servs., 489 U.S. 189, 195 (1989).

66. *See, e.g.*, Shipp v. McMahon, 234 F.3d 907, 913–14 (5th Cir. 2000), *cert. denied*, 532 U.S. 1052 (2001); Soto v. Flores, 103 F.3d 1056, 1066 (1st Cir. 1997). *But see* Navarro v. Block, 72 F.3d 712, 716 (9th Cir. 1995).

67. Linda G. Mills, *Killing Her Softly: Intimate Abuse and the Violence of State Intervention*, 113 HARV. L. REV. 550, 559 (1999).

68. Wayne A. Logan, *Criminal Law Sanctuaries*, 38 HARV. C.R.-C.L. L. REV. 321, 373 (2003).

69. Angela Corsilles, Note, *No-Drop Policies in the Prosecution of Domestic Violence Cases: Guarantee to Action or Dangerous Solution?*, 63 FORDHAM L. REV. 853, 854–55 n.8 (1994).

70. Holly Maguigan, *Wading into Professor Schneider's "Murky Middle*

Ground" Between Acceptance and Rejection of Criminal Justice Responses to Domestic Violence, 11 AM. U. J. GENDER SOC. POL'Y & L. 427, 431 n.16 (2003) (citing studies).

71. *Id.* at 442.

72. Susan L. Miller, *The Paradox of Women Arrested for Domestic Violence: Criminal Justice Professionals and Service Providers Respond,* 7 VIOLENCE AGAINST WOMEN 1339 (2001).

73. Corsilles, *supra* note 69, at 857.

74. Hanna, *supra* note 48, at 1863.

75. Crawford v. Washington, 541 U.S. 36 (2004).

76. Thomas L. Kirsch II, *Problems in Domestic Violence: Should Victims Be Forced to Participate in the Prosecution of their Abusers?,* 7 WM. & MARY J. WOMEN & L. 383, 402 n.126 398–407 (2001).

77. Francis X. Clines, *Judge's Domestic Violence Ruling Creates an Outcry in Kentucky,* N.Y. TIMES, Jan. 8, 2002, at A14.

78. Laura Bauer, *Reticent Accuser Gets Three Nights in Jail,* K.C. STAR, Mar. 19, 2005, at A10.

79. Hanna, *supra* note 48, at 1865.

80. Emily J. Sack, *Battered Women and the State: The Struggle for the Future of Domestic Violence Policy,* 2004 WIS. L. REV. 1657, 1673–74 n.85 (citing studies).

81. Mills, *supra* note 67, at 556.

82. Pub. L. No. 103-322, § 40701, 108 Stat. 1902, 1953 (1994).

83. 18 U.S.C. §§ 2261, 2247, 2265(a) (2000).

84. 8 C.F.R. § 204.2(c)) (1999). VAWA gives no relief for abused spouses who are married to either non-U.S. citizens or nonlegal permanent residents. See 8 C.F.R. § 204.2(c)(1)(iii).

85. 42 U.S.C. § 3796gg (Supp. 2002).

86. Jennifer R. Hagan, Comment, *Can We Lose the Battle and Still Win the War? The Fight Against Domestic Violence After the Death of Title III of the Violence Against Women Act,* 50 DEPAUL L. REV. 919, 969 n.364 (2001).

87. 42 U.S.C. § 13981 (2000).

88. 529 U.S. 598, 628–29 (2000) (Souter, J., dissenting).

89. 529 U.S. 598, 613.

90. Antioch College Sexual Offense Prevention Policy, http://www.antioch-college.edu/Community/survival_guide/campus_resources/sopsap.htm (last visited Apr. 10, 2005).

91. Baker, *supra* note 34, at 687.

92. *See, e.g.,* WIS. STAT. ANN. § 940.225 (2005).

93. *See* Neal A. Gordon, Note, *The Implications of Mimetics for the Cultural Defense,* 50 DUKE L.J. 1809, 1827–28 (2001) (discussing People v. Moua, No. 315972 (Cal. Super. Ct. Feb. 7, 1985)); Holly Maguigan, *Cultural Evidence and*

Male Violence: Are Feminist and Multiculturalist Reformers on a Collision Course in Criminal Courts?, 70 N.Y.U. L. Rev. 36, 37 (1995) (discussing People v. Dong Lu Chen, No. 87-7774 (N.Y. Dec. 2, 1988)).

94. SUSAN BROWNMILLER, AGAINST OUR WILL: MEN, WOMEN AND RAPE 15 (1975).

95. Camille Paglia, *Feminism Has Concealed the Truth About Rape*, AT-LANTA J. & CONST., Feb. 17, 1991, at H1.

96. Jerry A. Coyne & Andrew Barry, *Rape as an Adaptation*, NATURE, Mar. 9, 2000, at 121.

97. RANDY THORNHILL & CRAIG T. PALMER, A NATURAL HISTORY OF RAPE: BIOLOGICAL BASES OF SEXUAL COERCION (2000).

98. EVOLUTION, GENDER AND RAPE (Cheryl Brown Travis ed. 2003).

9

Feminist Legal Theory and Globalization

[A]ll the nations and people are too closely knit together today for any one of them to imagine that it can live apart. Peace has been said to be indivisible; so is freedom, so is prosperity now, and so also is disaster in this One World that can no longer be split into isolated fragments.
                                                                    Jawaharlal Nehru[1]

A. Introduction

Picture Carly Fiorina, a few years back, approaching the dais to address the NEC IEXPO technology conference in Tokyo, Japan. A woman still in her forties with intelligent eyes and a California smile, she was then the celebrated chief executive officer of Hewlett-Packard, a powerful company with 140,000 employees (6,000 in Japan) who do business in forty-three currencies and fifteen languages and "work[] in every time zone on Earth."[2] Fiorina, who spoke often of her company's responsibility to the world's rich and poor, told her Japanese audience that "our world today is on the cusp of . . . some of the greatest advances in history—advances that have the potential to change the way we live, work, and relate to one another."[3]

Now picture a young girl from Romania sitting quietly on the London subway.[4] She wears a red-flowered dress, a plastic jacket, and pink socks. She's thirteen years old, but with short hair and a slight frame, she easily passes for nine or ten. She is a prostitute. Six months ago the girl was flown from her home in Romania to London's Heathrow Airport. Her ticket was paid by a criminal gang promising financial opportunity. Once in London she was collected by other gang members and told she must repay their investment by having sex for money with twenty to thirty men every day for an indefinite period of time. Young girls like her do well in this city, she is told, because the clients—who are often traveling business executives—believe young girls like her are less likely to be infected with AIDS. For this child and others like her, "the greatest advances in history" cannot come soon enough.

Carly Fiorina and our nameless Romanian girl represent two drastically different views of how globalization affects women. Which is accurate? If the answer is "both," how can feminism take advantage of globalization's sunny side, while avoiding the shadow side? Is there such a thing—could there ever *be* such a thing—as global feminist legal theory? This chapter addresses that question.

B. Globalization and Its Discontents

Globalization describes the increased bonding of economies and cultures throughout the world. This evolution affects almost every aspect of life, including the status and welfare of women. The joining of national economies affects economic growth, consumption of natural resources, the mobility of workers, workplace standards, and access to foreign goods, technology, and medicine. Much of this development is positive. At the top end of the world's economy are a growing number of top-ranking female professionals involved in global economics and international relations. Count Ms. Fiorina among these. At lower economic levels, the Internet and other technological advances have greatly expanded the so-called informal labor sector, which includes cottage industries, tool and garment making, and small-scale manufacturing. More than 60 percent of the world's workers are employed in this sector; more than half of them are women.[5] Because of such changes, the global pay gap between men and women, which had remained stable for nearly a hundred years, is suddenly beginning to narrow.[6]

Advances in communication and the expansion of foreign travel now broadcast progressive values—democracy, equality, prosperity—to people once less familiar with those ideals. One example of this spread of information was the 1995 World Conference for Women in Beijing, which attracted thousands of activists from all over the world, including Uganda, Guyana, and Papua New Guinea.

But globalization has its downside, too. The same supercharged market that distributes medicines, technology, and jobs also propagates illegal trade, cutthroat competition, and cultural erosion. Women, who often represent the most vulnerable group in their countries, are particularly threatened by such ills. Thus the expansion of U.S. oil companies in Nigeria has led to the destruction of village forests and creeks, which women rely upon to provide resources for their families. (In 2002, Nigerian women occupied a Chevron-Texaco terminal for ten days in protest.) Throughout the developing world, the situation of farmworkers grows increasingly desperate as these women—for the large majority are women—attempt to compete internationally with heavily subsidized American and European agricultural goods.

C. In Search of a Global Feminist Theory

The plight of women in the world is disturbing. Women make up 70 percent of the world's 1.3 billion absolute poor. Women account for two-thirds of the world's working hours, but they earn only one-tenth of the world's income and own less than one-tenth of the world's property. Other aspects of human welfare are also compromised, as women often do not receive their proportional share of food, medicine, or education (most women in the world are illiterate).[7] Add to this, sex-based infanticide in rural China, dowry-related deaths in India, episodes of violence against women everywhere, and one begins to wonder whether being female, itself, threatens one's survival in the world. Indeed, Harvard economist Amartya Sen finds that the global population ratio of females to males is significantly *lower* than biology would suggest. According to Sen, this is because more than 100 million young women and girls die before their existence on the planet can even be counted.[8]

How can feminist legal theory address these concerns? Global conceptions of feminist legal theory are just taking shape, but the central questions are already clear. And they resemble the same questions we have seen in other contexts. What do we mean when we speak of women's equality (similar treatment, preferential treatment, something in between)? How can the public-private distinction transform legal thinking to improve women's welfare? How can feminists pursue the universal interests of women (assuming they exist) while at the same time respecting a variety of cultural and religious beliefs? Consider each question in turn.

1. Defining equality and women's well-being

In the West, feminist theory is sometimes split between those advocating equal rights and those advocating equal welfare. This contest arises in global feminism, too, but against a backdrop of cultural variety. From the rights perspective, one would focus on global standards of formal equality between men and women based, perhaps, on treaties or other forms of international law. Western human rights activists have taken this tack by using international human rights laws to challenge ritualized genital cutting, domestic abuse, and other forms of physical violence.[9] The strategy has succeeded for two main reasons. First, the universality of violence against women has united feminists from around the world and channeled their energies toward particular goals. Second, the movement has been able to take advantage of an already developed legal structure (international human rights law) to further goals specific to women.

But the international movement against gender-based physical violence distracts us from what is perhaps a larger, but less defined, problem—economic impoverishment in developing countries. How can legal equality on its own free women from the yokes of poverty and ignorance? For some global feminists, the negotiation for "equal treatment" cannot begin until Victor removes his jackboot from Maria's neck. In this way some global feminists take up the banner of dominance theory.

2. The public-private distinction

To say that something is public or private is to make a statement about jurisdiction. American law, as we have seen, is more likely to regulate public than private activities. Generations ago, when sexual harassment was seen as a personal issue between two workers, law's jurisdiction was limited. When, at last, courts acknowledged the connection between sexual harassment and economic discrimination, law's jurisdiction expanded. This same jurisdictional debate exists within other countries. But globalization gives rise to new jurisdictional debates in which "public" and "private" assume two other levels of meaning.

On one such level, the public-private distinction can describe the line between sovereign nations and private corporations. International law does not typically apply to the actions of the latter. Rather, as it is sometimes said, international law is a tool *of* nation-states, *by* nation-states, *for* nation-states. In this sense, the global economy is becoming increasingly privatized. The influence that multinational companies have on the world is growing, while the practical ability of public governments to regulate corporate action is shrinking. Consider that just over half of the world's one hundred largest economies are corporations, not countries.[10] Unregulated, private markets tend to disadvantage marginalized people, driving them further into poverty and practical servitude. In the "new" economy, this supporting class is often made up of women, particularly women of color.

The welfare of workers, once seen as part of the public mission of individual nations or public international law, is increasingly becoming more of a private (and essentially voluntary) responsibility of global companies. In 1996, when the public learned that clothing marketed under Kathie Lee Gifford's name was being produced in sweatshops in the United States and in Central America, consumers responded with threats of boycotts, not lawsuits. To address the welfare of female workers in the apparel industry, the Clinton administration then helped initiate a private code of best practices, which private corporations were encouraged to adopt.[11] In this sense, globalization poses important challenges to feminists by eroding the power of government and, by extension, the power of *law*, which has become a crucial tool for improving the lives of women.

On a second level of meaning, "public" might instead represent the "international community" (made up of nations, corporations, and nongovernmental organizations), and "private" would refer to a single nation. In 1995 the Fourth Conference of Women emphasized the power of nations and global nongovernmental organizations to establish universal standards for women's rights, incorporated in multinational treaties, which would transcend the laws of a particular nation or culture. If such universal standards are adhered to long enough by an adequate number of countries, it is possible in some circumstances that they could evolve into "customary" international law, applicable even to countries that have never accepted these standards. Essentially this is a debate about the sovereignty of a nation, just as the issue of, say, spousal abuse, was once seen by some as a debate about the sovereignty of the home.

3. Feminism and multiculturalism

As discussed previously, American feminists often address multiculturalism through the principle of antiessentialism. According to this principle, feminists should be sensitive to different experiences and needs of women across lines of class and gender so as not to marginalize their sisters in the movement. The challenge of building a "feminism for all" grows exponentially when once considers the even greater diversity of women throughout the industrialized and developing world.

At the international level, feminist concerns for diversity are not just larger, but often reveal a difference in emphasis as well. In the United States, multiculturalists often complain that feminism excludes and ignores outsider women. Sojourner Truth's "Ain't I a Woman?" narrative captures a sentiment perhaps felt by generations of women who for various reasons found themselves outside the mainstream feminism of their eras. Third world women also complain that Western feminism pays little attention to their circumstances. But an equally important debate concerns the complaints that third world women raise when those Western feminists *do* pay attention. Too often, these critics say, Western feminists treat third world women as victims of backward, violent, and patriarchal cultures, whose societies need to be rehabilitated, which is to say "Westernized." This view is often popularized in the Western press with stories of third world immigrant women being abused by their husbands out of what is suggested to be cultural tradition.

Third world feminists do not deny that sexism, including gender-based violence, exists in the developing world. Rather, they argue that these injustices should not be used as shorthand to define their entire cultures. Practices and belief systems in the developing world may have much to contribute to feminist action in these regions and beyond. Besides, blatant sexism and cultural oppression are hardly alien to the West, which is after all the birthplace of Botox, breast implants, and stiletto heels.

D. Case Studies

The best way to understand these issues against the backdrop of globalization is to put them into context. Thus we examine feminist legal theory as it applies in three often-discussed global feminist issues: female genital cutting, international trafficking in women and girls, and economic development.

1. Female genital cutting

Before going further, we must define the object of discussion, a step that itself raises controversy. The World Health Organization refers to the excision of parts of the female genitalia as "female genital mutilation," a term with obvious negative connotations. The phrase replaces the more euphemistic "female circumcision," a term human rights activists reject as both medically and metaphorically inaccurate. Some feminists, particularly those in non-Western countries, prefer the more value-neutral "female genital surgery." Still, Jomo Kenyatta, a pan-African leader and anthropologist, suggests Westerners use the Kikuyu word *irua,* as a way of acknowledging the practice's cultural context. Mindful that no term will please everyone, we will refer to "female genital cutting," or "FGC," a term increasingly employed by sociologists and journalists.

Although FGC takes several forms, most discussion focuses on two types, which together make up 80 percent of all FGC practiced in the world. The first type involves excision of the prepuce with or without excision of part or all of the clitoris; the second type involves excision of the prepuce and clitoris together with the partial or total excision of the labia minora. It is estimated that worldwide between 100 and 132 million girls and women have been subjected to FGC. An additional 2 million girls are believed to undergo the procedure every year. FGC is most widespread in twenty-eight African countries, including, most notably, Nigeria, Egypt, and Ethiopia. The procedure also occurs to a lesser extent in the Middle East, Asia, Australia, New Zealand, North America, and Europe.

Communities that practice FGC do so for a variety of stated reasons, including cultural initiation, religious demand, family honor, hygiene, the protection of virginity, the prevention of promiscuity, improved fertility, and enhanced sexual pleasure for the husband. While

FGC is most common in Muslim communities, it is also practiced in some Christian and Jewish ones. Methods of FGC range from the medically primitive (more likely) to the medically advanced (less likely) and can include the use of special knives, scissors, pieces of glass, razors, or scalpels. Medical complications from FGC are common and include uncontrolled bleeding, infection, extreme pain, shock, damage to the urethra or anus, and future psychological disorders.

What does globalization have to do with FGC? Globalization, it is fair to say, has not expanded the practice of FGC or intensified its woeful effects. But globalization is certainly the reason that activists, medical professionals, and feminists from all over the world are now talking about this practice, which, after all, has been a feature of some societies for many generations. It was not until large waves of immigration from African countries to Western countries, stirred by an international economy, that Westerners were forced to confront the issue legally. Usually this occurred when a female immigrant would cite the fear of FGC upon return to her native country as grounds for political asylum or when Western officials would discover FGC being performed in their own communities. Thus globalization can be credited with raising awareness about the prevalence of FGC and igniting the debate about whether it is appropriate to try to force change of other countries' cultures and traditions.

Many Western feminists argue that FGC constitutes a violation of international human rights, as expressed in global treaties and other sources of international law. This view holds that FGC is morally wrong because it breaches universally recognized principles, which include the right to equal treatment on the basis of sex, a child's right to security, the right to bodily integrity, the right to health, and freedom from torture.[12] Following this rationale, the 1995 Platform for Action of the World Conference on Women in Beijing urged governments and human rights organizations to initiate laws, educational plans, and medical programs to eliminate FGC throughout the world.

The international campaign against FGC suggests a number of themes we have seen before. First, it shows how a practice that might initially be seen as a private aspect of family or culture can be transformed into an issue of public and even international concern. Keep in mind that FGC is not required or performed by any government actor, and that most procedures are performed by other women with the consent of the subject. These distinctions raise questions about whether international law should attempt to reach beyond a government's official behavior and attempt to affect the behavior and customs of a government's private citizens.

Second, the campaign shows how the principle of "equal treatment" can be used to build an international coalition against a practice that, while painful and unsafe, might otherwise have been ignored by Western nations. FGC is not only physical mutilation, the argument goes, it is physical mutilation targeted *on the basis of sex*. Note that the success of this argument depends on activists' ability to differentiate FGC from other types of excisions or "mutilations" that are directed exclusively toward males. (While male circumcisions do not approach the invasiveness of FGC, what of more extreme male initiation rites like the ingestion of hallucinogens, physical scarring, or dangerous confrontations in the wild?)

Third, the international campaign against FGC uses the concept of human rights to *universalize* a rule against FGC, regardless of tradition, culture, or geography. The universalist approach presents both strengths and weaknesses. The upside is that universalism provides moral clarity, which helps build and energize international coalitions. This explains why more than ten conventions and treaties now voice disapproval of FGC. The attempt to impose a single tradition invites charges of oversimplification and moral arrogance, factors that breed resentment among the very women Westerners are trying to help.

For instance, a common complaint of African feminists is that Western human rights activists have essentialized the motivations behind FGC to either superstition or passive submission to male control. Such oversimplification, they argue, undervalues the sophistication of their cultures and ignores important connections (such as the connection between FGC, marriage, and economic well-being) that must be understood to change long-term behavior. A second complaint argues that human rights activists have focused on the right against FGC at the expense of the broader and more critical rights to health care, education, and clean water.

In response to this criticism, some Western feminists have begun to advance an "integrationist" approach, which seeks eradication of FGC through a slower, more culturally sensitive process that emphasizes grassroots coalitions between Western and non-Western activists and that attends to the broad needs of individual communities where FGC is practiced.

2. International trafficking in women and girls

The international trafficking of persons represents a complex human rights issue. In international law, the term refers to the illegal and highly profitable practices of recruiting, transporting, or selling human beings into all forms of forced labor or servitude. The U.S. State Department estimates that each year seven hundred thousand to four million persons—most of them women and girls—are trafficked worldwide. An estimated fifty thousand women and children are trafficked annually into the United States. Noting that more than thirty million children have been traded over the last few decades in Asia alone, UNICEF's Kul Gautman has called such trafficking "the largest slave trade in history."[13] Many of these people are forced to work in brothels, prostitution rings, or the pornographic film industry. Others are funneled into nonsexual markets to serve as domestic laborers or textile workers.

Typically the victim of trafficking is an economic refugee who has paid to be smuggled into another country with promises of a better life, only to find later that her fortunes have taken a terrible turn. In the sex trade, trafficked women are often beaten and raped before being transferred from one master or brothel owner to the next. Asian prostitutes in the United States and Japan may sell for up to $20,000 each. The wheels of human trafficking are greased by the new global economy. As the global demand for cheap sports shoes and sexual entertainment escalates, so does the need for illegal and often forced labor. Old-fashioned government corruption also plays a role: it is not uncommon for state officials to facilitate human trafficking by accepting bribes or falsifying travel and work documents. The trafficking industry undoubtedly also benefits from the desperate status of women in many parts of the world.

How do national and international laws address this tragedy? As already noted, virtually every country in the world considers human trafficking a crime. Why does that not solve the problem? Feminists offer two explanations. First, the laws of many countries focus on finding and punishing the illegal laborer, rather than the illegal trafficker.

In Japan, for example, Thai sex workers who have been trafficked into the country are regularly detained as illegal aliens, deported, and prohibited from reentering Japan for five years. In some ways Japan's legal response is easy to administer—seizing the laborer is usually easier than seizing the trader. But its strategy does little to control the industry's suppliers (traffickers) and consumers (Japanese and foreign businessmen). More significantly, Japan's policy ignores that sex laborers are themselves the greatest victims of the sex trade. As feminists must continually assert, "Women are people too." Human trafficking therefore represents a global human rights problem.

The transformation of human trafficking from "social nuisance" to "human rights abuse" follows directly from dominance theory, which emphasizes the role of sexual oppression in human activity. With this insight, it is a short step for feminists to identify a second weakness in law's traditional handling of human trafficking: the lack of global uniformity in attacking the problem. If human trafficking is a violation of *universally* accepted rights, than surely it is deserving of a *universal* standard of law enforcement.

To this end, the General Assembly of the United Nations recently approved the Protocol to Prevent, Suppress and Punish Trafficking in Persons, Especially Women and Children ("Trafficking Protocol"), which is now open for ratification. The Trafficking Protocol treaty requires ratifying countries to criminalize human trafficking under a uniform definition, to share law enforcement information with other countries, and to strengthen border controls. Significantly, the treaty holds that a victim's consent to trafficking abuse is irrelevant in defining the crime. In a provision that proved controversial with wealthy nations, the treaty encourages destination countries to allow trafficking victims to remain in the country either temporarily or permanently. (Poor nations wanted this provision to protect their citizens, who are more likely to be victims of trafficking; wealthy nations feared the provision would encourage more illegal immigration.) In addition, the United States adopted the Victims of Trafficking and Violence Protection Act in 2000.[14] This law requires the U.S. State Department to each year evaluate the antitrafficking efforts of eighty-nine countries whose citizens are at special risk.

Solving problems through international law almost always raises issues of national sovereignty: by definition, whenever a country promises to meet an obligation by treaty, it is giving up its sovereign right to do otherwise. With human trafficking, nations that join the Trafficking Protocol or that wish to be seen as responsible friends of the United States under the Victims of Trafficking Act must expose at least some of their lawmaking activities to outside opinion.

It is here where difficult privacy and cultural issues come into play. Greece, for instance, claims to be adamantly against sexual trafficking, but it resists the United States' definition of the practice, which includes "forced marriage," a cultural mainstay the Greek government is not prepared to criminalize. In addition, Greece does not agree that *nonsexual* servitude—indentured laborers in textile mills, young girls forced to sell flowers on the street—should be treated as harshly as the sexual variety. In its view, the United States and the United Nations go too far in attempting to regulate the internal laws and familial customs of Greek citizens. The feminist response to this charge is that where human rights are at stake, the personal (or, in the case of a nation, the "domestic") becomes the political.

3. Economic development

Beneath these issues is the problem of economic resources. It is women's comparative lack of financial resources that limits their choices in family and economic matters and that forces them to endure the indignities of forced labor, physical abuse, and intellectual impoverishment. Thus it is not surprising to see many feminists now emphasizing global economic development as the key to women's liberation.

This emphasis indicates a recognition that in the developing world, "equal rights" are, by themselves, unlikely to improve the lives of most women. One reason is that among the very poor the promise of rights may not be as immediately important as the promise of material goods. What benefit does the right of equal pay bring to an Indian widow who may not leave her house under penalty of stoning? What is the right to education to a Bangladeshi girl who spends ten hours each day preparing meals and collecting water?

A second reason lies in the deep chasm between "the law on the books" and "the law as applied." India's constitution, for instance, bans sex discrimination in all forms, officially extending equal rights much further than does the U.S. Constitution. But after more than fifty years of formal equality, women and girls in India have yet to receive anything near their proportionate share of food, medical care, job opportunities, or education. Today the literacy rate among Indian women is 40 percent as compared with 64 percent for Indian men. The promise of formal equal treatment has not translated into substantive equality.

Globalization itself provides some benefit by facilitating the transfer of jobs, goods, medicine, and technology from one country to another. The information and service economies have brought jobs to millions of women—the customer service representative you talk to on the phone is now almost as likely to be stationed in Mumbai as in Topeka. Saskia Sassen, of Columbia University, credits globalization with a "growing feminization" of job markets and business opportunities. This trend, which has particularly helped immigrant women, leads to more wealth, greater social autonomy, and stronger influence over family decisions—when mothers earn more, fathers *listen* more.

But globalization's rising tide has not raised all boats. Instead, the global economy more accurately resembles a system of locks in which some boats rise swiftly and others continue to sink. According to UN figures, 70 percent of all direct investment in developing countries goes into fewer than a dozen countries, most of them middle-income countries. Only 6 percent of direct investment goes to Africa, and only 2 percent goes to the forty-seven poorest nations. And while wealth within a country is never divided equally among males and females, countries with equivalent wealth can vary significantly in their degree of gender equity. India and Kenya, for instance, have the same gross national product per capita, but the share of earned income that goes to women in India is 26 percent, compared with 42 percent in Kenya.

In the face of such challenges, reformers have proposed an array of solutions that draw from different strains of feminist legal theory. To begin with, the Convention on the Elimination of All Forms of Discrimination Against Women ("CEDAW") requires all ratifying nations to guarantee equal pay for equal work and encourages member states to craft budgets that direct equal amounts of spending to the needs of men and of women. (CEDAW has been ratified by more than 160 countries, but the United States is not among them.) Both of these approaches—one emphasizing equality of opportunity, the other equality of result—follow principles of equal treatment theory.

But the problem appears more complicated than this. Law professor Barbara Stark observes that the new globalized labor force is really a combination of two labor forces: the hypermobile professionals who tote Blackberrys, sip lattés, and put up at the nearest Intercontinental Hotel, and the class of local support staff who sweep the floors, serve the espresso, and make the beds. This latter set of workers, most of whom are women, labor in a market nearly invisible to the eye of government and as a result are often poorly paid and poorly protected. Within this second economy, we must also include the expanding, but equally neglected, class of women now profiting only modestly from the sale through intermediaries of home-based handicrafts (sold on the Internet!) and small-scale farming. The first, professional economy, to which Carly Fiorina contributes, seems amply suited to take care of itself. But the second, shadow economy could become another tool of oppression if societies fail to provide protections for such workers and for their capital investments (their tools, inventory, and machinery).

Thus many international women's groups have begun projects to help indigenous women form farming or crafts-making co-ops where they can collectively pursue personal goals and leverage business assets. UN agencies, such as the United Nations Developmental Fund for Women ("UNIFEM"), and private organizations, such as OXFAM, sponsor extensive "microcredit" programs that allow women to secure business loans. In countries like Bangladesh, poor women have pooled their meager resources to form "microbanks" to enable each other to make capital investments. Such programs perform a kind of modern-day alchemy—transforming women's unrecognized assets in the informal economy into income-generating capital. This recognition—even celebration—of the homespun economy should remind us of cultural feminism, which seeks to reward women's significant contributions to home and community even when those contributions have not traditionally appeared on the (male) accountant's balance sheet.

But perhaps one of the most fascinating feminist projects to come out of the globalization debate draws on postmodern feminist theory. Recall that postmodern theory emphasizes practical effects in a local context over universal principles. This perspective has already swung the spotlight from issues of violations of universal human rights (FGC, human trafficking) to the broader and more basic challenge of satisfying women's practical and material needs (economic development). In comparing the universal rights approach to the practical well-being approach, we have identified important weaknesses in relying only on official rights, namely, that official rights are not always enforced and that they do not, without serious prodding, extend into private or unofficial areas of life. Cultural feminism provides the argument for extending protective rights into the unofficial economy and for developing international support groups to invigorate the unofficial economy.

But an important question remains: How do we know if these reforms are making progress? Or, put another way, how do we measure improvement in women's practical well-being? Traditional economic approaches fall short when measuring women's quality of life in developing nations. As previously noted, gross national product fails to account for income distributions between men and women. Even if the distributions were known, differences in material needs and buying power across nations would not allow us to compare accurately a woman's quality of life in Toronto against that of her counterpart in Nairobi. What is needed is a more localized and contextual approach.

Philosopher and law professor Martha Nussbaum has helped fashion such a model, called the "capabilities approach," which attempts to measure women's well-being based on their practical ability to do or enjoy certain essential activities. The capabilities approach is now regularly employed by the Human Development Reports of the United Nations Development Programme. Professor Nussbaum's list of minimal capabilities includes (among others) the ability to obtain food and shelter, to control one's body, affiliate with others, seek employment, and own property. This list suggests protection not only from extreme poverty, but from many other ills as well, including FGC and human trafficking. Despite the model's internationalist perspective, it eventually circles back to a concept of universal rights based very much on Western tradition. Whether such an approach amounts to an improved measure of women's well-being or an inappropriate endorsement of a particular cultural perspective will no doubt be the subject of future debate.

E. Questions for Discussion

1. Feminists still disagree about what to call FGC. Why does it matter? What values are suggested by the terms "female genital cutting," "female genital mutilation," "female circumcision," "female genital surgery," and *irua*? What would *you* call it?
2. What would a substantive understanding of equality require in terms of governmental policies that a procedural guarantee of equality would not reach?
3. Is there a way to develop a concept of universal rights or basic principles of respect without imposing Western political ideals on non-Western cultures?

SUGGESTED READINGS

Jim Chen, *Globalization and Its Losers,* 9 MINN. J. GLOBAL TRADE 157 (2000).

Martha Chen et al., *Counting the Invisible Workforce: The Case of Homebased Workers,* 27 WORLD DEV. 603 (1999).

THOMAS L. FREIDMAN, THE LEXUS AND THE OLIVE TREE (1999).

MARGARET E. KECK & KATHRYN SIKKINK, ACTIVISTS BEYOND BORDERS: ADVOCACY NETWORKS IN INTERNATIONAL POLITICS 171–72 (1998).

Hope Lewis, *Between Irua and "Female Genital Mutilation": Feminist Human Rights Discourse and the Cultural Divide,* 8 HARV. HUM. RTS. J. 1 (1995).

MARTHA C. NUSSBAUM, WOMEN AND HUMAN DEVELOPMENT: THE CAPABILITIES APPROACH (2000).

SUSAN MOLLER OKIN, IS MULTICULTURALISM BAD FOR WOMEN? (1999).

Amartya Sen, *More Than 100 Million Women Are Missing,* N.Y. REV. BOOKS, Dec. 20, 1990, at 61.

Barbara Stark, *Women and Globalization: The Failure and Postmodern Possibilities of International Law,* 33 VAND. J. TRANSNAT'L L. 303 (2000).

Symposium, *Feminism and Globalization: The Impact of the Global Economy on Women and Feminist Theory,* 4 IND. J. GLOBAL LEGAL STUD. 1 (1996) (featuring articles by Saskia Sassen, Zillah Eisenstein, and Aihwa Ong).

Leti Volpp, *Feminism Versus Multiculturalism,* 101 COLUM. L. REV. 1181 (2001).

UNITED NATIONS DEVELOPMENT FUND FOR WOMEN (UNIFEM), http://www.unifem.undp.org/.

ALICE WALKER, POSSESSING THE SECRETS OF JOY (1992).

WORLD HEALTH ORGANIZATION, GENDER AND WOMEN'S HEALTH DEPARTMENT, http://www.who.int/frh-whd/FGM/index.htm.

NOTES

1. Speech delivered in the Constituent Assembly, New Delhi, India, Aug. 14, 1947, on the eve of independence, *quoted in* MARTHA C. NUSSBAUM, WOMEN AND HUMAN DEVELOPMENT: THE CAPABILITIES APPROACH 9–10 (2000).

2. Carly Fiorina, Remarks at NEC IEXPO, Tokyo, Japan, Dec. 12, 2002. Ms. Fiorina stepped down as Hewlett-Packard's CEO in February 2005.

3. *Id.*

4. The description is a fictional composite based on true accounts.

5. Saskia Sassen, *Toward a Feminist Analytics of the Global Economy,* 4 IND. J. GLOBAL LEGAL STUD. 7, 524 (1996)

6. Zafiris Tzannotos, *Women and Labor Market Changes in the Global Economy: Growth Helps, Inequalities Hurt and Public Policy Matters,* 27 WORLD DEV. 551, 567 (1999).

7. About UNIFEM, http://www.unifem.und.org/about.htm (quoting Noeleen Heyzer, Director of UNIFEM) (last visited Sept. 12, 2005).

8. Amartya Sen, *More Than 100 Million Women Are Missing,* N.Y. REV. OF BOOKS, Dec. 20, 1990, at 61.

9. MARGARET E. KECK & KATHRYN SIKKINK, ACTIVISTS BEYOND BORDERS: ADVOCACY NETWORKS IN INTERNATIONAL POLITICS 171–72 (1998).

10. Sarah Anderson & John Cavanagh, *The Top 200: The Rise of Global Corporate Power* (1996), http://www.ips-dc.org/downloads/Top_200.pdf.

11. *See* Steven Greenhouse, *Groups Reach Agreement for Curtailing Sweatshops,* N.Y. TIMES, Nov. 5, 1998, at A20.

12. These rights are expressed specifically in the United Nations Charter (sexual equality), the Convention on the Rights of the Child, the Universal Declaration of Human Rights (bodily integrity and health), and the Convention Against Torture, and Other Cruel, Inhuman or Degrading Treatment or Punishment. Many of these rights are also guaranteed in other sources of international law.

13. *Asia's Sex Trade Is "Slavery,"* BBC NEWS, Feb. 20, 2003, http://news.bbc.co.uk/2/hi/asia-pacific/2783655.stm (quoting Kul C. Gautman, Deputy Executive Director, UNICEF).

14. Pub. L. No. 106-386, 114 Stat. 1543 (2000).

Index

Abortion: anti-abortion violence, 138–140, 158n26; Freedom of Access to Clinic Entrances Act, 10, 27, 47–48, 58, 74, 80, 95, 108, 111–112, 128, 131, 139, 144, 201, 226; mandatory counseling, 131–132, 157; minors, 136, 144–145; Nuremburg Files website, 139–140; "partial birth" abortions, 136–137, 142, 158; pro-life feminism, 143–144; right-to-life movement, 135–36, 138–139; spousal notification, 131, 140, 142; statistics, 159; TRAP laws, 134–135; Voices Brief, 141–142; waiting period, 131–132

Accommodation, 21–22, 62, 84, 92, 113

Affirmative action, 28, 95, 112

African Americans, 91, 96, 110, 120, 145, 157, 194, 209

Alfieri, Anthony, 28, 43

American Association of University Women (AAUW), 89, 100, 116, 121, 123, 126

American Civil Liberties Union (ACLU), 8, 16, 21, 62, 93, 152, 155

Anthony, Susan B., 3, 5, 144

Assimilation, 22, 121

Athletics, 98, 107, 110–113, 115, 120, 125–126

Atwood, Margaret, 44, 55, 148, 161

Autonomy and choice, 9, 19–20, 65–66, 81, 107, 141, 150, 152, 154, 176, 186, 188–189, 201, 209, 224

Baby M., In re., 148, 151–153, 161

Balkin, Jack, 35, 44, 83

Bartlett, Katharine, 46, 52, 55–56, 81, 121

Bell, Derek, 28, 40, 72, 84, 158

Bender, Leslie, 15

Biological differences, 17, 18–19, 21–22, 28, 64

Boys: minority race, 90, 102; socialization of, 86–92, 116–114

Bradwell v. Illinois, 4, 47, 58

Brown v. Board of Education, 84, 93

Butler, Judith, 37, 44

California Federal Savings & Loan Association v. Guerra, 13, 21

Caregiving, 20, 22, 25, 61, 75, 84, 175

Choice, 39, 66, 74, 151. See also Autonomy and choice

Class and economic disparities, 37, 50–53, 57, 87, 144–145, 150–151, 160, 196, 216, 225

Cohen v. Brown University, 111–113
Comparable worth theory, 76–77
Consciousness-raising, 13, 25, 45,
    49–50, 54
Conservative political groups, 6–7,
    58, 64, 118, 142
Contextual reasoning, 13, 45, 48, 50,
    53
Coverture, 4, 163–164
Craig v. Boren, 41
Criminal law, and self-defense, 19
Critical legal studies, 27
Critical race feminism, 8, 26–27, 40, 54
Critical theory, 41
Cultural feminism, 8–10, 12, 18, 20,
    23, 66, 119, 141, 144, 150, 186,
    225–226

*Davis v. Monroe County Board of Ed-
ucation*, 117
de Beauvoir, Simone, 15
Declaration of Sentiments, 2
Deconstruction, 36–38. *See also* Post-
    modern feminism
Derrida, Jacques, 36
Dershowitz, Alan, 193, 208
Dewey, John, 34
Difference theory, 18–22, 66. *See also*
    Cultural feminism
Domestic violence, 23, 26, 43, 49,
    55–56, 132, 142, 180, 189,
    193–199, 201–202, 205, 207–210;
    battered intimate partner syn-
    drome, 190–194, 205, 208–209;
    battered intimate partners who kill
    their abusers, 192–194; cultural
    defenses, 203, 210; immigrant
    women, 194, 201, 205; lesbians
    and gay men, 195; mandatory ar-
    rests and prosecution, 198–200;
    police response, 195–201, 205;
    racialized effects, 196; self-defense,

189; survivor theory, 191, 193. *See
    also* Violence Against Women Act,
    196, 201, 210
Dominance theory, 8–9, 12, 22–25,
    40, 119, 150, 186, 215, 222
"Don't Ask, Don't Tell" policy, 11,
    25, 30, 79, 85
Dothard v. Rawlinson, 60
Dress codes, 81
Due process, 79, 131
Dworkin, Andrea, 13, 24, 153, 156,
    162

Ecofeminism, 8, 12, 31–33, 43; envi-
    ronmental justice movement,
    32–33, 40, 44, 54, 56
Economic development, 218, 223,
    226. *See also* Female genital cutting
Education: coeducation, 86–89, 92,
    94–96, 99–100, 102, 105,
    120–121; Department of Educa-
    tion, 98–100, 105, 110, 113, 117;
    diversity, 96, 98, 100, 119, 122;
    higher education, 62, 87, 91,
    120–121; inequalities in, 89, 91,
    94, 109; segregation in, 91, 93–95,
    102–104, 109, 121, 124; test
    scores, 89, 101–102; the Young
    Women's Leadership School, 93,
    101. *See also* Schools
EEOC v. Sears Roebuck & Co.,
    65–66, 113
Employment: discrimination, 58–60,
    62, 64, 66–67, 70–71, 73–75, 82,
    85; occupational segregation,
    73–77; unemployment compensa-
    tion, 62; wage gap, 57, 75–76, 82,
    84; work-family conflicts, 62–63.
    See also Title VII
Environmental justice (EJ), 32–33, 40,
    44, 54, 56. *See also* Ecofeminism
Equal pay. *See* Employment, wage gap

Equal Pay Act, 75–77
Equal Protection Clause, 11, 55, 98–100, 106–107
Equal Rights Amendment, 6, 7, 58
Equal treatment theory, 8–9, 16, 18, 21, 23, 35, 61, 154–155, 186, 188, 224; male norm, 19
Equality, 1, 2, 6–7, 9, 11, 13–19, 21–23, 28–31, 34–35, 39, 41–42, 74–75, 131–132, 213–215, 224, 227–228
Essentialism: anti-essentialism, 32, 160, 217; gender essentialism, 25
Ethics, 32, 41, 54

False consciousness, 25, 39–40, 143
Family and Medical Leave Act, 21, 41, 57, 63
Fathers' rights, 140
Female genital cutting, 218–221, 227
Femininity, 29
Feminism: definition of, 1; feminism, 1, 8–12, 15–16, 18, 20, 22–23, 26–27, 36, 54–56, 141, 143–144, 159–160, 186–188, 217, 225–227; methodology, 35, 45, 53–54, 141; "power," 188. *See also* Cultural feminism; Dominance theory
Feminist Anti-Censorship Task Force, 13
Friedan, Betty, 29
Frontiero v. Richardson, 8, 41
Frug, Mary Jo, 36

Garrett v. Board of Education of the School District of Detroit, 96
Gay legal theory, 29–31
Geduldig v. Aiello, 55
Gender: biases, 37, 45–48; socialization, 124; stereotypes, 20, 46–47, 58, 64, 71, 74, 103, 155. *See also* Biological differences

General Electric Co. v. Gilbert, 55
Gilligan, Carol, 9, 19–20, 41, 55
Ginsburg, Ruth Bader, 16–17, 40, 98, 121
Girls: minority race, 90; socialization of, 86–92, 116–119
Glass ceiling phenomenon, 74–75, 91
Globalization: global feminist theory, 214–226; labor force, 225; sovereignty, 217, 222. *See also* International
Grimké, Sarah, 2
Griswold v. Connecticut, 145, 165

Harris, Angela P., 26, 42–43
Harris v. McRae, 130, 157
Hate speech, 27
Heterosexuality, 25, 29, 42. *See also* Lesbian, gay, bisexual, and transgender legal theory
Hispanic, 57, 91, 124, 208
Homosexuality, 30; Defense of Marriage Act, 30, 43, 167. *See also* Lesbian, gay, bisexual, and transgender legal theory
Housework, 24–25, 80

Interest convergence thesis, 72, 84
International: abortion policies, 143; Convention on the Elimination of All Forms of Discrimination Against Women, 224; economic development, 218, 223, 226; European Union courts, 77, 85; globalization, 215–219, 221–223, 227; human rights law, 215; Third World, 217; trafficking in women and girls; workers, 221–223; World Conference on Women in Beijing, 219. *See also* Female genital cutting

Intersectionality, 206; discrimination claims, 66
Irigaray, Luce, 18

James, Henry, 45, 55
Johnson v. Calvert, 151–153
Judges, 54

Karst, Kenneth, 56, 77, 85
Kirstein v. University of Virginia, 93
Kohlberg, Lawrence, 19

Lawrence v. Texas, 79
League of Women Voters, 8, 13, 62
Lesbian, gay, bisexual, and transgender legal theory, 30. *See also* Heterosexuality; Sexual orientation
Liberty, 128, 131, 141, 144, 167, 171
Litigation, 8, 13–14, 20, 63, 65, 94, 141

Maathai, Wangari, 33
MacKinnon, Catharine, 13, 22, 24–25, 27, 38, 42, 44, 46, 54–55, 66–67, 109, 125–126, 130, 153–157, 161–162, 205
Maher v. Roe, 130, 157
Marcosson, Sam, 30, 43
Married Women's Property Acts, 4, 164, 180
Masculinity, 24–25, 29, 103
Maternity leave, 9, 13, 21, 61–63. *See also* Family and Medical Leave Act
Matsuda, Mari, 27, 42, 48–49, 55–56
Media coverage, 103, 185
Meritor Bank v. Vinson, 67–68
Military: "Don't Ask, Don't Tell" policy, 11, 25, 30, 79–80, 85; women in combat, 77–79
Minor v. Happersett, 5
Minow, Martha, xii-xvii, 22, 48, 55, 176

Mississippi University for Women v. Hogan, 9, 41, 95–96
Moral reasoning, 19
Motherhood, 43, 48, 150–152, 157, 161. *See also* Surrogacy
Mott, Lucretia, 2
Multiculturalism, 217, 227
Multiple consciousness, 26–27, 42

Narratives, 27–29, 38, 120, 186. *See also* Storytelling
National Organization for Women, 8, 120
Neal v. Board of Trustees of the California State Universities, 114–115
Newberg v. Board of Public Education, 95
Nineteenth Amendment, 5–6
No Child Left Behind Act, 93, 99
Nussbaum, Martha, 226–228

Okin, Susan Moller, 33, 81, 88, 94, 160, 163, 165, 176–177, 227
O'Loughlin, Ellen, 31–32, 43
Oncale v. Sundowner Offshore Services, 71–72, 83

Paglia, Camille, 187–88, 204, 207, 211
Patriarchy: definition of, 23–24; unmasking, 13, 45, 50
Pierce, Charles Sanders, 34
Planned Parenthood of Southeastern Pennsylvania v. Casey, 131–132, 142, 157
Pornography, 10, 13, 24, 128, 153–156, 162; anti-pornography ordinance, 24, 26; First Amendment law, 155
Postmodern feminism, 8–10, 36–44, 119. *See also* Deconstruction

Power: between lawyer and client, 15, 37; between sexes, 9, 12, 22–23, 67, 74, 84, 181

Pragmatic feminism, 8, 11–12, 34–35

Pregnancy: Pregnancy Discrimination Act of 1978; 55, 62, 148; trimesters, 130, 133–136; viability, 130–131, 133, 137, 156. *See also* Reproductive rights

Price Waterhouse v. Hopkins, 64

Privacy, 78, 96, 130–131, 145, 160, 180, 206, 223

Property: ownership, 2, 4, 8, 17, 29, 35, 163, 166, 169, 171–175, 178–180, 214, 226. *See also* Married Women's Property Acts

Public-private distinction, 12, 106, 176, 180, 181, 214–217

Race: biological views of, 18; social construction of, 28, 30; women of color, 10, 26–28, 56, 110, 129, 145, 160, 181, 196, 206, 216. *See also* African Americans; Critical race feminism; Hispanic

Radical feminism, 22–26. *See* Dominance theory

Radin, Margaret Jane, 34, 150, 161

Rape, 179–189, 198–202; acquaintance rape, 187–188; evidentiary rules, 185–186; evolutionary biology theories about, 204–205; forcible compulsion, 182–183, 206; historically, 27–28; marital exemption, 180, 206; media coverage, 185–187; myths, 183–184, 186–187, 207; nonconsent, 182–183, 186; resistance, 182–183, 186, 206; statistics, 184

Reed v. Reed, 8, 41

Reproductive rights: condom distribution, 146; contraceptives, 146–148, 160–161; emergency situations, 147; insurance coverage, 147, 161; Comstock Act, 129; gag rule, 146, 161; RU–486, 137–138; teenagers, 133, 146–147. *See also Roe v. Wade*

Rights, retrenchment, 72

Robertson, Pat, 1

Roe v. Wade, 7, 29, 39, 135, 137, 142–143, 156, 159; McCorvey, Norma, 142, 159–160

Roiphe, Katie, 187, 207

Rostker v. Goldberg, 78

Sanger, Margaret, 128, 157

Schools: charter schools, 104–106, 124; law schools, 88–89; medical schools, 88; single-sex, 92–106, 119, 123; vouchers, 104–107. *See also* Education

Schanck, Peter, 36, 44

Schlafly, Phyllis, 7, 76, 85, 155

Seneca Falls Convention, 1, 3

Sexual harassment, 66–72; Clarence Thomas hearings, 67; employer liability, 67; in schools, 117–119, 126; reasonable woman standard, 70, 83; same-sex harassment, 71–72; unwelcomeness requirement, 68

Sexual orientation, 11, 26, 29–30, 42–43, 46, 71, 82, 116, 194–195. *See also* Lesbian, gay, bisexual, and transgender legal theory

Sexuality, 11, 24–25, 29–30, 40, 42, 44, 120, 154–157, 188, 204

Sommers, Christina Hoff, 187–188, 207

Special treatment theory, 9, 18–22, 34, 41, 92. *See also* Cultural feminism

Sports, 98–100, 105, 107–111, 113–115, 117–120, 125–126; coaches, 24–25; health benefits of, 108–109, 112; participation of girls and women, 102, 108. *See also* Title IX

Stanton, Elizabeth Cady, 1–3, 5, 144

Stenberg v. Carhart, 137, 158

Stereotypes, 13, 20–21, 46–47, 58, 62, 64, 71, 74, 81, 103, 107, 155, 184, 209

Storytelling, 11, 28, 43, 50, 142, 180; Voices Brief, 141–142

Suffrage, 2–3, 5–7, 14, 16, 39, 56, 87

Summers, Lawrence, 91–92, 122

Surrogacy, 28, 128, 148–151, 153, 156, 161; reproductive freedom, 149

Taylor v. Louisiana, 9

Title VII, 6, 9, 21, 55, 58–59, 62, 65–67, 70–72, 74, 76–77, 81, 83, 117, 147; bona fide occupational qualification, 60–61; disparate treatment, 59–60; disparate impact, 59–60; EEOC, 59, 65–67, 73, 81, 83; history, 58. *See also* Employment

Title IX, 98–100, 105, 107–111, 113–115, 117–120, 125–126; gender ratios, 113–114

Truth, Sojourner, 3, 14–15, 217

UAW v. Johnson Controls, 60

United States v. Morrison, 202

United States v. Virginia, 96–98, 106, 120, 123

Violence Against Women Act, 196, 201–202, 210; *See also* Domestic violence

Virginia Military Institute, 96, 120

Vorchheimer v. School District of Philadelphia, 94–95

Wage gap, 57, 75–76, 82, 84. *See also* Employment

Walker, Alice, 31, 43, 227

Walker, Lenore, 190–191, 208

Webster v. Reproductive Health Services, 131, 157, 159

Welfare: Personal Responsibility and Work Opportunity Reconciliation Act, 80

West, Robin, 41–42, 159

Williams, Joan, 22, 41–42, 62, 83–84

Williams, Patricia, 27, 42

Williams, Wendy, 16

Williams v. McNair, 94

Wills v. Brown University, 118

Wolf, Naomi, 187–188, 207

Women's Rights Project, 8, 16, 21

Zelman v. Simmons-Harris, 107

About the Authors

Nancy Levit is the Curators' and Edward D. Ellison Professor of Law at the University of Missouri—Kansas City School of Law. She is also the author of *The Gender Line: Men, Women, and the Law* and coauthor of *Jurisprudence—Classical to Contemporary: From Natural Law to Postmodernism.*

Robert Verchick holds the Gauthier-St. Martin Chair at Loyola University New Orleans School of Law and is a Scholar at the Center for Progressive Reform in Washington, D.C. He lives with his family in New Orleans and on Whidbey Island, near Seattle.